Enlightenment
And
Wellness

Florette Kingston

INTRODUCTION

My mother left myself and my family a legacy of spiritual enlightenment and awareness, which I would like to share with anyone else who is seeking spiritual knowledge. I have reached the pathway in my life where I can acknowledge my 'self' and understand the reason why I have incarnated with my family and friends on this life's journey. I will share the knowledge that I have gained throughout this life in the hope that it may help others to understand more about the circle of life/death. The spiritual journey is a personal quest we undertake to reconnect with our Soul to find our authentic life purpose. Everyone and everything are evolving at their own speed. Everyone's destiny is enlightenment. Spirituality is not a religion but a way of life. You may ask yourself *'How will I benefit from reading this book'*

Hopefully you will find something that resonates with you that will help you to find some answers.

Florette wishing you peace light and Love.

A spiritual enlightenment and wellness journey

covering the purpose of the soul

Guardian Angels

The contract of the soul-family

How to heal your life

The souls Journey

Death and re-incarnation

The circle of Life and Death

This book offers insight into finding inner peace. Understanding life's purpose and a guide to your own spiritual awakening

Earth is a school of learning, and the spiritual journey is a personal quest that we undertake to reconnect

with our soul and find our authentic life purpose

"Who am I"

"Why am I here"

"Where am I going"

Everyone's journey is quite unique

We are not human beings having a spiritual experience, we are spiritual beings having a human experience

With awakening comes confidence and deep feeling of self-worth

Awaken your spiritual energy and remove the fear of death by understanding the

circle of Life

A SPIRITUAL WELLNESS JOURNEY

Where to begin….

By embarking on a spiritual journey, you can discover who you truly are. A spiritual journey is a very individual and intimate quest to consciously deepen your insight about life. I was fortunate to be born into a very spiritual family and therefore I began my journey very early in life. My Mother impressed upon us that we are not human beings having spiritual experiences, but we are spiritual beings having human experiences. This enabled me to build and follow my spiritual pathway through this life. Each one of us is living an entirely different life. We all come from different backgrounds and have different pasts. We make different experiences during our lifetimes. Even further, every one of us believes in totally different things. *Your life* is absolutely not comparable to mine. Therefore, one needs to understandable that *everyone's journey in life is quite unique.* What is important is that you find YOUR path.

"Who am I?" "Why am I here?" "Where am I going?"

Firstly: Our soul keeps returning to learn many lessons that we ourselves and our team of guides have chosen for us. Depending on what we need in order to grow spiritually. When a soul decides it is ready to return to the earth plain, it meets with these guides, some of whom have been with them for *many lifetimes* and some new guides as well. The other group is a council of our elders or master teachers, who help with the process of achieving what our new lessons will be in this earthly time, and how to assist the soul with its return to the earth plain. We go through the process of looking where our soul could grow and the experiences necessary for our soul's growth. Past-life karma is looked at and evaluated on many levels. Your soul wants to experience many different scenarios with families, economic conditions from poor to rich or vice versa, social status, spiritual and individuals' beliefs. Your soul goes through many lifetimes in the hope of spiritual and soul growth. Your soul's evolution is looked at, and the planning starts. Figuring out the needs for growth, your guides, teachers and you will look at many scenarios and choose the one that will fit you best. It's like watching many movies and choosing the one you want to be in. It's hard to imagine that we choose the life we are currently in, but that's the way it works. You chose your parents, siblings (yes, your siblings!) and the circumstances that create your world now. If you look at each adventure or mishap that has happened in your life, you can take on a new outlook. Ask yourself how you can handle each situation in a loving way, knowing there is a lesson to be learned and you did indeed choose to learn it. Can you believe you choose your body, including what type of body – male or female, handicapped, gorgeous, not-so attractive? All with lessons to learn. Imagine being a model or actress who is judged by appearance, constantly having to submit to this judgement of onlookers.

Maybe the lessons they came with include *finding the beauty within themselves* and not to be burdened with what others think or say about them. Imagine wanting to be born with a disability so that you might teach others compassion. When it's time to reincarnate is totally up to you. You might wait until your soul family is ready to reincarnate with you. Your soul family can include your parents, siblings, co-workers, family and friends. I know my family and myself have been together in many lifetimes and in many different scenarios. (I will elaborate later) When we reincarnate, *we forget all the other lives* we have lived and what lessons we choose for this lifetime, but that's only so we can have a fresh start this time around and experience all the joy and sorrows that we may encounter for the *purpose of our soul's growth*. Enjoy life and find the joy that is ours. Let go of hurts, anger slowly, and laugh a lot. Earth is just our schoolroom, not where we will live forever. We chose to reincarnate often to balance Karmic debts.

Karma simply tells us that what happens to us in the *present* is the causes *we ourselves have set in motion in the past*, whether ten minutes ago or ten lifetimes ago. These days we call it – '*what goes around, comes around*'. Or '*what you sow, so you reap*'. Karma tells us that whatever we do will come full circle at some point. Karma and reincarnation go hand in hand. *Karma* means accountability and *payback*, while *reincarnation* is another word for *opportunity*. It gives us another chance to make good on the Karmic debts we owe others. *Karma and reincarnation tell us that our soul is evolving through many lifetime experiences.* When you realise this, it can help you to understand the reasons *why* we have certain experiences and *why* certain people come into our lives and even the challenges that some present. People may ask:

why was I born to these parents? Why did I give birth to the children I have? Why am I afraid of water or heights? Why am I here?

Karma isn't fate. We weave karmic threads *through each lifetime.* Everything is energy, including your thoughts and emotions, which are *energy in motion*. So, in essence, everything you do creates a corresponding energy that comes back to you in some form. To put it simply, *everything you do creates either a positive or negative consequence.*

Therefore '*you reap what you sow*' and '*what goes around, comes around*'. Karma picks up where the golden rule leaves off. Do to others as you would have them do to you – *because someday it will be done to you*. The Sanskrit word Karma means "*act*" or "*deed*". Our thoughts, words and deeds, both positive and negative *create a chain of cause and effect*. Karma will also return the good that we have done for others. It allows us to learn from our mistakes. Send your enemies Love and Light and pray for them. Accepting **all** people and by **not** judging them, you are learning an important lesson in Love. If, in this life you have fears or phobia's that you cannot explain, then it may be 'baggage' that you are carrying from a former incarnation. Something that you haven't yet dealt with. *During our lifetime we are tested again and again. We need to show how much love and forgiveness we can infuse into a situation to heal both ourselves and others.*

"What is the Soul's purpose, and indeed – what is the soul?"

Your soul: is an ethereal counterpart to your human form that is infused throughout every cell of your body.... The soul is your *higher self* and mirrors much of your personality; in other words, even after your soul leaves your human form after death, *you are still you!* Each soul is a part of a larger scheme.

We choose the precise moment to incarnate to Earth, and we do this time and time again until we have learned the lessons that our soul needs to progress spiritually. There is a reason that we choose our parents, our life and the purpose for being here this time around. Life on Earth is a team game. It is vital to learn the rules so that you can participate. Earth is a plane of free will, and we can choose whether or not to follow the rules/laws. Your higher self makes certain decisions before you come to Earth. Your soul makes these choices based on experiences you need for your progress. As I mentioned above, we choose our parents. We may choose to be born to difficult parents because they embody the challenge that your soul needs. People come into our lives, *not by chance* but either we have Karma to repay or because they bring happiness to our lives. Either way, *it is not by coincidence.* You may have many challenging experiences throughout your life, but many of them are pre-life decisions, which are inevitable. You have free will to choose how to handle each circumstance and make decisions about everything in your life. I like to describe this a train journey: You book your ticket with certain *pre-booked* stops along the way. The '*planned*' stops are agreed before you set off on your journey. However, you may choose to get off at a different destination (*this choice is yours*) The choices you make along the way and the way in which you deal with them, determine whether you will need to board the train again (in another incarnation) to complete your journey. So, if you do not complete the journey (planned lessons/tests) you will keep having the same lessons/tests present themselves until you do, whether in this lifetime or the next. The Soul is said to be the *mind, will and emotions* where we *think* and *feel*. Without a soul there is no – '*Self.*'

The Soul: Our soul is our *mind, will and emotions*. This is the part where we think and feel. Your soul is the immaterial essence and totality of who you are at a core level – *it is your true nature.* It is the *sum of all the lives that we have lived previously.* It is our soul that provides us with our '*inner voice*'. *We are not human beings having a spiritual experience. We are spiritual beings having a human experience."*

Body: Our body is the easiest part to understand because it's the part we see. Our body is the flesh and bones we walk around in. Everything physical is our body. Our skin and bones, muscles, nerves, blood, hair, etc., all make up our bodies. This is the part of us that decays over time and will eventually cease functioning when we die. (Our soul is encased within this body) We experience life as a human so that we can learn and grow and evolve spiritually.

Life on earth is about learning lessons, and balancing Karma. So, as I have said, if we do not learn the lessons that we have chosen to learn, then we may choose to return (incarnate) to have another chance. Human life consists of four aspects: the physical, mental, emotional and spiritual levels of existence. Our *physical body* needs to learn the ability to *survive and thrive* in the material world. The *mental level* of our existence consists of our *thoughts, attitudes, beliefs and values.* The *emotional* aspect is the part of us that seeks *meaningful contact and connection with others.* Our spiritual aspect is our inner essence, *our soul,* the part of us that exists beyond time and space. It connects us with the *universal source* and the oneness of all life.

BASIC LAWS OF LIFE

Firstly, it is important to know that the universe loves you no matter what mistakes you think you have made on Earth. Think of Earth as a school, a place of learning. Lessons are presented to us, and it is how we deal with these lessons as to whether we '*pass the exams*' presented or if we choose to come back in another life and *re-sit.* We have the same lesson pop up throughout life giving us extra opportunities to learn from it. If we continue to fail, this is when we can return in a different life in order to learn what the soul needs from the *experiences presented*. Life gives us constant opportunities to learn about ourselves. When we, who have *signed up* for this course on Earth, wish to change something in our lives, we must look within to alter our beliefs and attitudes so that our outer world can change. Always listen to your *inner guidance and intuition*. Your '*gut*' instincts. You have permission to walk away from anything that doesn't feel right. Trust your *instincts and listen to your inner voice*. When we trust and follow our intuition (instincts) we are living authentically. We are making choices that are aligned with *who we are*, and the path that we have chosen.

Trusting your life choices

As humans we all make choices. It depends upon the experiences and the lessons we learn from each choice that moves us forward. We may feel that we have made mistakes in our choices, but ultimately, we will have gained a certain knowledge from that choice. You may feel that you lost an opportunity from 'a mistake', but maybe you were just not ready to take on the challenge at that particular time. Listen to your intuition and be guided by that.

Intuition is seeing with the soul.

It is ok to say no and set boundaries.

All too often we feel afraid to say no as we don't want to upset the other person. Some people can be very clear with their boundaries and will just say no without feeling the need to explain their reasons why. Often, we can feel that setting ourselves a boundary is going against someone else. I think we just need to be honest about who you are and what you want, what you can do and what you can be. Then it is up to the other person to see if they can accept your boundary. Some of us feel that we can easily be manipulated as we feel uncomfortable saying no. The thing is that life will send you a whole lot of experiences and people that will challenge your boundaries. We often see boundaries as being a negative. I for one, struggle with this, even today when I know that what I am saying is true. Children who are given boundaries, show more respect and find life easier to deal with. They feel safe with boundaries. There are people that will 'use' you (maybe not intentionally) but because they know that they can. Again, we need to find balance otherwise we end up feeling stressed or cross that other people are taking the time from us that we don't necessarily want to give. There are certain people that will throw a wobbly if you say no when you have always said yes, but the people that respect you will understand and accept. The ones that don't accept will either move away from you and find someone else that they can manipulate, OR they will respect the new you that says, "*Sorry but I can't today*" We are supposed to have some relationship changes throughout your life. You will stay together for as long as is needed, and then you will go on your own pathway. We need to grow and change with each relationship.

Forgiveness and Karma

The way to achieve harmony with all parts of the psyche is through forgiveness. We are all human and have all done things that we are not proud of. So, we must *forgive ourselves* for making human mistakes in life. Forgive yourself for the errors and Karma of your previous lifetimes, whether you remember them or not. We all must go through experiences in the best way that we knew how at the time. It may not have been the perfect way, but that is the process of learning, experiencing, going through trial and error, and then finally coming out on top. Don't condemn yourself for your shortcomings and what you feel are mistakes. *Just resolve to do better next time.* Your soul is worthy of Love and forgiveness. Forgiveness is an important part of balancing Karma. It is also important to *forgive others*. When you forgive others, you are freeing yourself from entanglements of this and previous lives. Most of us have difficult people in our lives. Sometimes we can't seem to resolve things with them and to disentangle ourselves. Often this is because we have *never forgiven old hurts and old wrongs,* some from previous embodiments, and so they hang on. Non-forgiveness hardens the heart and ties us to people that can make us feel bitter. Therefore, forgive and forget, and move on. You can ask your *higher self* to show you how to forgive. You can meditate and set yourself an affirmation. Imagine a sphere of Violet light surrounding those that you want to forgive, dissolving all negativity and filling their souls with the light of forgiveness. You could say their name…. Followed by – is a being of Violet fire.

Forgiveness quotes:

"To forgive is to set a prisoner free and discover that the prisoner was you." Lewis B. Smedes

"There is no love without forgiveness, and there is no forgiveness without love." Bryant H. McGill

"To forgive is the highest, most beautiful form of Love. In return you gain peace." UN-Known

Are you tired of letting anger from past mistakes, hurtful breakups or toxic family relationships occupy space in your heart and mind? There's an extraordinary healing power in taking the steps to forgive someone, or even yourself. When you hold resentment toward another, you are bound to that person or condition by an emotional link. If you allow other people to have a negative influence over the way you think, feel, and behave, then you are giving away your power. Grudges won't do anything to diminish the other person's life, but it can wreak havoc on your own. Whether someone hurt you yesterday or 10 years ago, holding a grudge *allows that person to take up more space in your life*. You are also giving away your personal power when you change your mind every time someone tugs at your heart strings, and you give others power over your behaviour. If you really don't want to do something, be strong enough to stick to your choices, even when someone tries to take you on a guilt trip. Not everyone is going to like you. You don't have to let one person's opinion define *who you are or how you feel about yourself.* If you allow someone else to cause you to get so angry, you may say or do things you later regret, or you succumb to pressure to do something against your values, therefore *you give away your power.* It's important to behave according to *your values*, no matter what is going on around you. Every minute you spend thinking about someone you don't like or complaining about someone you don't want to be around; is 60 more seconds you give that person. When you dwell on negative people, *you give them power over your thoughts.* Decide that *you are going to be in control of how you think, feel, and behave* regardless of the situation you find yourself in. Forgiveness as a conscious, deliberate decision to release feelings of resentment or vengeance toward a person or group who has harmed you, regardless of whether they actually deserve your forgiveness. Forgiveness does not mean forgetting, nor does it mean condoning or excusing offences. Though forgiveness can help repair a damaged relationship, it doesn't obligate you to reconcile with the person who harmed you or release them from legal accountability. Instead, forgiveness brings the *forgiver peace of mind and frees him or her from destructive anger.* Hurts can run deep, even if at first glance they don't seem to make a big impact. It's important to give yourself permission to acknowledge the pain that's very real for you. Notice where you feel it in your body and ask yourself, "*What do I need right now?*" Maybe you need to feel supported, take more time, or do something kind for yourself. Allowing space for the pain in this way can help you know whether you're ready to release it from your heart and mind.

Love is the ultimate goal

Love is where your spiritual pathway begins. The state of love is the *highest energetic frequency* that we can reach for. When we operate with love, we vibrate a signal which brings us into harmony with the blueprint of love at the core of all creation. *We are beings of vibration,* and the *frequency of Love* carries the harmonic wavelengths that represent the very essence and presence of life. When we fear the loss of love, we begin the journey towards endless suffering. This is the opposite of how the creation process works. Opening the heart to receive, paves the way for all other relationships. Loving attitudes create loving outcomes. Love is the ultimate soul-food: the very sustenance of our heart. With it, we can attain the seemingly impossible. Without it, we become lost, destabilized and uninspired. *So, love yourself.* When we give with loving kindness, the heart truly comes alive. Develop tolerance, patience and deep understanding for all people and you will know the true essence of love. The Dalai Lama said that the purpose of life is to be happy and that we experience this state of being through our inner development. So, it isn't something we get, or something we seek…it's something we develop, which takes practice. A spiritual practice. In order to truly know love, we must allow it to enter our being and invite it to remain as a permanent state of our presence. *Love is the key to a happy life.* I was fortunate indeed to have loving parents that taught me invaluable lessons in life. My mother taught me the spiritual truths and answered my many questions about each subject. She taught me love, kindness and respect. My father taught me laughter and love and introduced me to music and the arts. I had a happy childhood without too many misdemeanours. Throughout life I have learned many lessons and I give gratitude for them all, knowing that I have dealt with many challenges, both learning to forgive and forget, and indeed – move on. I believe that forgiveness is the key to abundance as it unlocks the resources of the universe. I give gratitude to my parents for giving me life, and I always *try* to look for the positive in any situation. My mother always taught me to see the best in others. She explained that we are all on different pathways and have different levels of understanding, and therefore we should try not to judge others by our own standards but accept that other people may not act towards us as we wish them to. Some people are younger souls and maybe need to reincarnate many times before they can become more understanding of life and learn how to love. As I said, we go through many incarnations, taking on different personalities, etc. until we become the best that we can be. We are all here to learn and experience life with all of its challenges with each other. I have experienced many challenges (and there will be more no doubt) but finally I am in a '*happy place*' within myself, knowing that I am doing the best that I can for myself and for others. There have been people in my life that I haven't always been happy with, and there has been conflict, and many challenges, but through the art of sending thoughts and blessings and asking forgiveness through meditation, matters have been resolved with a happy outcome. This is one of the reasons that I can 'preach' about the positivity of forgiveness to another. Sometimes it can be hard to stay positive in life when you are drowning in the waters of negativity. Happiness isn't the only type of positivity definition. There are many ways to stay positive in your life, even when you're experiencing anger, sadness, or challenges. The definition of being positive is having hope and confidence in one's ability to handle what's tough, along with remembering that nothing is all negative all the time. You can't always control what happens to you, but *you can control how you respond.* Meditation will improve your focus, attention, clarity and will keep your mind calm. It keeps you from getting stressed out and keeps you happy in the long run. It is beneficial for both the body and mind. We continually go through changes, because this is how life is meant to be. You can experience the worst phase of your life, but you should look for the positive aspect and find a solution to your problem. If you think of each *challenge that is sent to you as a lesson on your life's journey* and think of how to handle the problem in a positive manner, and with love in your heart, then you will pass the exam and will have no need to re-sit! Love is a beautiful feeling and emotion which can really change people positively. A little love, kindness, trust can spread positive vibes and make people feel good about themselves. When you treat people with love, then you know what it feels like to be really loved. Life is about accepting the challenges along the way and choosing to keep moving forward. The more difficult the victory, the greater the happiness in winning. Sometimes the greatest thing to come out of all your hard work isn't what you get for it, but what you become for it.

What we give out, we get back

Life in reality is very simple: What we give out, we get back. *We* are responsible for what we do with our free will. Every thought that we think is creating our future. *We* create our own experiences by our thoughts and feelings: *The thoughts we think and the words we speak create our experiences.* If we create peace and harmony in our minds, we will find it in our lives. *Our subconscious mind accepts whatever we choose to believe.* We need to train our minds to think and speak positively and not negatively. If we constantly think negative thoughts, then that is what we will attract, negative situations and negative people. The inner attracts the outer. If something in your outer world is not what you want it to be, look inside and shift how you feel about yourself. You will then automatically draw different people and experiences to you. Always, *embrace* the *positive* rather than *resisting* the *negative.* If you have lived with people who were very unhappy, frightened, guilty or angry, then you will have learned a lot of negative emotions. You may then think, "*I never do anything right*" or "*it's my fault*" "*If I get angry, I am a bad person*". Beliefs like this create a frustrating life. When we grow up, we have a tendency to recreate the emotional environment of our early home life. We also tend to recreate personal relationships we had with our parents. We treat ourselves as our parents treated us. We hear their words in our head. As I have already said, I was loved and encouraged as a child, and I feel happy with the person that I have turned out to be. I know that I still have lessons to learn from life, but I can address my failings and still love myself non the less.

As parents we need to tell our children often that we love them. I mentioned earlier that we choose our parents. Each one of us decides to incarnate to this planet at a particular point in time and space. We have come here to learn a particular lesson that will advance us upon our spiritual journey. We choose our sex, colour our country and the parents that will mirror that pattern we are bringing into work this lifetime. All the events you have experienced in your lifetime up to this moment have been created by your *thoughts and beliefs you have held in the past.* What is important in this moment is *what you are choosing to think and believe and say right now.* If you are having negative thoughts, **stop and think**, do you want this thought to be creating your future. Just be aware of your thoughts. We can choose what we think. *Your mind is the greatest power of all.* You can stop what you are thinking at any point and change the thought. We do have to deal with and express all emotions at some point. We are all learning at different levels and even though it is helpful to look at the positive opposed to the negative, we still have emotions that come with different experiences. If we can think about how the experience makes us feel and then take a step back and look at it from a 'bigger' perspective and see how best, we can deal with the situation with a more positive view. We can all act on impulse and then look back and think how we could have possibly reacted differently. We do have choices to how we think about a problem, and then how we deal with it. Sometimes life and life's lessons can be overwhelming. We just need to give ourselves a moment to sit back and reflect and think about how this lesson serves us and how best we can deal with it. We often listen to other people's opinions and then feel confused about what we feel we should or shouldn't do. What I would say is, if what that person advises you to do, if you feel comfortable with it then that's a good way to think about it. On the other hand, if it puts you in confusion and you maybe feel manipulated, then take a step back and trust your instincts to show you the way. There really isn't a right or wrong way, it is how you feel that you want to experience and deal with challenges. All lessons are a part of life, and we learn through growth how they best serve us. When we can let go of anger, we can think logically and then maybe the way we react to a problem, may serve us better. Life in general can be very chaotic and we must figure our reactions. We can lose ourselves in other people's negative talk. If we can focus on what is important to us and deal with our emotions from our heart, we can often find that we can work through the lesson without a clouded vision. I can talk about this from personal experiences that have taught me to stop and think before I act. I have experienced, grief and trauma through many actions that I have played out in the past. All of cause, learning curves. By reflecting now, I can see how things could have played out differently if I had chosen to act rationally, and not on impulse and sometimes in anger. We choose lessons and challenges before we incarnate, and it is how we deal with these challenges/lessons that help us to find the balance and be our 'best self'. We need to come out of the 'victim' state and stop the blaming game, by realising that we all play our part in life's lessons. Life can be extremely challenging, and it can often take us to the depths of despair. We can stay there wallowing in our dark feelings for some while, before we then decide that we don't want to be in this place any longer.

Dis-ease (disease) comes from Disharmony

Whenever we are ill, we need to search our hearts to see who it is we need to forgive. *Usually, the very hardest person you find it hardest to forgive is the one you need to let go of the most.* It does not mean that you condone their behaviour, but we must be *willing to forgive and move on from the negative situation.* We also must learn to love and approve ourselves exactly as we are. Disease/illness means that disharmony has crept in. Our inner child (*soul*) stays with us until the day that we die. *The child is who we are*. We need to love and cuddle our inner child and release any painful memories that we may have. Any past life governs the way we perceive and receive life.

For example: If you lived a past life of enslavement you may naturally come into this life with an unconscious feeling of not being valued or needing to be independent. Negative choices made in a *previous lifetime* may require you to clear up what's been *left unsettled* like an open case yet to be closed. It's just up to you to use that knowledge to make different choices. It's an *opportunity* for you to learn and grow within the current experience and balance Karmic debts. If you choose not to, then those same patterns will follow you into your next life. When you're in a relationship with someone you've been in a past life with, it's very possible for them to create uncomfortable feelings inside of you without knowing it. These "uncomfortable" feelings go beyond the surface. They're more like deeply rooted fears and insecurities that you never had with any other partner before. When you feel '*triggered*', it's showing you where there's an opportunity for growth and healing. Relationships can be some of the biggest teachers in life and your partner can be shining the light into a dark corner, helping you discover what's yet to be healed.

It's not always easy to see it this way when you're feeling charged, angry or hurt, but it's possible to shift your perspective and see your partner and what they may be providing *for* you. Knowing and understanding Karma, can help us to understand "*why*" things happen to us. Many will ask "*why does this keep happening to me*"? The reason will be that you haven't learned from the experience what you need to learn, and so therefore, *the same challenge or similar will keep showing up in your life.* So then, Karmic debt describes something that occurred in a past life that you are now making amends for in this lifetime. when you haven't mastered a karmic lesson, it'll repeat itself repeatedly until you master it. When we have '*irrational fears*' it is often something that is rooted in our past lives. Whether it's a fear of open water, an aversion to joy, a distrust of authority figures, etc., if there's nothing from this lifetime that can explain a feeling or behaviour, it will probably stem from a past life. (I will describe my aversion to frogs and how that maybe a bad memory from the past) in another chapter. You may be repeatedly drawn into a relationship with one particular person, for example, who seems to be teaching you the same lesson. These relationships can be toxic, but they can also be necessary for us to work through our karmic debt. A karmic relationship is a relationship meant to help with the lessons we need to learn in this lifetime surrounding love and partnership. More likely than not, we'll each have one of these karmic relationships in our lifetime. It's the love that pushes you to grow. But these relationships aren't exactly smooth sailing. So, as I have explained earlier in this book, the two of you made an agreement before your souls entered this lifetime, to help each other on your respective paths. Very often, there are *numerous unresolved issues from past lives*. When people open to learning rather than try to control each other, then much healing can occur. Again, I say that once you can understand the bigger plan, it makes it easier to deal with the challenges. Often these relationships are not intended to last a long time. This is because you are coming together in this life to clear karma between each other. It's often a balancing out of a bad experience from a past life. This is the same with people that you may find 'challenging'. You have come together to work through your previous karma. If drama is connected to any of these relationships, then you can guarantee that it is due to Karma. If you feel frustrated and misunderstood, then this is one example. Often there is miscommunication between you. Those highs and lows tend to *repeat themselves, over and over.* You have issues that are carried over from a past relationship, indicating that these are the lesson that needs learning. The relationship will bring all your fears to the surface: about love, your future, and your relationship together in general. Any past traumas will be brought to light—there's no running from it. We may experience a lot of negative 'stuff' and maybe think that we are not good -enough and have a *lack of self-love*. How do we come from being the tiny baby who knows the perfection of itself to being a person who feels unworthy, and unlovable *Self-love* is very important here? You may want to visit a medium, psychic, energetic healer, or past-life specialist to learn more about the karma you're working to balance and clear. There are many healing therapies that can help us to heal. (I will mention them later in this book). We need to do some mental housecleaning. Some people will find the cleaning process very painful, but it need not be. If a thought or belief does not serve you, *let it go*! Make a list of all the negative things that were said to you. *Limiting and negative things said are what have created disharmony.* We can often repeat these negative comments to ourselves, and then wonder why our lives don't work. When you have made your list, acknowledge that these are *beliefs* and *not truths*. We learn our belief systems as very little children, and then we move through life creating experiences to match our beliefs. Look back in your own life and notice how often you have gone through the same experience time and time again. Your limiting decisions have shaped everything you do.

Limiting Beliefs and Karma

Limiting beliefs have prevented you from seeing opportunities and maybe even discouraged you from trying at all. Time to bring them out of hiding. We can all be hard on ourselves in a judgemental way. Limiting beliefs set by others can still have an impact on our lives today. Maybe your father 'put you down' and said derogatory things e.g.: You will never make anything of yourself. Or a teacher may have told you something similar or very negative about an aspect of you. These beliefs get stuck in our system and can hold us back from making important decisions now. A little voice in our head, says "I don't think I can do that; I don't believe that I am confident enough" These thoughts then are coming from a place of fear. Subconsciously we are protecting ourselves so that we don't get judged or criticised by others. So, you stay in that fear, the stuck limiting beliefs. If you feel that this resonates with you, you will need to do some deep searching back into your memory and find where the limiting beliefs began. Ask yourself if these thoughts and beliefs serve you now, or do they hold you back from doing the things that you feel you would like to do.

That fear will hold you back, and you may be afraid to move away from it because you don't want to experience more self-doubt. It may be painful to let the emotions flood through you, but unless you let go, you won't find the happiness within that you so deserve. What you believe, becomes your truth. When you know your worth, no-one can make you feel worthless! You may choose to think, "But, *my* limitations are *real!*" Here's the place where choice comes in. Which are you more interested in: defending your limitations to the death or achieving your goals and desires? If you avoid taking any steps to change your beliefs, you will just feed your old limiting belief. Taking action, even the smallest step, will help solidify your new UN-limiting decision. Your first steps don't have to be perfect, just headed in the right direction. Be sure to acknowledge yourself when you've taken that step. We are all beings of light, sent here to reincarnate until we merge with the vibrations of *love and forgiveness* that are the true nature of the universe. Your life purpose is to find your spiritual pathway, which requires honesty, integrity and commitment to all that distracts you from spirit. A sign of progress is when you no longer fight the nature of life. Instead, *you work with it.* You stop pretending that life is supposed to be a certain way and accept it on its own terms. *There will always be pain in life and challenges.*

This is something we learn as we progress spiritually. If you are spiritually happy you naturally want others to be happy. You can't help but help. Spirituality is not a religion; it is a way of life. It is the gift of love. *Service to others is the discipline of love.* If you reach out often to those in need, not because you should but because your heart leads you more and more deeply into the hearts of others, then keep on going. It has taken me years to realise '*why*' I have returned to Earth this time around. I am here to do service by showing compassion, empathy and love without wishing for anything in return. My mother played a very important role in my spiritual teachings, and I can now pass on the same to my family and friends (*those that desire spiritual knowledge*) I have realised also the Karmic debts that I have needed to pay back. So as I have said, if there is something in your life that *keeps re-occurring and makes you feel uncomfortable* then these are triggers to memories of a past life somewhere back along. Karma isn't just about our current life choices, but also about our past life choices. The body we inhabit when we return is indicative of *how many more lessons* need to be learned to bring ourselves into completion in our spiritual journey. It is also essential to know that if you are owed Karmic debt from others, *your path will continue* until you receive payment. *Good* deeds equate to a *positive* "credit," and *bad* deeds equal a "*debt.*" There is a numerical value attributed to it, and your payment *may not* occur in this life, *but rather in the next.* You may currently be paying a debt from your previous life. It is essential to understand that your credit or debit isn't calculated by just your actions, but also by the *morals, thoughts,* and *intentions behind your actions.*

An example: *Donating to a school to manipulate the school system to overlook specific actions by your child will not be seen as a karmic credit, but rather a **debt**. On the other hand, making the same donation to a school because you genuinely believe that children should be provided with a science lab for their better learning will equate to Karmic **credit**.* Karma has no timeline' The universe will bring back any acts you committed, or feelings you caused in another person. This Karmic boomerang helps teach you how your actions impact others and to teach you to find compassion. I 'signed my contract' before incarnating to do service for others. Having realised this, and accepting that this is so, it has made a difference to how I view the *challenges* that have been sent my way. I look at them as the lessons that *I chose before this life* and that instead of feeling upset, angry and negative about them, I look for the positive in the lesson.

I mentally tick a box in my head and tell myself that I have completed one of the tasks that I set myself and I can move on to the next challenge with a different perspective. I can still feel upset by hurtful comments/actions, but I can deal with them with a better understanding. To accept your challenges means to acknowledge what you're experiencing. We can all run away from our problems or stuff them under the carpet believing they will disappear — out of mind out of sight they say. Yet, what you stow away is likely to build energy and come back to trouble you later, when you least expect it. *The greatest challenge in this life is discovering who you are, and your life's purpose.* Then to being happy with it. Once you realise that challenges are what *you* have chosen to help you to grow, then you can find a way to deal with them accordingly. Don't wait for others to make you happy, find your happiness from within. We continue evolving and changing – *that's the nature of life.*

 So, what is spiritual enlightenment? It is the understanding of the inherent qualities of Pure Soul *(Self)* and the non-self (Ego). Once you become aware of the inherent qualities and differences of the Self (*your own soul*) and the non-self, you have acquired Enlightenment.

The contract:

Before we take birth there is a certain incubation period. Imagine that in this period, you huddle together with your companions for a meeting. *These are the people you share your life with today.* From a person you talked to for a brief moment in the lift, a beggar on the street, your parents, your ex, to your life partner and everyone else in between. The purpose of this spiritual round-table conference is to decide the *lessons* you will *learn in the life to come.* These are *'soul contracts'*, being written for *you* as you get ready to pursue the next ride to Earth. Your spirit guide and council are also a part of this conference. I will talk about our spirit guides later. *Everyone that you meet, or encounter plays a part in your contract. All decided before incarnation.* So then, maybe you need to return this time around to learn forgiveness. Something that you haven't reconciled in a previous incarnation. To learn the act of forgiveness, *someone must take the responsibility to deeply hurt you.* Thus, providing you the choice to *either forgive them or stay resentful.* To know how to be independent and strong, *someone must ensure they abandon you at your worst hour.* This gives you the opportunity to *either stand up for yourself or fall down and succumb to your circumstances.* So, everyone you meet has signed-up to help your soul's evolution as *YOU* have signed-up too, to deal with them. *Even the annoying and challenging ones*! It is a Karmic balancing act. Understanding *why* we encounter challenges, helps us to deal with them in a positive way rather than a negative approach… which has I have explained adds to the Karmic balance sheet. You may ask, "*what about the soul that has taken on the challenge to hurt you*" "*Aren't they then creating negative Karma for themselves*?" The answer is, "*they will be the soul that is paying back Karma from a former lifetime with you*" It is all a chain of *positive/negative karma.* How you learn things will be unique, designed to suit your soul's personality and requirements as you progress. You may become the parent to a differently able child, so that you can learn to take care of and love someone unconditionally. You might have to keep taking care of them for several years, before you truly understand this. Someone else might learn the lesson of unconditional love by having to deal with difficult siblings, or a stubborn partner who makes a lot of bad choices. Once we realise that we are all on *our own individual spiritual pathways* and accept that other people act differently to how we *think* they should, then we become less judgemental and critical of others. We allow ourselves to understand the working of our soul, how we interact with others and how they affect our lives, and we theirs. Life becomes less stressful, and we find more joy in our everyday lives. We are *ALL* balancing Karma at whatever level we have chosen before incarnation. None of us are perfect, *otherwise we would not be here.*

There are some lessons you have already mastered in the past, and there are others that will come to you when it's your time. All souls' have different maturity levels. Don't be fooled by the human relationship or age you're in! *Your soul has taken many lifespans to acquire a holistic and all-encompassing flavour of humanity. Karma is the luggage your soul carries on its trip from life to life.* Unfortunately, unlike luggage at the airport, this particular baggage *never gets lost,* which means you're stuck with it until you open it up and sort through its ancient contents. Without even knowing it, you may be experiencing karma that originated *several lifetimes ago*. Humankind follows a spiral projection upwards, and although sometimes it may feel that we are not progressing…. We are. *With each re-birth and afterlife reflection, we find ourselves on a higher plane*. Your soul is the higher aspect of you, which holds *all the experiences of your journeys* through many existences. Many people do not believe in the existence of an afterlife because it defies science. Because there is no specific proof that it is possible to live without our 'solid' body, some think that it cannot exist. Our soul exists long before we are born into this world and continues to do so after we leave. The soul is pure energy and is not reliant upon a physical body. When we incarnate onto planet earth, and assume very dense and primitive physical forms, we forget all of this, and then suffer from intense amnesia. Yet, as I said earlier, our soul has assumed many physical forms in other dimensions, existences, and in galaxies, and star systems all over the cosmos. It is not attached to the earthly sphere and neither does it need to incarnate here.

It is basically a soul's '*free will*' and choice whether it wishes to assume a physical form on planet earth – *or not*. When we do choose a physical body, it is like putting on a coat. We wear it until we pass over and then we discard it as it is not necessary to the soul energy.

The Soul is pure Energy: It can be difficult to understand the concept of our soul being pure energy, and that all the records of the soul (and indeed all of life and life forms – the whole of Creation) is stored in one vast central *Energy field*, which is enormous, yet compact, and this is pure spiralling energy. At its very core lies the *Divine Core Creative Energy Force*. In essence then our soul can never be separate from the very same energy field in which it is stored. The Higher Self is an extension of yourself.

It is part of you and part of the Source—the ultimate higher power, the universal source of cosmic energy. This energy links us to everyone and everything. We are *all interconnected through shared energy*. And as this universal energy—this higher consciousness—is contained within each one of us, we can use the Higher Self to access this universal wisdom and knowledge from within. The *lower* self is in essence our *material body and mind*. The *higher* self is in its essence your *spiritual body and mind – or heart*. If you could for a moment view your *'self'* as a spirit being, with all the powers of the conscious universes within you, (which you do have), you will see this '*self*' on a different level completely. The '*self*' being your *material body* (or new soul) which *you as a spirit are trying to teach,* to become enlightened. This could be likened to having a new pet that you are trying to teach how to behave in your home. Unfortunately, we, unlike or pets, have a very large ego. It can take *many lifetimes* to attain this enlightenment. *Acknowledging the good that you already have in your life is the foundation for all abundance.* Be grateful for every experience, both the good and the bad. Act with love towards everyone no matter what they've done. Check your motives and make sure they come from a place of love for self and others. Watch your attitude, because negative thoughts create angry energy directed at you. Forgive! This can be the hardest thing to do, but the most important in balancing Karma. If you're a generous person who's having a streak of bad luck, the Universe is not punishing you. *Karma has no timeline*. It ebbs and flows and not on our schedule. But it does come around. We're faced, every day, with stress, anxiety, and an overwhelming number of problems. Our bodies, our minds, and our spirits absorb each of our experiences and store all of them in some capacity. Sometimes 'self-trust' can be confused with thinking you need to have all the right answers or that you will always make the best decisions. However, 'self-trust' is believing in and being kind to yourself regardless of outcomes. We sometimes, and often, refuse to even recognise our full potential, and so we lose ourselves. Our work on this earth plain is to create and improve our *'self'*. Our lower self can sometimes lean to the side of destruction where this feeling of destruction can make the negative side of us feel powerful and controlling. *Vanity and ego* drive this on and on. We must learn to listen to our *Higher Self* and learn to accept guidance. Vanity and ego can make us choose to get off at a *different stop on our train journey.* In order to get back on '*track*' we need to listen and look for guidance. One thing we can expect when our sixth sense becomes more heightened, is increased awareness of the *loving, white-light-infused spirit beings* that are around us all the time. We have a team of spirit guides and helpers, and I will explain about them and how to ask for guidance from them.

Spirit Guides and helpers: Spirit Guides are *highly evolved beings* that remain as an energy being long after they have served their '*life purpose*' to act as a guide or protector to a living, incarnated human being, imparting their knowledge when needed. '*Spirit Guide*' is a general term that covers all types of guides including, but not limited to, guardian angels, archangels, ascended masters, enlightened beings, and more. Your main *spirit guide* stays with you from birth until death. This guide is your spiritual protector. Other guides come into your life to help with whatever you need specific help with. *Angels* are a different from "spirits." Spirits have the capacity to incarnate into human form, and *angels do not,* plus angels are at a *much higher energetic frequency* than spirits.

Choosing to listen to your guides and connecting

When you are ready to tune into your guides and spirit team, they will know it. We live within the realms of spirit, and they are besides us every day. When you ask for them to connect, you will be aware of a different voice in your head. It will be different to your own thinking patterns. We are all familiar with the voice of doubt, the voice of judgement, the voice of self-blame etc; but the voice of your guides will be of encouragement and love. Your guides are a team, which connect with the source energy. They will relay messages to you, mostly through your main guide, but they also connect to other groups. Some who have incarnated on Earth and some that have not. They work with us on a soul level, soul energy and they see our broader journey. When I first became a medium/channeller, I would often question what I was given and wondered if it was my own thinking that was creeping into the messages that I was receiving. My mother told me always trust what you are given. (Which I will explain later) when I talk about mediumship.

My main guide is '*Fast Cloud*'. I have learned that he was my father in one of my former incarnations as a Dakota Indian girl. I was the only girl, with five living brothers. Originally there were nine, but the others died. '*Fast cloud*' gives me my strength and inspiration. His first message to me: *"Florette, you have my fire in this life. You are a strong warrior. I try to keep balance." "Let the stars watch over you while you sleep.* " I have called upon '*Fast Cloud*' many times to give me strength where I have needed it. I feel his very large, but gentle energy whenever he draws near. Our spirit guides can be with us throughout many incarnations. They will inspire, guide and teach us as well as direct us towards our destiny. Within our 'team' there is also a *gatekeeper or protector guide.* This *being's* main role is to protect your space from any negative energies that can take possession of you. This guide along with your main guide will protect you if you decide upon being a '*medium*' or '*channeller*' as multitudes of different energies can bombard a mediums magnetic field. Some mediums can travel 'out of their bodies' to connect with spirit for development. There are a multitude of guides that work alongside of us. Our guides tune in with other guides to make sure we receive the correct help and information. They always inspire us to be the best that we can be.

Mediumship and Empathy

I sat in a *development circle* for a time. A group of five, together with our 'teacher' and protector, met every week at the same time and place. My niece, Joanne was one of the members, and has developed her own skills and achievements, since then. (I have asked her permission to list her therapies in the therapy section of my book in case anyone would like to get in touch with her) It was during these 'sessions' that I developed my psychic abilities and learned how to use my healing gift. A medium channels energy between our deceased loved ones and the person seeking truth and knowledge. I am what is known as a *clairsentience* medium. *Sensing and feeling energies.* This is commonly described as *'gut feeling' or intuition.* I have the ability to sense and feel emotions from spirit both positive and negative. These feelings are being transmitted through my guides and are clearly different from my own feelings. I don't see spirit when I connect, but I sense their energy and am able to *'hear'* in my head and sense what the spirit wants to impart. Like many, I do see *flashes of light when a spirit is around* and what you could call a *vision* or a *glimpse* of things that can help the 'sitter' to understand who it is that is trying to reach them. I was taught by my mother, to *always give exactly 'what I saw'* or felt as even though the message may seem odd or obscure to me, it could mean something to the 'sitter'. I remember one service where I was tuning in to spirit and I heard some-one (in my mind) singing… *'Polly put the kettle on'.* I asked if anyone in the room could understand this, and a lady put her hand up and said, "yes… my grandmother was called Polly and we always joked with her, saying… Polly put the kettle on". I was then able to connect with her and give her further information to conclude that this was indeed her departed grandmother that was wanting to connect. She was very happy with the information that she received, and it helped her to know that her grandmother was often nearby. Another was when I was drawn to a couple sitting towards the back of the room. I saw a light over their heads and visually saw a motorbike on its side and knew that the young man had passed to spirit. When I asked them if they could understand or accept this, the lady began to cry softly, and she said, "that would be our son". "He was 17 and had not long been riding his motorcycle when he had the accident which took his life". Again, I was given information to them through thought connection that gave them comfort. This is what I see medium ship to be, the ability to impart information from our loved ones in the spirit world to the people that are wanting contact. After I had done some 'live channelling' and psychometry readings, I began to get validation that messages I was able to relay resonated with people and gave some of them closure, or enlightenment and most of all love from their deceased relatives and friends. Eventually I came to trust that what I was receiving was coming from a higher energy source and not from my ego. Spirit do not '*fortune tell*' but they can give guidance through the medium. They do not see themselves as superior to us, but they are coming from a place of pure loving energy. Their aim to help you to connect to your higher energy to help you find guidance.

Why mediums channel spirit energy

Channelling is just the art of communicating with the energies There is a lot of misunderstanding about channelling and mediums. We get inspiration through either clairvoyance, clairaudience, clairsentience. We can all channel energy through music and dreams. So often we wake up with a dream that has a clear meaning. Or we have part of a song that keeps going round in our head. When we focus on it, we can hear the message in the words. I will write a chapter on these later. Channelling lets us connect with the higher realms. We up-shift our energy to connect with our loved ones that have passed to other dimensions. By communicating with the energies of our loved ones, it brings peace to many knowing that their loved ones are still around, and their energies can still be felt. Many channeller's work in the general field of wellness, by channelling "energy." this can help people discover what they want out of life. A true medium will connect and will be able to give the 'sitter' something that the medium could not have possibly known. This is the 'proof' that they are connecting. Of cause there have been know charlatan's that are 'out there' for monetary gain.

These people have given the rest of us a bad name and made people sceptical. A true medium will tell you that your loved ones and spirit guides don't fix your problems, they will help you to find solutions, by understanding what is going on and helping you to uncover the truth that you seek. A medium/channeller can help you to understand why you may have made poor choices and how not to repeat them. They can help you begin your journey to self-awareness. By channelling we can begin to find our true purpose. understanding of our path to self-discovery. We can learn to ask the right questions and find the answers to guide us in our purpose. We can achieve full potential and live the life we were meant to have, by connecting to the higher energies and balancing our own.

Sensitives and empaths

Those of you are very tuned in on energy will be able to use your strengths to help others in need. Empaths have a high level of feeling and sensitive connection to others and their mission in life to help alleviate suffering and raise the vibration of the planet. They have heightened senses which are increased further by different challenges or traumas they've experienced in their own lives. (Some past and some present)

They extend themselves outwardly, taking on and empathizing with the emotions of others. Empaths are also here for themselves to learn to protect their own energy and embody both their shadow and light aspects, while maintaining the ability to tap into, care for, love, and identify with whoever they encounter. They can soak up the negativity from another person or take on their emotions. Empaths like peace, harmony and good feelings. They are usually people that are here to do service, as they will put others before themselves so that they can help them. Being an empath can be very draining on their energy. Even if the empath feels tired and someone asks them for their help, they will be there for that person, no matter how much they would really love to curl up on the sofa and be peaceful. It is all part of doing service. You become an 'agony aunt' if you like, as everyone wants to tell you their woes and you make them feel good because you listen! I realised some while ago that I am an empath, and yes it can be extremely draining when I am around negative people. Empath's can often sense someone's intentions or where they're coming from. In other words, empaths seem to pick up on many of the lived experience of those around them. I find that I can feel what other people are feeling when they are near and because I feel as if I am experiencing their emotions by absorbing their thoughts and feelings. I accept that I do have a high level of empathy towards others. I can see and feel tiny changes in expression, body language and even the tone of voice that some people might miss. I can sense their feelings. Being an empath, I am sensitive to the 'feel' or atmosphere of surroundings, and this can be overwhelming as I, (like many) are happiest when the atmosphere is calm and peaceful. Chaotic and depressing environments, or indeed people, drain my energy and can make me feel miserable as it upsets my emotional balance. I feel that I understand where people are '*coming from*' and can empathise with their emotions because I feel what they are feeling and trying to express. Empathy, after all is fundamentally about connecting and understanding others. With this insight, empaths are frequently sought out by their friends for advice, support, and encouragement. It helps that they also tend to be good listeners and will often patiently wait for someone to say what they need to say and then respond from the heart. If this sounds like you, you probably know that it can be hard at times as people don't always realize how much of your energy it takes for you to be the listener an advice-giver, and some people may take it for granted. However, I feel that I have been given this insight as part of my *challenge to do service in this life.* An empath isn't some special human being because of this, it is part of their journey. However, there must be a balance, or the empath can burn out! Everyone is designed to be on this planet for different reasons. It is a complex network. We all need to find our sense of purpose. It is looking within and asking yourself, what makes you feel the feelings that you are feeling. What motivates you? I feel accepted, I guess when people say to me that they like to be in my company as I show empathy and listen, without being judgemental. Those of us that are Empaths, get benefits also as we can feel satisfaction for being able to help others, also the ego likes to be liked. Maybe we may be healing something within ourselves from a past incarnation. This could contribute to why we feel uncomfortable being around someone that is negative or pessimistic. This then shows a need for balance within the empath. We all need to 'let people be themselves' and not try to change them. We, can listen, give empathy and care (which is inbuilt in our spiritual DNA) and therefore we are not able to NOT be an empath! We can offer some healing for people that come to us for support. But I also think that we are here this time around to learn to protect our own energy and embody both our shadow and light aspects, while maintaining the ability to tap into, care for, love, and identify with whoever we encounter. My 'life service' is to help spiritually and give support. I am sensitive. I love deeply, and I think deeply about life. I own the fact that

I am different in many ways. It is OK for people to judge me. So, what if I want to dance barefoot in the sand, or gaze longingly at the stars or sunsets. I am a little bit crazy (my family tell me so) but I recognise '*who I am*', and I am comfortable with my '*self.*' To have found peace without, I had to find peace within. I know that I will have more challenges to face in this lifetime, as I am still learning and balancing Karma. We are always learning. That is the reason for our existence. *The whole of life, from the moment you are born to the moment you die, is a process of learning. "The nature of humanity, its essence, is to feel another's pain as one's own, and to act to take that pain away. There is nobility in compassion, a beauty in empathy, a grace in forgiveness."*

A few life lessons

People will treat you how you allow them to treat you. Respect and love yourself and others will do the same. *Remember that everything that happens to you, is a lesson to be learned.* Forgiveness is a gift you give yourself. It allows you to be happy and find peace within. You do not forgive because you are weak, but because you are strong enough to realise that only by giving up on resentments will you be happy. Stop fighting against life and accept that you have chosen life challenges and experiences to grow. *Life is your journey.* Remember that we are all inhabiting a human body and the human side of us makes mistakes. Every one of us is balancing Karma, and that we are all growing in spiritual knowledge. This life is meant for the realization of one's Real Self (*our own soul*) Give up on saying '*life is unfair*', and that bad things always happen to you. *You attract in this life, what you need to experience.* We focus so much on outer things and not what is within us. Listen to your intuition. Your '*gut*' instinct will lead the way. This world is trapped in the well of suffering. What is this suffering due to? This suffering stems from ignorance of the 'Self'. All suffering in this world is because of ignorance in one form or another. Have you ever wondered why people suffer? Why do bad things happen to good people? Why everyone around you seems to succeed and all you do is fail? Why you don't feel special? Why people disappoint you? Why you can't get the job/offer/position you want? Everything in your life is programmed and orchestrated before you incarnate. However, you have a level of control over your life at any point in time with your decisions We are born with free will and we can decide on who to relate with, what to eat, where we live, what job to do, and how we behave. When to get off the train! Though sometimes, these decisions are being affected by external factors, it depends on how you deal with these factors. Having a negative mindset, adds considerably more stress to your life. There is a serenity prayer which says: '*Grant me the serenity to accept the things I cannot change; courage to change the things I can; and wisdom to know the difference'.* You don't have to have religious beliefs to understand the message. Instead of immediately going to "*that's unfair*" in your head whenever something negative happens, think about whether you have control over it, and if you did, what you could have done to change the outcome. If in fact if you could change your mindset, you can change your mental direction. Therefore, If you don't like something, change it. If you can't change it, change the way you think about it. You have chosen your life lessons, now you are the one who chooses how you decide to react and respond to these challenges. That includes how long you grieve, how long you brood, how long you stay angry, and how long you choose to be happy. Stop playing the blaming game. Viewing yourself as a victim tends to keep you in the past and promotes a sense of powerlessness. Recently someone asked me: "*why is it that every-time I feel that I have got over a challenge and all seems well in my world, something else crops up to either set me back or give me another challenging experience*"? The answer is simply this: "*You chose the challenges that were necessary for your soul growth before you incarnated.*" "So, as one challenge (*think of it as tests at school*) is completed, your 'self' will be getting ready for the next test." So, depending on what challenges you need to pass all your exams/tests, they will present themselves at the appropriate time. IF you do not accept the challenge, or deal with it in the way it was intended for your growth, then you will keep getting the exam paper returned to you (*you will keep getting the same challenge*) over and over. If you do not find a way to deal with the challenge, then you will need to sit the exam again in another incarnation. So, on this note, remember that each challenging experience that comes your way is what *you* have chosen because of something *your soul* needs in order to progress. *Don't see every challenge as a problem, see every problem as a challenge. Obstacles don't block your path…. They ARE your path.* To run away from your problems without facing the real issue only delays the healing process. Challenges can be difficult, especially when they emerge out of nowhere, whether it be: personal, professional, health-related, financial or relationships. They cut deep into your psyche and can leave you feeling vulnerable. As I said, putting off the challenge doesn't make it go away. Challenges are opportunities to grow. To answer the question: "Life is full of its ups and downs". "One day, you may feel like you have it all figured out and then in a moment's notice, you've been thrown a curve ball". "Everyone has to face their own set of challenges". "Learning how to overcome challenges will help you stay centred and remain calm under pressure." You will be understanding by now that everything about your life really is optimally suited for your soul's growth. Every challenge you face and every difficult person you encounter are all part of the plan. It is the time in between lives when you meet with your soul group to determine the lessons you are here this time around to learn from life lessons. Accepting spirituality can help you to understand life and therefore help you to recognise the things you can change within yourself to find a happier outer.

Spiritual Vibrations/Energy

The two most common spiritual dimensions of reality that people on Earth are familiar with are their *waking state of consciousness* and their *dream state of consciousness*. Overall, the lower dimensions are typically described as being dense, heavy and rigid, having lower vibrations or energies. The higher dimensions are described as being light, transparent, flexible, less complex, more broadly encompassing, having higher frequency vibrations, and an increasing sense of universal oneness and less individuality. (And humans tend to think of them as "heaven". The "Lower" and "Higher" refers to *rates of vibration.* The overall frequencies of *Higher* dimensions are *faster* than Lower dimensions. It is similar to how a higher note on a piano keyboard vibrates at a higher frequency than a lower note. In order to better understand how dimensions work and what it means to be living in the third, fourth or fifth dimension, think of a dimension as a point of perception rather than an actual place to travel to. By seeing things this way, it gives us a better understanding of how we can identify what dimension we are mostly resonating with. Energy cannot be destroyed, it simply changes. We change energy with our surroundings. Your "light," that is, the essence of your energy (not to be confused with your actual consciousness) will continue to echo throughout space until the end of time. Your aura is an electromagnetic frequency that surrounds your body. (*I will explain more about the aura with the chakras*) It can be seen, but it can also be felt. When someone says they are getting a "*bad vibe,*" they mean they are somehow connecting to another person's *aura* and picking up on his or her *frequency.* Light itself is energy, and that is how we become when we return to spirit. My book cover sort of describes how we appear within the energies, when our soul returns to the spirit spheres. Right now, your body is composed of energy-producing particles, each of which is in constant motion. So, like everything and everyone else in the universe, you are *vibrating and creating energy*. Vibrations are a kind of rhythm. Rhythms are like seasonal changes and tidal patterns and happen within your body. Your heartbeat and breathing rates are examples of rhythms. There are vibrations within each one of your cells also. Anxious thoughts trigger the release of stress hormones that stimulate your heart rate to speed up or slow down. The sound vibrations of music, likewise, affect thoughts, emotions, and body systems. By changing your thoughts, it is possible to speed up or slow down vibrations. Certain emotions and thought patterns, such as joy, peace, and acceptance, create *high frequency vibrations*, while other feelings and mindsets such as anger, despair and fear vibrate at a lower rate. Everything created is energy, and energy vibrates at different levels. Just as a singer has a vocal range of notes that she can sing, human beings have a vibrational range. In other words, you *move up and down a vibrational scale*. The more you work on loving and accepting yourself, the higher your vibration rises, and the easier it is to connect with the higher vibrational beings that I refer to as spiritual helpers and guides. These beings vibrate at different places on the vibrational scale. Each level is not good or bad; it just simply is. Let's begin with where we are, *at the lowest level of vibration.* Physical beings are you and me and everyone you see with a body and a heartbeat. While we are able to raise our vibration temporarily in order to communicate with those on the higher planes, we aren't able to sustain this permanently and must come back down after a while. The only way to ascend to a permanently higher vibration is through death. Spirit guides once inhabited a physical form and had the same journey or purpose as us physical beings that they are now guiding. As I mentioned previously, upon leaving their physical bodies, spirit guides choose to become teachers or guides to those of us still in the physical realm. They offer guidance, comfort, and, at times, warnings and protection. Humans that have transitioned to the higher vibrational spheres, can become guardians or a spirit guide. Remember, they don't have a body any longer, so they are not limited to being in one place at a time. *They are energy* and can be everywhere and anywhere, all at once. As we move up the scale to a different dimension, we *vibrate at a higher rate.* There are many levels in the astral world. A drop of water becomes vapour, which is invisible, yet vapour materializes into billowing clouds, and from clouds rain falls back to earth, forming river torrents and eventually merging into the sea. Has the drop of water died along the way? No, it undergoes a new expression at each stage. Imagine *your soul*

as a drop of water which can transform itself.
To try to define things exactly are very complex, and I am not able to go into too much depth on this subject, but I am trying to produce a picture for you to try to understand how our soul continues after the body dies. After death we arrive in the Astral, which has been described by some as a place akin to the material world. [*Heaven, hell, and purgatory*] lie in some distant region beyond the sky or under the earth. However, these aren't actually a place as such but a *state of awareness*. Different planes exist simultaneously. One way to try and understand is, that there a set of vibrations or frequencies, you can call them the *physical plane*, the *astral plane*, the *causal plane*, and that which is beyond the beyond. There are an almost infinite numbers of astral planes, divided into a higher and lower astral world, and even the lowest ones vibrate at a higher frequency than the material world. *Our soul is pure energy, and we vibrate at the level we have gained through the lessons learned in our material body.* I also want to add that, I believe we have more than one escape route planned into our life path before we get here so that we can leave at various times during our lifetime. I don't believe there's ever an accident. More about that later, after a little more clarification on the Astral planes.

To reiterate: There are a set of vibrations or frequencies, which are higher states of consciousness, one being the Astral plane where we are before we are born and where we return after death. The Astral plane has no limitations like here on Earth.

The Astral Plane

Also known as the Astral Sea, it is a [space between everything]. It has been described as a silvery horizon that extends all around you like you are inside a silver orb, to a dark plane with twinkling lights in the distance like stars and stretching out before you is a sea of silvery cloud-like mists. Spending time in the astral plane is exactly like living within the earth plane, but on the higher planes *thought* is more evidently a force. There is more learning done on the Astral plane and some souls spend centuries on this plane of study. Communication becomes increasingly *non-verbal as* we ascend to *higher levels.* The astral dimension is the place of light and indestructible life force. This is the realm of vibrational energy. By connecting again to the astral dimension, you realize your *'true self', the essence of who you really are.* So, our soul is in the Astral dimension before coming to this physical life, and we return to the Astral when we leave our material body. When we return to the astral plane, we become free from the limitations of the physical world. The Astral plane is the plane that vibrates at a higher rate than the Earth plane (which is the physical plane) We will be *EXACTLY* the same person there as we were here upon our first arrival. We take memories of all of our desires and emotions with us. The '*hell*' of this plane is any desires that require a physical body to satisfy cannot be satisfied. Thus, the strong frustrations. As I have mentioned, *Hell* is not a place but a *state of mind.* Many who die and first arrive on the Astral plane do not realise that they are dead as so they try to behave as if they still had a physical body. The Astral body form creates its own life on the Astral plane, much as we do down here. If groups of Astral plane forms say they want to go to the opera, or the theatre, they simply wish it. The Astral Plane entity literally creates its own environment on this plane, such as parks, mountains, streams, buildings, or whatever *just by thinking* about the item. It is on this plane that we completely destroy all the gross emotions and all the base desires it created while on the physical plane. The soul then proceeds to the sub-planes of the mental plane which we call '*Heaven*', which is a dimension. We will graduate to the higher levels/planes as we lose our 'base' desires. What we call dimensions represent states in which reality is perceived. You perceive reality in three dimensions, and you have a glimpse of reality in a fourth dimension. There are many dimensions which merely represent *various capacities of consciousness*. Our guides operate within the *fifth dimension*, which is a higher rate of vibration, where pure love, unconditional acceptance and ultimate healing exists.

More about our Guides and messages

Spirit guides have many 'guises' and come from many sources. One of your guides might be a deceased relative who communicates with you in a way that you recognise, or the energy feels familiar. They could appear in dreams, bring messages and ideas directly into your mind or assist you to feel '*urges*' which guide you one way or another on the physical or spiritual path ahead. You may have an advanced soul guide, that may come from a plane where your soul once resided. In every case we will feel a sort of authority and wisdom from our guides, a knowing that they have more information than we, and are able to assist us on our earthly journey. Our spirit guides are wiser and kindly beings who have volunteered to help us on our path knowing their reward is to witness and share in our spiritual growth. They love to help us in the same way a parent would help a child. Your spirit guides have a greater understanding about your *life purpose* and will work hard to make sure you are in the right place at the right time to achieve your goals; the things you planned to do during your current lifetime on earth. Their role is a greater responsibility of *guiding and steering us, cheering us on and helping us out*. Sometimes it seems as if they literally hold our hands and lead us to where we need to go. They might arrange for '*coincidental*' meetings or help us to be in the place we are meant to be so that important life lessons can happen. They might whisper words of reassurance or help us to find the information we need to get the job done. They are wonderful and our lives would be so much harder if they weren't around. Your life path might involve the opportunity to become more patient, kind or maybe help others. (I know that this is my path) I am here to do service to help others, and I also need to learn patience. Our spirit guides will help as much as they can to ensure we get the opportunities to experience whatever we need to grow in these areas. Some more advanced earthly souls right now (maybe you), are here to help mankind. As our soul slips into our physical bodies at birth we forget '*why*' we are here and what our mission is. We don't need to worry; our guides are around and ready to '*awaken*' us when the time is right. Your mission is probably something you already feel excited about doing! People become aware of their guides in numerous ways. You might feel a sense of your guide being by your side if you feel sad or lonely.

For example: In your mind you might cry out for help and suddenly feel calm or as if someone is now holding your hand or placing a reassuring hand upon your shoulder. This might well be your guide. Another time you may be struggling for a solution to a problem, 'wish' that someone could give you some guidance and then get a strong feeling to take one path over another. You may find it works best if you ask your guide (*or guides*) if you need a little help. They are restricted by how much they can help and when they can step in but have more power to *assist* us if we tell them that they can, if we give them permission. Remember, that *their role is to help us not to do the job for us!* You don't need to use fancy words or a specific ritual. Just chat to your guide in your mind as if you were talking to a friend. I prefer to thank them before I receive help, this signifies gratitude and that I know that they will help where they are able. Either way, *always thank them*. They can use a variation of any of the signs to help you or you might feel or sense your guide assisting you with a feeling. When you feel strongly that a particular action is a bad one or a good one, you may literally feel it in your gut. Some people call this gut instinct or intuition. You could feel a fluttering of excitement (like butterflies) in your stomach to show you that you are in the right direction; or a tightening or sickness, when something is wrong for you.

The more you follow these signals the stronger they become. You and your spirit guide will work more closely together as you learn to recognise what each feeling means to you. Occasionally, their guidance might be less subtle. So maybe you can't decide which direction to drive when lost on a country road at night and one way seems brightly lit up and the other is dull; that's an easy choice.

Maybe a song comes onto the radio and the words really stand out for you. The words are just what you need to hear at that moment. You'll pick up a magazine in the doctor's surgery and when randomly flicking through you come across an article which gives you the information you were seeking. Or a friend turns up unexpectedly at the door and they can help you out.

As I said before, I don't believe in coincidence. *Everyone* that comes into your life is *there for a reason* and our lives are *mapped out to include these people and experiences.* In the same way that others come into our lives to help us, we in turn are in their lives to help them. Our guides will direct us when we are ready to meet the *'right people'* at the *'right time. I get my messages in songs, dreams and feathers, which I will also discuss in another chapter.*

Soul mates:

You'll meet *many 'soulmates'* in your lifetime. A soulmate is someone with whom you can be yourself but is not necessarily a perfect fit. A true soulmate is like a mirror, reflecting to you the aspects within yourself that are holding you back from being your true self.

> *You have crossed paths before.*
>
> *Your souls meet at the right time.*
>
> *Your quiet space is a peaceful place.*
>
> *You can hear the other person's silent thoughts.*
>
> *You feel each other's pain.*

You know each other's flaws and the benefits in them

> *You share the same life goals.*

Spiritually speaking, it is said that even before you were born, the name of your spiritual half has been determined. Each soul has a perfect match… *your soulmate*. Although most people think of a soulmate as a perfect harmonious union of bliss, your true spiritual soulmate is the person who is intended to help you "*complete yourself.*" Soul mates complete each other. A person is unable to complete his mission in life alone. Everyone needs someone to help them become a better person. This is not always a blissful experience. Often soulmates appear in disguise. You might not be physically attracted to each other when you first meet, but there is a mysterious force pushing you forward that tells you this is "*the right one*" for you. Being quiet together is comforting like a fluffy blanket on a cold winter night. Whether you are reading in the same room, or driving in the car, there's a quiet peace between you. You feel each other's feelings: sadness, worry, and stress. And you share each other's happiness and joy. We have more than one kind of soulmate. A soulmate is someone that your *soul recognises or resonates with*. There are different types of soulmates that we come across in our life and each one plays an important role in our personal, emotional and spiritual growth. Some stay with us forever, while others leave more quickly than me may want them to. What some of us struggle with is feeling that deep, soulful connection with another person and then having to go through the process of accepting that their purpose in our lives has been served and it's time to let them go. This is why people may have more than one partner in their lives.

Once we have achieved the reason that we have been together, we will move on to the next person that is meant to be in our lives for the next step on our soul journey.

Friendship soulmates: Sometimes we meet a person and just 'click' from the moment we lay eyes on each other. It's as if we've known them our entire life, even if we've only known them a few minutes. You tell each other everything. You could talk to this person for hours on end and never get bored. You share everything about yourself, and they don't judge you. These types of soulmates actually know you better than you know yourself, which is why they are extremely important in your life. My friend, Marion is one such soulmate. They "get you" in ways nobody else does and help you navigate your way through all of life's trials and triumphs. The friendship soulmate is a gift and one you should treasure your entire life. Because they are here to stay! Then there is the soulmate that comes into our life to shake things up. They challenge us and make us question everything we thought we knew about life. There is a clear "before them" and "after them" distinction when we look back on our lives and realize that we are now a completely different person than the day we met them. This type of soulmate can come in many forms but it's normally a romantic relationship that leaves us feeling as if we've been swept up like a tornado, taken for the ride of our life, and then dumped from the sky with no warning in a heap. Despite feeling like we don't know what the hell happened since the ride was so fun when it first started, the beauty of this type of soulmate is that like a tornado hitting and leaving mass wreckage behind, we're forced to rebuild from the ground up and can now make the changes that we want/ need. This is showing that we don't always stay with the partner that we began with. *Each soulmate is in our lives for the time that it is necessary for the important lessons that we need.* Even when it is time to move on, we may be able to stay on good terms with the other person. When this happens, we can acknowledge how much we have learned from each other, and the 'soulmate' relationship lasts.

The divine Love soulmate: that everyone wishes to have are the ones that remain with us for the rest of our days on earth. You will experience the familiarity, the feeling of having known them for an entire lifetime moments after meeting them. The intense bond never goes away, the deep friendship and the extraordinary, deep-seated love.

Why we have difficult people in our lives

The people we term as difficult, or challenging, have specific and valuable lessons to teach us. So, one of the great on-going questions for anyone who wants to live an authentic spiritual life without going into a cave is this: how do you deal with difficult people without being harsh, or putting them out of your heart? How can you explain to your friend who keeps drawing you into their own dramas, that you are drained from the negativity, but remain friends? How do you handle the boss whose tantrums terrorize the whole office, or situations that

keep popping up time and time again to drain you? Should we chalk this up to Karma or are the things that we don't like about them reflections of our own disowned or shadow tendencies. Parts of us that were in previous incarnations. [The process of incarnation is unique to every soul]. Either way, the next time that someone does something that annoys or infuriates you, force yourself to pause for a few seconds and place your attention on your breathing. Then go ahead and respond from a calmer place. The thing *not to do* is react with anger in that moment. When you do this, you are exiting the present moment and handing control over to your ego. Remember, things said in anger cannot be undone. This was a lesson that I have had to learn myself as I have responded negatively on many occasions in the past. Now I *try* to pause, stand back and weigh up the situation before I react. The same lessons will crop up time and time again, until you learn to change the way you deal with negativity and also realise why you are experiencing the same challenges over and over. If we don't pay attention in class, or 'bunk' off, and fail the tests, we'll keep having the lesson put in front of us until we learn the lesson and pass the exam. The *'tests'* are those *situations where you have the opportunity to do the right thing by yourself. Where you have the opportunity to make a different choice or continue to do the same thing (or variances of it) and expect a different result.* If you keep finding yourself in the same situation again and again, ask yourself *"What am I supposed to be learning from this?"*. Over time we do evolve and change, but we must personally adapt and take charge of your own life. As we gain in spiritual development it becomes possible to recall some aspects of our previous lives. For example, if you have an "unknown" magnetic pull for a particular country, such as Egypt, there is a good chance that you had an incarnation previously in Egypt. This could well be the explanation of why someone would undergo sexual or gender transgender operations. A woman in a previous life who does not *"feel right"* in a new man's body, or vice versa, might wish to regain a previous gender body. Even though you chose this body before you incarnated, you have the choice of free will to make any changes. Those who have a special talent in a particular field is probably the result of having acquired such a talent in a previous life. In each reincarnation we rotate between the sexes, human relationships, and various civilizations and locations. We each literally create our own lives and lifestyles by the choices and decisions we made before incarnation. Every decision has a consequence according to the Law of cause and effect. Or "*Whatsoever ye sow so shall ye reap.*" To become totally responsible for oneself, and to consciously and deliberately choose our every thought, our every emotion, our every action, requires many lifetimes of experience. I know of five of my previous incarnations which I will explain in another chapter.

Surroundings in the spirit world and what happens there

So, as I mentioned earlier the spirit world is comprised of various levels of *consciousness and states of vibration*. As we move along the spirit world, we pass through these various stages. There are even varying levels of vibration within each of the afterlife stages. In fact, we experience a sort of death, as we proceed from one level to another. I mentioned the Astral plane, where we spend a good time assessing our most recent earthly life. Here we go through a sort of life review where we are confronted with either what we have achieved, the positive and the negative actions. Free will is inherent to all spirit and we experience transformation only to the degree that we are willing to confront and change. Our guides are with us here and many helpers to inspire us along the pathway of spiritual healing and transformation. Changes only come about through our *own desire to change* and our willingness to work through that that needs to be changed. So really it is better that we should endeavour to make the changes now, while on the Earth plane. People ask, "*where is the spirit world?*". *It is right here, where we are.* We do not have to travel to get there. It is not separated by distance, as we perceive distance. What separates the Earth plane from the spirit world is *dimension*. It is through the doorway of *consciousness and dimension* that the spirit must pass in order to enter the spirit world. That is the doorway that we will pass through (some call it the veil) at the time of our death. The spirit world exists in a *higher rate of vibration* than does our three-dimensional Earth plane. From time to time, people experience a heightened or extended sense of perception, and they catch a glimpse of this amazing world. Some people have outer body experiences where the spirit or consciousness separates itself from the confines of the body and brain, thus becoming free to experience other planes of existence. If you have ever felt that you have been visited by a departed loved one in a dream, *then you have.* We do not have to die to visit the spirit realms. Some visit in dreams, while others meditate. I realise that I have gone over a few things on more than one occasion, but I am just highlighting things that I feel I need to clarify within each chapter.

What happens in the spirit world?

In spirit we do not go to jobs, we do not have to earn money, or worry about mortgages and food. These are aspects of Earthly life. Whatever motivates us on earth, motivates us in spirit. Death allows us to shed the *solid earthly body* and move through the doorway/veil. We do not become all knowing or perfect. We remain the same person as on the earth plane. Death does not automatically remove problems and all ignorance. We seek to communicate with our loved ones. We will meet our already departed loved ones, and there is a grand re-union of sorts. People who suffer long term illness will often see their deceased loved ones before they pass over and it gives them joy to know that they will be waiting to help them to pass when their time comes. A person that has suffered a long illness, will rest on the other side until they are ready to assess the recent Earth life. As I mentioned earlier, we view our successes and failures, and we do so with unclouded vision. There are special spirit helpers to assist us. Some memories can be very painful. These helpers *do not judge us* and there is always love and guidance even for the poor unfortunate souls that may have led an evil life. There are halls of learning in spirit where we are given the opportunity to learn and become wise souls. Like on earth the spirit world has halls in which knowledge can be obtained and like our schools and universities we would visit these to expand our understanding of life and how to move forward on our journey. Anything and everything can be learned in these Halls. We are also helped in our healing process. Eventually we move to higher planes/frequencies which takes us further away from the dense Earth plane. We can always draw back closer to earthly conditions in order to communicate with our loved ones, and so we are never separated. This is where a medium is used to help with communication. As a soul in the spirit world, we choose what is needed for our spiritual growth. Thoughts are transmitted to communicate with each other. Thoughts instantaneously react to whatever we wish to project. So, if we think of someone, we will instantly see them. Wherever we wish to be... *we are*. We are able to live in houses of *thought forms*, or on a grassy hill slope, whatever we desire, however these are not necessary because we can be wherever we *think* we want to be. Some souls may feel comforted by feeling as they have the comforts

that they had in a physical form. Little by little
we adjust to the spirit form. Some are known as
Earth bound spirits. These are the spirits of
people who have passed over but for various
reasons cannot accept that they have passed and
so they do not move forward into the spiritual
life. They are locked into the vibration of the
Earth Plane *until* they finally see the light and
move forward. If a person whilst on earth has
committee horrendous sins against another (*this
being the only true sin*) then the soul will lie
fallow for a long time, unless it so beset on evil
that it returns to trouble those left behind. *This is
what we on Earth term as a haunting.*
Sometimes the soul does not realise that it has
passed over and so hovers around the earth
plane. He will wonder why no-one can see him
or pay any attention to him. Others who pass
over suddenly, feel great shock on learning that
they are in the spirit world. On the astral plane,
the soul with the greatest amount of materiality,
and coarsest nature, is stopped by the screen of a
certain grade or plane and cannot pass on to the
higher ones; while one which has passed on to
the higher planes, having cast off more
confining sheaths, can easily pass backward and
forward among the lower planes, if it so desires.
Souls often do so, for the purpose of visiting
friends on the lower planes and giving them
comfort, and in the case of a highly developed
soul, spiritual help may be given in this way.

The plane of *soul slumber* is sacred to the souls occupying it, and it is of a nature which is a distinct and separate state than the great series of astral plane, and sub-planes. Only the pure and exulted souls who have gained a high degree of evolution may visit this plane.

To try to explain a plane in simple terms: A plane is a level of *existence, thought or development*.

PHYSICAL PLANE/EARTH PLANE: The Physical Plane refers to the visible reality of space and time, energy and matter: this is the lowest or densest of a series of planes of existence. These descriptions may simplify the planes of vibration to you. We are all familiar with our *dense physical body*, but we also have subtle bodies, collectively called the '*aura*', which surrounds the physical body. Both are made of *energy* but *vibrate at very different frequencies*, so the physical appears solid and the subtle are invisible to normal sight.

ASTRAL PLANE: The astral plane, also known as the emotional plane, is where consciousness goes after physical death. The astral plane can be visited consciously through astral projection, meditation, near-death experience. This is the first plane that we go to after death. The Astral plane is almost a duplicate of the physical world.

MENTAL PLANE: The mental plane, also known as the causal plane, is the third lowest plane. The mental plane, as its name implies, is that which belongs to consciousness working as thought; not of the mind as it works through the brain. All of the planes are working on a different frequency.

ETHERIC PLANE: This is where the ascended masters and other 'light' beings reside.

COSMIC PLANE: Archangels and cosmic beings reside here.

ETERNAL PLANE: Ultimate and Absolute truth.

THE SUBTLE BODY AND THE SOUL:

Try this simple exercise and feel your subtle body:

Gently rub your palms together. Now hold your hands with palms facing each other. Slowly move the palms apart and bring them back towards each other. At some point, you may notice a slight resistance or change in temperature between your palms. What you are feeling is your subtle body or your aura. Everything that happens in the physical body first happens in the subtle body. Spiritual energy flows from the subtle to the physical. We are energetic beings, running off the fuel of this energy. Energy being that which gives us life and consciousness, which allows us to move and do. Right now, your '*Soul*' is in your body. It is full of infinite knowledge and infinite vision. But our human selves are unaware of our true identities. Who you are now is just as important as who you once were and who you will be? Experiences from different lifetimes intertwine to bring new levels of understanding to our higher beings. Sometimes, those experiences crossover and create problems with different lives. As our soul progresses lifetime after lifetime, we lose the memories of who we once were. So, owing to the not knowing, we mistakenly believe the body, or the name given to body, as our 'Self'. Once you realise that you have chosen this life and the experiences that go hand in hand with your journey it becomes easier to steer your life in the right direction. Blaming others for where your life is will get you nowhere – if anything, it will make you feel stuck. *Every journey comes with obstacles*. Your fears, phobias, anxieties, and other emotional states have their origins in past-life events. (Explained in a later chapter) It's so crucial to understanding other people's feelings, their intentions, as well as beliefs. It's an invaluable social skill, and it will help you on your journey towards reaching all your goals. You just need a clear and open mind, *one without prejudice*, and you will be able to put yourself in someone else's skin.

To re-cap on your life's journey:

"I realise that I have already talked about our life journey, but I feel that it is good to bring this back to focus every now and then, where I feel it is necessary to understand what I am trying to explain".When your soul decides it is ready to return to the earth plain, it meets with guides, some of whom have been with them for many lifetimes and some new guides as well. The other group is a council of our elders or master teachers, who help with the process of achieving what our new lessons will be in this earthly time, and how to assist the soul with its return to the earth plain. We go through the process of looking where our soul could grow and the experiences necessary for our soul's growth. Past-life karma is looked at and evaluated on many levels. Your soul wants to experience many different scenarios with families, economic conditions from poor to rich or vice versa, social status, spiritual and individuals' beliefs. Your soul goes through many lifetimes in the hope of spiritual and soul growth. Your soul's evolution is looked at, and the planning starts. Figuring out the needs for growth, your guides, teachers and you will look at many scenarios and choose the one that will fit you best. It's like watching many movies and choosing the one you want to be in. It is just a reminder for you to realise that our journey in life is of our own making, and so we need to take responsibility for it. Stepping up and taking responsibility for what is going on in your own life, is one of the most important things that you will ever do, and one of the best. As you now know, once you own what is going on in your own life you can begin to shape your future. Other people's factors do have an impact on our lives, but we are responsible for our own decisions. Being accountable for your actions, is crucial to having good relationships with others. Try to stop running away from problems and challenges that are presented to you and think of it as part of the contract that you signed to balance your Karmic debt. It sounds like I am continually harping on about Karmic debts, but in fact when you can shift your thoughts to understanding that challenges and people that affect your life are there for a reason, you can shift your thought pattern and make life easier to understand, and deal with. Much like blaming other people, stop making excuses, as this is shrinking from your responsibilities. Your life may seem stuck in some ways, but if all you ever do is complain about it, nothing much will change. Look at the reasons for your life is not going as you would like it and address the situations. Once again, I say, try to remember that everything in your life is a plan. You can accept this plan and work with it, or you can get off 'the train' and wander about aimlessly. You will 'get lost' within yourself and lose direction. Remember, life isn't meant to be easy, YOU have chosen the challenges that your soul needs. If you can't take this on board, then you may go through life continually struggling with your emotions. It's not that most people sit around all day pointing out the negative in life, most of us may even actively seek to notice and talk about everything we must be *thankful* for in life. We may even frequently share special moments with loved ones, follow our passions in life, write about gratitude in a journal, or engage in other positive activities. But we can still find ourselves complaining more than we need to—and more than is healthy. Most of us do need to vent frustrations from time to time and, hopefully, this is done in the context of finding solutions. It is important to deal with all feelings and try to find a balance. We should talk to loved ones about feelings, both positive and negative. Maybe we could seek the opinions of those we trust when facing difficult choices or situations. And this can be positive, but it can also often involve sharing stories about problems. Sometimes that slips into excessive complaining or gossip—and that can be a slippery slope. Believe me, I have been in situations where I have moaned about the situation and felt cross with certain outcomes that have been a product of the situation. I haven't always make the right choices, and I have struggled to cope with problems that have been presented to me. However, Once the light switched on inside my head, and I began to look at '*what*' I was experiencing through these challenges, and '*accepted*' that each challenge was a lesson that my soul needs to experience. I know see '*why*' certain people present challenges and '*how*' I can deal with more understanding. I will include some questions and answers on all subjects throughout this book. Please see the lists in the back of the book.

MAKING CONNECTION WITH OUR LOVED ONES IN THE SPIRIT REALMS

All too often, people think that you have to be religious, and that communication can only happen through prayer. This is not the case. Firstly, *spiritualism is not a religion*, it is a way of life. You don't have to pray, just open your heart. We can make connection by simply just thinking about our loved ones. *Spirit energy connects with our thoughts.* When a loved one passes, we naturally go through the grieving process. We can often cry out for contact with the departed and put all of our emotional energy into doing that. If we do not get a sign from them that they are around, right away, we can become negative in our thoughts and depression can take over which will cause a blockage of our energies. It is not always possible for our loved ones to make contact with us right away. Sometimes they have passed traumatically or have been ill for a very long time. They then need to rest before they can learn to work with the energy vibration that is necessary for contact. As I have said previously, when they are ready and able, they can visit us in our dream-state, or connect with thought. As well as our loved ones, there are helper guides and our angels that guide us and watch over us. They can help heal in our darker times. We must give them permission to help and so this is why we 'cry out' for help sometimes when we are in a negative place. They can help us to feel more grounded if we give them authorisation to do so.

Meditation

Through meditation, you can connect with the higher frequencies/energies thus allowing our loved ones and guides to connect with us. A meditation practice can improve our ability to regulate emotions, let things go, and raise our vibration at the same time. How do you learn to meditate? In mindfulness meditation, we're learning how to pay attention to the breath as it goes in and out. When we pay attention to our breath, we are learning how to return to, and remain in, the present moment.

1) Take a seat

Find place to sit that feels calm and quiet to you.

2) Set a time limit
If you're just beginning, it can help to choose a short time, such as five or 10 minutes.

3) Notice your body
Sit in an upright position with your feet on the floor. I prefer to be barefoot as I feel more grounded.

4) Feel your breath
Follow the sensation of your breath as it goes in and as it goes out.

5) Notice when your mind has wandered
Inevitably, your attention will leave the breath and wander to other places. When you get around to noticing that your mind has wandered—in a few seconds, a minute, five minutes—simply return your attention to the breath.

6) Be kind to your wandering mind
Don't judge yourself or obsess over the content of the thoughts you find yourself lost in. Just come back.

7) Close with kindness and give thanks
When you're ready, gently open your eyes. Take a moment to notice how your body feels right now. Notice your thoughts and emotions. I make a point of saying thank you, guides and the highest truth for connecting with me and for revealing solutions to problems.

When you have mastered the art of meditation and want to connect with your guides and loved ones, always ask for only *truth and light* to connect with you. The second step in connecting to your spirit guides is to listen. As I mentioned above, when you meditate, you quiet your mind so that you can hear the wisdom of the guidance that's within you and around you. Everything created is energy, and energy vibrates at different levels. Just as a singer has a vocal range of notes that she can sing, human beings have a vibrational range. In other words, you move up and down a vibrational scale. The more you work on loving yourself, *the higher your vibration rises*, and the easier it is to connect with the higher vibrational beings. we all possess the ability to reach the highest level through appreciation, forgiveness, joy, mediation, and love. You might be wondering why you need to raise your vibration. Energy attracts like energy; The more you stay in a higher, lighter, clearer vibration, the more you will be able to connect with the spiritual realm. While we are able to raise our vibration temporarily in order to communicate with those on the higher planes, we aren't able to sustain this permanently and must '*come back down*' after a while. The only way to ascend to a permanently higher vibration is through death. It can be difficult for our loved ones in the spirit realms to lower their vibrations to fit ours until they have mastered it and have gained more knowledge and maybe reached a higher plane, and so our Guides usually relay the messages. To show gratitude for the connection, you can say in your mind: *"Thank you, guides of the highest truth and compassion".*

Or "truth and light". "Thank you for showing me what I need to know".

"Thank you for leading me in the right direction". "Thank you for whatever it is that I need."

When you connect, you may get thoughts or pictures in your mind (*this is what is known as the third eye*). Some of you may hear spirit. When you pay attention to the guidance you receive, you're letting yourself be in the awe and wonder of all the love that is around you. This beautiful feeling is available when you truly let yourself connect. *The feeling of love is all encompassing.* Your guides are loving and wise, and they want to offer you guidance. As humans we often try to control situations. In the past I've obsessed over how I have wanted things to go and have tried to manipulate outcomes to get what I thought would be the best outcome. Now I realise that *if you must manipulate a situation and fight for it to be as you think it should, then it is not the right path.* If, and when things *are meant to be*, you will notice, that things fall into place without you having to try. You will find yourself in the *right place*, at the *right time* and with the *right people*. I like to think of it like a jigsaw, every piece must fit into place before it can be complete. We cannot force pieces into any space, *they must fit*. Another thing to do when you ask your guides for help, is *trust*. Believe in what you are receiving. The more you trust, the more you will receive. Loved ones or family members who've passed on may choose to be one of your spirit guides and actively support you by helping you in very practical ways, like sending you the thoughts that will push you onto the next step of your journey. One of your grandmothers could be an important spirit guide for you, whether you knew her well in life or not. In fact, any human who has passed on might become a spirit guide for you. If you're a dancer, you could have a spirit guide on your team who was once a dancer and performer too and now want to help guide and inspire you as an artist. Spirit guides will often enter your life by sending you *signs*, also called *synchronicities*. Carl Jung defined *synchronicity* as "a meaningful coincidence." An example would be realizing you need to improve your romantic relationship after having a fight with your partner before bedtime, and out of the blue the next day you notice a book about communication in romantic relationships sitting on a co-worker's desk. Spirit guides also like to communicate with you through numbers or number sequences like 11:11, or you might have a lucky number, and when you go for a job interview, your lucky number is in the company's address. Spirit guides can talk to you by sending *musical messages*, like a song that always inspires you playing on the radio when you get in the car. Or you may wake with a piece of music that is playing in your head. Sometimes you will get a small part of the music that will keep playing over and over. Until you realise what the words are and the message it relays, it won't go away, and you will keep humming it to yourself throughout the day. They might send you a *dream* that gives you an idea about how to handle a situation, or a guide could even appear to you in a dream. Or they send helpful people and opportunities your way. They will often give you cryptic messages. You will see 'something' that stands out and will give you that a-aha! moment. Part of getting more guidance from your spirit guides is *recognizing the messages they are already sending*. Many times, the messages our guides send are lost on us because our lives are too busy or our minds are too busy. This is where meditation helps because it slows your mind and leaves space for communication. When you're frustrated about a situation, confused about the best next step, or feeling that you don't have enough control, surrender an issue over to your guides. Even if it's just to give yourself a little break. This can allow fresh insights to come to you as well as let your guides have more freedom to do their thing and help.

Clairaudience: You can *hear* gentle voices in your mind *Clairvoyance*: You *see* guidance as images in your mind C*lair cognizance*: *know* guidance as breakthrough thoughts or mental downloads *Clairsentience: feel* guidance as energy, emotions, or physical sensations.

Proof of communication and spirit connections

When I began my spiritual journey, I kept a journal and wrote everything down. Any feelings, thoughts or sensations. I would ask questions and keep a note of them. I also recorded messages that I received from my fellow 'mediums' in a journal. Week by week, we would sit together at the same time and the same day, and we would all channel together to lift the vibrations, thus allowing our guides to connect with us. It will happen when you are ready to receive and not necessarily when you want it to happen. The more intuitive you get, the more you open and the clearer the information will come to you. I have had so many inspiring messages and connections for myself, and others. I always tell people to ask for their own proof that our loved ones communicate with us. My partner listens to me and shows a kind of interest in what I believe, but until recently had not asked or even felt the need for proof. We had been having a conversation about his deceased parents and I suggested that he 'asked' in his mind for proof that they were around him still. He did this, and the *very next day* he was having his lunch up at his allotment. Two very rare birds flew down and sat right beside him. The following day the same two birds flew down and did the same. Not only were the birds rare, but my partner and his father bred birds together. Mike accepted this as his proof that both of his parents had sent him a message by sending the birds. Now months later, he has not seen those particular birds again. As a medium, I hope to bring comfort to others by bringing proof of their loved ones through messages. I love and absolutely believe in the messages, and it is a privilege to help people to come to terms with their loss. I ask spirit to communicate and give me something for the sitter that no one else could possibly know. Also, I ask if they can give a little insight into something to help direct them. Or information concerning their past, present or that insight which could include obstacles that they may have to encounter. Spirit will *never* tell you what to, but they can give you the insight and support, helping you to make up your own mind. You don't necessarily need a medium to channel, you can learn to tap into your intuition by silently asking your guides for help when you need it. Either just ask or meditate. You then need to be able to open your mind and heart to receiving the signs. So, how do you know whether something is truly a sign? There is no definitive answer to that. *You must use your intuition.* If you think you have received a sign but aren't confident that it is one, continue to ask and meditate. Ask for more help, more signs, more assurance, and see what happens. One sign can be through electricity. Spirits are energy currents, so it is easy for them to manipulate electricity and cause mobile phones, televisions, computers, and lights to flicker. Of cause, when a lightbulb burns out, it can simply mean the lightbulb was old. But if you are sitting on the edge of your bed looking at a photo album, reminiscing about a grandma who has passed, and a light pops off, I would bet it's her letting you know she's there. All spirits are different, and spirits' methods of communicating with you may vary greatly. Nature is another way. They can manipulate nature and your awareness to get your attention. Some people may be thinking of their mother for instance and have a butterfly or a robin come close. Spirit are able to manipulate the energy of the butterfly or robin to get your attention.

Angels will send us small signs and signals to let us know that they are near and will always be there to love and support us. These signs can be anything from a subtle flash of light, a rainbow on a gloomy day, or even an unexpected, sudden feeling of love and warmth within you. One of the ultimate signs your Angels are with you is finding a feather. Coming across a feather in your path or finding a feather in an unexpected place. The spirit world is naturally a higher vibration that we are in the physical world. Spirit love to connect with the vibration of music. How many times have you been missing your loved one, only to hear their favourite song or a song that connects you to them throughout the day? Since spirits don't have a physical voice, they like for us to focus on the lyrics. As I mentioned earlier, you may just have a few words of the song in your head, and they keep repeating until you realise what the words are saying to you. Some people might argue that these types of signs are nothing more than coincidences. I understand and respect that opinion but do not agree. I do not believe in coincidences. I believe that everything in the universe happens for a specific reason and that such synchronicity is often triggered by spirits. If you are open to that belief, the spirits will be open to giving you the signs and guidance you seek. These will enlighten you to a new way of living and thinking and will empower you to build your own communication system with the spirits. If your mind is closed to the spirits, they will likely recognize your attitude over time and will respect that you do not wish to communicate. I have had many messages that have answered my questions and have brought comfort when I have needed it. I will list some of my meaningful dreams, music and feather messages throughout the chapters.

Negative Energies and protection

A spirit is a person who is not now in a material body, i.e. the body we have on the Earth Plane.

While we have our loving spirit energies, there are also negative energies that still hang around. Negativity is toxic to your entire system, so clearing negative energy is an important strategy on your journey of holistic well-being. Negativity can make you feel heavy, dark, and gloomy. You may feel emotionally reactive and defensive and view the world through a mixed filter of fear, anger, and paranoia. As I have explained earlier, some people pass over that remain with a lower form of energy based on fear, doubt, shame of anger. Remember, energy attracts the same energy and so if we are in a negative mindset, we attract negative energy to us. The negative energy spirits can attach their energy to ours. Be it accomplishing some unfulfilled tasks or taking revenge from someone, these negative energy spirits are always looking for an opportunity to work through our energy, and 'live' through us. They often will not accept that they have passed over. We need to be careful not to attract these spirits (some like to call ghosts) into our lives. Some people are curious and think it is fun to play with a Ouija board. This is simply dabbling with the occult and without protection it is easy to attract trouble. *Negative energies feed off negative energies.* I learned this for myself in my teenage years, and it can be a very frightening experience. Perhaps one of the most popular terms most of us have heard when it comes to ghosts, is the word *poltergeist* which means "noisy ghost" because it is said to have the ability to move or knock things over, make noise and manipulate the physical environment. Loud knocking sounds, lights turning on and off, doors slamming, even fires breaking out mysteriously have all been attributed to the type of a spiritual disturbance that the poltergeist energy emits. Another frightening aspect of the poltergeist is that the event usually starts out slowly and mildly, then begins to intensify. And while many times poltergeist activity is harmless and ends quickly, they have been known to become dangerous. Some experts explain it as a mass form of energy that a living person is controlling unknowingly. *Emotional stress and negative emotions can attract the negative spirit.* Your home should be your safe haven — the place where you feel relaxed, happy, and at peace. But when bad energy is lingering around, your home can quickly become the complete opposite — a place of hostility and negativity. And when you have this negative energy in your home, it can affect every other aspect of your life. That's why house cleansing can be an important part in your personal well-being.

Excessive complaining: If you or your family members catch yourselves complaining, even when things are okay (or worse, when they're actually pretty good), you may have negative energy in your home. The same can be said, that by excessive complaining you will draw negative influences. The same is true if you're struggling to find positivity in life.

Negative relationships: When the people around you – spouses, children, family, and friends – are negative, it's worth looking at the kind of energy you're putting out there. *Negative energy attracts more negative energy, and it becomes a vicious cycle.*

The blame game: Household members always pointing the finger? Negative energy in the home could be preventing them (and you) from looking inward to place responsibility where it really belongs.

Criticism: If there's a lot of criticizing going along with all the blame, your home could be swamped with bad energy. When you or others in your house send out negative vibrations, you're increasing the bad energy in your home.

Clutter: One of the biggest ways of creating negative energy in a home is clutter. Clutter blocks the way energy flows through a home, so it could be keeping bad energy in and making things worse. De-clutter your house, open all your windows and let in as much light and fresh air as you can while cleaning. Don't forget to dust, vacuum, and check for cobwebs – you don't want the negative energy to have any reason to stick around. As you clean your home, know that keeping broken items in your house is bad feng-shui – and items that don't bring you joy can only drag you down. If you have an item that's irreparably broken, it's time to get rid of it and move on.

When you've cleared away the clutter and removed broken items from your home, you can finish removing negative energies with smudging. The ancient Native American technique of *smudging* can help remove bad energy in your home. The Native Americans used it for millennia because they knew it worked – and fortunately, the same materials they used are readily available in health food stores and online.

Burning *sage* – particularly white sage – is a simple and fast way to clear out bad spirits and negative energy. Add *frankincense* or *patchouli*, or other herbs recommended for house cleansing. Follow this step-by-step guide to smudge your home with sage (or other herbs)

Stand in the centre or at the front door of the room you want to cleanse. Most people begin in the kitchen, as it's the heart of the home. Light the sage bundle like you'd light incense, and let the flames die out (they will, very quickly). Fan the sage carefully to encourage a steady stream of smoke. Visualise the smoke absorbing bad energy and carrying it away. Cleanse yourself first by lightly fanning the smoke around your body, beginning at your feet and working up toward your head. Walk clockwise around the room, swirling the sage bundle in circular motions. Pay special attention to the walls, corners and floor, and don't forget the ceiling. This process will help manifest positive energy in your home. Your home should bring you joy and be a source of positivity. Negative thoughts in the form of jealousy, criticizing others, being quarrelsome, and more should be avoided, as negative energy attracts more negative energies. To remove negative energies within the body it is good to know how to cleanse your chakras. Chakras are the energy centres within the body. They allow energy to flow through the aura and the nervous system. I will explain more about the chakras in the '*Opening up*' section.

More about Spirit Guides and protection

As I mentioned earlier, some spirit guides have been with you for your entire life, even since before you were born. Others came on your team as you needed them at different times in your life. Your particular 'spiritual guidance squad' the team of spirit guides assigned to you, could include any or all of the following:

Archangels

Archangels are leaders in the angel world and have a powerful, very large energy signature. *If you're an empath* or are sensitive to energy, when you call on an archangel you might feel an energy shift in the room. Each archangel has a speciality, like Archangel Raphael's speciality of healing, and can work with countless humans at once.

Guardian angels

Guardian angels are yours exclusively, and we each have more than one! *Guardian angels* have devoted their lives to helping just you. Call on them anytime for immediate assistance. They love you unconditionally, forever. Remember that angels are non-denominational and work with people of all faiths and spiritual beliefs.

Ascended masters

Ascended masters like Buddha were once human, living journeys of deep spiritual growth and influence. Now they have a special place as leaders in the spirit world and as guides/teachers to us humans.

Highly Evolved Spirits

The level of love that a spirit has within themselves is how they are viewed in the world of spirit. A highly evolved spirit is one who has removed most of the negative energy from themselves, so anger or judgement of others is not part of their personality.

Departed loved ones

Loved ones or family members who've passed on may choose to be one of your spirit guides and actively support you by helping you in very practical ways, like giving insight into where you should be on your journey. They can manipulate your thoughts to put you on the pathway that you are meant to be following. They can orchestrate meetings that are needed for you to meet the people that you need to meet along the way. One of your grandmothers could be an important spirit guide for you, whether you knew her well in life or not. In fact, any human who has passed on might become a spirit guide for you. If you're a dancer, you could have a spirit guide on your team who was once a dancer and performer too and now wants to help guide and inspire you as an artist.

Helper angels

Helper angels are "freelance angels," so to speak, who are just looking for humans to help with specific situations, like finding new friends.

Stay on the lookout every day for signs from your guides.

The more you watch for signs from your guides, the more you'll recognize the signs they send. I find feathers in specific places, and often, repetitive sequences of numbers.

In numerology, angel numbers are a repetitive sequence of three or four numbers that appear in seemingly random places in your life to convey a spiritual message.

One of my favourites that appears many times is 11:11. I often see it when I get into my car and turn on the ignition. Someone might phone me at 11:11 or I have telephoned them or even a text message and realised that the time was 11:11. The one that amazed me most was when I purchased a few cards and birthday/Christmas paper. My bill came to £11.11! I will explain the significance of this number and others that have meaning for me later. As your guides sense you are more aware of them and their helpful messages, they will send more. Remind yourself on your commute to work or while you're showering in the morning that every day your guides are sending you messages. If you're trying to make a major decision, or you're going through big changes or challenges, expect the guidance coming at you to increase to help you navigate this situation. You may also get messages from your angels and loved ones in dreams. I will write a chapter on this later in the book.

Archangels

Archangel Michael is the angel of protection and the most powerful of all the angels. He is considered a leader within the angelic realm and a patron angel of righteousness, mercy and justice. As such, scriptural artwork depicts him as a warrior most often carrying a sword. Archangel Michael assists situations where you are afraid, confused or concerned for your safety. He helps to release fear and doubt and supports us in making life changes and is often said to work closely with those who perform healing work or provide spiritual teaching.

Archangel Raphael is the archangel designated for physical and emotional healing. Archangel Raphael not only helps in healing individuals but also helps healers in their healing practice.

He can help reduce addictions and cravings and is powerful in healing other injuries and illnesses, with cures often occurring immediately. Archangel Raphael aids in restoring and maintaining harmony and peace. He is also the patron of travellers, watching over them to ensure a safe and harmonious journey. Working in conjunction with Archangel Michael, Archangel Raphael helps to clear away fears and stressors that maybe adversely affecting your health.

Archangel Gabriel is One of the two archangels specifically named in the Bible in both the Old and New Testament, she is often portrayed holding a trumpet. As the patron of communications, Archangel Gabriel is the messenger angel. She helps writers, teachers, journalists and artists to convey their message, to find motivation and confidence, and to market their skills. She also assists in overcoming issues of fear and procrastination in communication as well as in all areas related to children, helping during conception, pregnancy, childbirth and child rearing.

Archangel Jophiel helps us to see and maintain beauty in life and supports us in thinking beautiful thoughts and in staying positive as well as in creating and manifesting beauty in our surroundings and hearts.

Archangel Ariel's role is to protect the earth, its natural resources, ecosystems and all wildlife and is always available with support and guidance for any activities that involve healing, rejuvenating, and/or maintaining our environment. Archangel Ariel assists in healing injured animals working closely with Archangel Raphael in these endeavours. It is believed she also works to oversee the order of the physical universe including all planets, the sun, and the stars.

Archangel Azrael is often referred to as the 'Angel of Death'. Azrael meets souls and helps them in the transition of death, in addition to helping newly crossed over souls adjust. He also helps loved ones who are still on the earth plane in dealing with their grief and processing the loss. Archangel Azrael helps ministers and spiritual teachers from all belief systems and religions in their spiritual counselling and assists grief counsellors to shield themselves from absorbing their clients' pain and to guide their words and actions. This archangel assists in all types of transitions and endings, not just those involving loss and death. He also helps with transitions related to relationships, career, addictions, etc., helping us to navigate as smoothly as possible through life's changes.

Archangel Chamuel has been called by many names throughout history and therefore is sometimes confused with other angels. His mission is to bring peace to the world and as such he protects the world from fear and lowers vibrating, negative energies. He is believed to have all knowing vision seeing the interconnectedness between all things. Archangel Chamuel assists us in finding the strength and courage to face adversity when it seems we have none left. He can also help to find items that are lost, to find important parts of our lives such as life purpose, a love relationship, a new job, and supportive friendships, and to find solutions to problems. Lastly, Archangel Chamuel also helps to heal anxiety, bring peace, and to repair relationships and misunderstandings. Angels are a fascinating aspect of our history as a culture. Whether you believe in angels or are a sceptic, your archangel can assist you whenever you call on them. Angels are extensions of the highest source (some people term this as *God*) whatever you term as your *God*. These Angels understand your life's mission and want to help you to accomplish it. Many have found connecting with an archangel who specializes in the area of their life where they would like to see improvement has accelerated positive progress and changes. I have called upon these angel guides from time to time to ask for their assistance. They can even help with the smallest of asks. One time, my son, Christopher and his family were coming to visit me, and Christopher phoned to say they weren't sure if they would make it as they had mislaid the car keys and had Looked everywhere! We were all disappointed at this thought. He asked me if I could '*tune in*' as he called it and ask for help. This I did, and I had the words '*sponge and water*' come into my head. I called back and told him this, and they found the keys which had fallen into the sink and had been covered up by a sponge! This is just a simple 'ask', but if you ask for help, listen and trust that help will be given, I can assure you it will be in whatever way it can be transmitted to you.

Who or What is God?

It is the idea that the universe began by exploding suddenly out of an ultra-dense singularity smaller than an atom. From this speck emerged all the matter, energy and empty space that the universe would ever contain, and all that raw material evolved into the cosmos we perceive today by following a strict set of scientific laws. Stephen Hawking and many like-minded scientists, have combined laws of gravity, relativity, quantum physics and a few other rules that could explain everything that ever happened or ever will happen in our known universe. The universe itself is a mind-boggling vastness and complexity. "*Who or what is God?*" *God* is the *cumulative consciousness of the universe* and the integrated Quantum energy. I understand *God* to be *everything that we can see, feel and touch.* So, I personally see *God* as the divine consciousness in the universe and not as an actual person. Say, you and your partner are bound by the energy of love, then *Love is your God.* A group of people are collaborating and are in perfect harmony by following a set of beliefs and rituals called religion, then these rituals and beliefs are their *God.* If you are dying and someone gives you a piece of bread, he/she is your *God.* If a constitution binds an entire country, the constitution is *God.* If you are giving water to a plant, you are it's *God.* That is how I explain *God.* However, everyone has their own idea's a belief about *who/what God* is to them, and that is absolutely your right to believe whatever you choose to believe.

Soul Energy and Reincarnation

As I mentioned previously, when we lose our heavy earthly bodies, we return to *soul energy.* Most people do not understand the concept of their souls being pure energy, and that all the records of the soul (and indeed all of life and life forms – the whole of Creation) is stored in one vast central *ENERGY* field, which is enormous, yet compact, and this is pure spiralling energy. At its very core lies the Divine Core Creative Energy Force. In essence then our soul can never be separate from the very same energy field in which is stored. When we start understanding this, we start to understand that our lives on this planet consist of a mere wink of an eye in eternity, and what our souls have come here to do, be and express is but one single fleeting moment in the infinite journeys of our souls. When we finally reconnect with our soul, we reconnect with our own *Higher Soul Selves*, and our true purpose and mission. Time after time we have experienced a cycle of birth and death. (*The circle of life*) Each time we are born into a new identity and cling to that incarnation as if it was all we had, until the moment we get a glimpse of something more. *We reincarnate many times*. Our soul keeps returning to learn many lessons that we ourselves and our team of guides have chosen for us. I explained earlier that when a soul decides it is ready to return to the earth plane, it meets with a team of guides, some of whom have been with them for many lifetimes and some new guides as well. The other group is a council of our elders or master teachers, who help with the process of achieving what our new lessons will be in this earthly time, and how to assist the soul with its return to the earth plane. We go through the process of looking *where* our soul could grow and the experiences necessary for our soul's growth. Past-life karma is looked at and evaluated on many levels. Your soul wants to experience many different scenarios with families, economic conditions from poor to rich or vice versa, social status, spiritual and individuals' beliefs. Your soul goes through *many lifetimes* in the hope of spiritual and soul growth. We are the result of all our past lives. Your soul's evolution is looked at, and the planning starts. Figuring out the needs for growth, your guides, teachers and you will look at many scenarios and choose the one that will fit you best. It's like watching many movies and choosing the one you want to be in. It's hard to imagine that we choose the life we are currently in, but that's the way it works. You chose your parents, siblings (yes, your siblings!) and the circumstances that create your world now. If you look at each adventure or mishap that has happened in your life, you can take on a new outlook. Ask yourself how you can handle each situation in a loving way, knowing *there is a lesson to be learned* and you did indeed choose to learn it. Can you believe you choose your body, including what type of body – male or female, handicapped, gorgeous, not-so attractive? *All with lessons to learn.* Imagine being a model or actress who is judged by appearance, constantly having to submit to this judgement of onlookers. Maybe the lessons they came with include finding the beauty *within themselves* and not to be burdened with what others think or say about them. Imagine wanting to be born with a disability so that you might teach others compassion. When it's time to reincarnate is totally up to you. You might wait until your soul family is ready to reincarnate with you. Your soul family can include your parents, siblings, co-workers, family and friends. When we reincarnate, we forget all the other lives we have lived and the experiences and challenges of those previous incarnations. We are given the opportunity to start over with a new human existence to experience all the joy and sorrows that we may encounter for the purpose of our soul's growth. Enjoy life and find the joy that is ours. Let go of hurts, and anger, and laugh a lot. Find positive ways to deal with the challenges that this lifetime will bring. *Earth is just our school room*, not where we will live forever.

Some of my past incarnations and family connections

I know of five lives that have had meaning to my soul progression. I have already mentioned that some fears, phobias, anxieties, and other emotional states have their origins in past-life events. Past-life regression can help you find your soul's purpose, which is your always ongoing path of growth and development. As we make our way through multiple lifetimes, we make unspoken contracts and decisions which are reflected in the current life. Some of this unresolved karma can manifest as illness and other difficulties. The soul can heal, through past life regression, by understanding the events of previous and how they have impacted our current life. I was able to regress to one of my former lives and could actually see myself as a young girl of proximately ten years old. I lived in a wooden hut with my grandmother. I saw myself picking herbs and putting them into a basket. My clothes were made out of a kind of brown sacking cloth, and I was wearing sandals. I could see purple heather all around me. I knew that I picked herbs and my grandmother would make herbal healing potions. *The year was 1465.* Today, I believe in herbal remedies for medicine and health benefits. There are so many herbs with different/natural healing properties. This is to say that you should not heed the advice of a doctor, but alternative medicine can often prevent the need for pills. However, just like conventional medicines, herbal medicines will have an effect on the body and needs to be used correctly. Therefore, they should be used with the same care and respect as conventional medicines. This life was obviously meaningful for me as I have carried back the importance of the herbs and the need for health, healing and well-being.

One of my earlier lives was in Egypt, and I was a male architect, named Nebanthum. My ex - husband Harry, and I shared a life in this time.

Other information given to us during one of our many sittings, was that our middle son Matthew is the soul energy of Akhenaton of the 18th Dynasty.

[Akhenaton]

From the heart of the galaxy, passing through the inter-dimensional gateway of our sun and reflected by the moon, we are continuously irradiated with divine light. Detecting this subtle spiritual energy requires a shift in our perceptual senses. This can come from spiritual initiations such as baptisms and special theurgical rites where this higher dimensional energy illuminates those who are open to receive it. During the reign of Akhenaton and Nefertiti, a religion was established that worshiped this holy light that they called Aton. We can see their reception and transmission of this spiritual energy in the countless works of art. In this life, uncannily, Matthew has the profile features of Akhenaton and the same body shape. Obviously, some aspect of the soul energy of Akhenaton still has something to balance. I actually stood in front of the statue of Akhenaton in Luxor temple, and shivers ran through my body, and so I believe that this connection is correct, even though to some it may sound a little far-fetched! Our spiritual teachers channelled with their guides to give us the information, and Malcolm's guide 'Edward' told me that the closeness that Mathew and I have in this lifetime is because of the one we had during a life in Egypt. When I was first introduced to re-incarnation, I was a little sceptical, I admit. One of the reasons I began to believe and understand about how and why this happens, is the fact that our spiritual teachers had written a list of the five lives that they said I had incarnated into. But before they told me what they had written down for me, I experienced regression and the life I described as the herbalist was just one of those that they had written down. So, neither of us knew about the other. Also, I knew who my guide was and his former culture. This information was mine and I hadn't shared it with them until they informed me through their spiritual guides that my main guide was indeed the energy of a Native American Indian. This also confirmed that what they had been given. I will explain about that life later in this chapter. You may have experienced extraordinary memories, feelings, and sensations that can point to the fact that reincarnation is legitimate and real. Beliefs for reincarnation focuses on the fact that most people have lived multiple lives before and might even remember them. Our past 'self' can identify with current situations. Are you attracted to a certain time period or culture that is unexplainable? If so, then, it is most likely that it will be some residue from your past life of that particular place or time. There have been thousands of case studies where former life experiences have been vividly remembered and correlated. As I explained, the soul is required to come into a body to complete the cycle of birth, death and re-birth. If you've only reincarnated a few times while on earth, this is reflected in your energy's age. You're going to appear more child-like and primitive. If your soulful energy has been reincarnated many times, you're going to display more wise and mature characteristics. Since experiences, memories, and certain timeframes can leave a residue on your life from the past. It's no wonder that it can leave fears and phobias that we have today. [I will explain about a fear/phobia's that caused me so much anxiety in this life until I addressed it]. You might experience an echo of a past trauma that shows itself as an unexplainable fear. Examples of this can be the fear of drowning, being scared of certain animals or places, or fearing specific objects. The life that my Ex-husband, Harry and I shared the life in Egypt, was not a romantic relationship, but we obviously needed to reincarnate together in this lifetime to bring our three children into being. We have shared many experiences that have taught us understanding, compassion and forgiveness. I retuned 1101AD as a soldier in China. At this time most of China was under control of the Northern Song dynasty, and the war lasted for two years. They were troubled times. In my life today, I hate any unkindness and feel sick in my gut area when there is any violence or cruelty. I cannot watch a television report, a movie or even listen to anything related to cruelty. So maybe some residue remains within my energy. I guess that I went through a troubled soul experience. I am probably feeling the effects from that incarnation, and most likely repaying the negative karma. Maybe this is why I have chosen to do service for others in this lifetime. Karma is the memory of our soul, which means it's often long-standing, stemming from prior lives. Indeed, the course of our current life is mostly predetermined by earlier lifetimes: *What we didn't finish then, we come back to finish now.* We have to find balance. Unpleasant situations are often the consequence of lingering karma, which can always be reversed and resolved. Obviously, there are certain issues that I haven't dealt with, OR that someone hasn't paid back to me. Karma places *everyone into your life for a reason*, and karmic relationships will play out as planned despite your best efforts. That's why it's important to acknowledge the role of each person in your life: *Why are they there? What have they come to teach you and vice versa? What is the karma you're meant to experience with this person?* The sooner you acknowledge the truth of the karma you share with someone (whether it's positive or negative), the sooner you can settle it. I know there are certain people in my life that bring me challenges, so maybe when we both have acknowledge this and learned how to deal with it, we can wipe the Karmic slate clean. One of the most fascinating facts about karma is that it often causes us to reincarnate in a reversed manner. This means that your parent may have actually been your child in a former life. Then, before reincarnating in this lifetime, the souls agreed to take on the opposite act. Souls switch genders, too. Positions shift throughout lifetimes based on karmic need. Whatever is needed to repair or heal karma will be manifested through changing roles in our cycle of lives on earth. The people you know now may have had a very different impact on your previous lives! There's a greater reason that karma repeats itself, and it's not to cause you pain. Instead, *it's to teach you to take different actions for different results*. If you're attracting the same type of partners into your life over and over again, it's time to stop and inspect your choices: Why do similar people keep coming in? What should you be doing differently? This calls for honest evaluation of your own faults and weaknesses, which is admittedly hard to do. Don't be afraid to look within. Recognize what must be changed inside of you so as to change what's outside of you. Then, you can modify your behaviour to end karmic patterns and progress in your potential. Past-life karma is hugely present in your current life. Mustering up the courage to open your karmic suitcase today can change your destiny for lifetimes to come. As already stated, we keep getting born again and again (reincarnated) in order to settle our give and take account. According to how we have lived in our past lives, and how we have used our wilful action in each of them, our personality has been shaped. The personality traits stored as impressions in our sub-conscious mind continuously get moulded/reinforced by our actions and thoughts in any given lifetime. In 1629AD I was a female born in the Dakota tribe. My father in that incarnation, is my guide today, '*Fast Cloud*'. I was the only girl with five brothers. There would have been nine, but the others died at childbirth. *Fast cloud* gives me my strength and inspiration. One of his first messages to me was: *"We have travelled many miles and many lives together and we mirror each other." "You have my fire in this life Florette." "You are a strong warrior." "I try to keep balance." "When we learn of our origins, much will become clear to you." "You will find much welcome" "I return next time in your home". "Let the stars watch you while you sleep."* He later told me that my Totem animal was an Owl. The owl spirit animal is emblematic of a deep connection with wisdom and intuitive knowledge. (Hence, being an empath) If you have the owl as totem, or power animal, you're likely to have the ability to see what's usually hidden to most. When the spirit of this animal guides you, you can see the true reality, beyond illusion and deceit. The owl also offers for those who have it a personal totem the inspiration and guidance necessary to deeply explore the unknown and the magic of life.

Owl Symbolism

Intuition, ability to see what others do not see -

Capacity to see beyond deceit and masks and Wisdom.

A wise old owl sat on an oak; The more he saw the less he spoke; The less he spoke the more he heard; Why aren't we like that wise old bird?" ~Unknown

My life as a Dakota girl is the one that resonates with me the most. The Sioux tribe believed that they would not die but would remained as spirits which could return anytime they wanted from their hunting ground to earth to visit their loved ones and roam on the land which they considered sacred. Religious visions are cultivated, and the people commune with the spirit world through music and dance. To this day, I love music and dance and obviously the spiritual aspect of life and so this is a part that I have carried back with me in this life. I love the Indian tribal dances and their music, along with so many different cultural dances. The music I often use when I am healing is a Native American instrumental compilation. I also play it when I am driving and there are two of the tracks that make me actually shiver as I can feel very connected when I listen to them. I also came across a very old postcard with a picture of an Indian chief with his granddaughter. I felt a sensation in my gut, and I have kept this post card as it puts a picture in my mind of what fast cloud and myself could possibly have looked like. I have watched the film 'Dances with Wolves' many times as I still feel the affinity with the Sioux. The connection with that life has a powerful impact on me. I feel that this was a happy time for me. In 1784- I incarnated as a South American traveller who dealt with frog venom (*hence my hatred of frogs)* in this life. (Until I had EFT therapy) which I will explain in another chapter. This then is how we can bring back fears/phobias from past lives. As we make our way through multiple lifetimes, we make unspoken contracts and decisions which are reflected in the current life. Some of this unresolved karma can manifest as illness and other difficulties. The soul can heal, through past life regression, by understanding about the events of previous lifetimes and changing the choices made in this lifetime. I have obviously had many more lives, but these ones were pointed out to me during one or two sittings. As explained previously, my ex-husband, Harry and myself met with two highly enlightened spiritual teachers once a week for some while and Malcolm's guide: *Edward* would talk with us. He told me that I was on the pathway of discovery. He said that I have realised the knowledge that there was for me to grasp and that I was in the correct place to gain it. He gave me information about our middle son Mathew and the lives we shared in Egypt, but he also said that Mathew and I were two parts of a pod, identical age spirits! Matthew's totem animal is the Frog! For as long as humans have walked the Earth frogs have been here. The frog as spirit animal or totem reminds us of the transient nature of our lives. As symbol of transition and transformation, this spirit animal supports us in times of change. Strongly associated with the water element, it connects us with the world of emotions as well as the process of cleansing, whether it's physical, emotional, or more spiritual. Frogs bring powerful emotions with me, even though through my EFT session I was able to let go of some of the fear. So then, is this not only a fear brought back with me from my former life, but the frog symbol is also deals with emotions, renewal and re-birth. Also, the fact that I was given the Owl totem animal for wisdom, connects with what the frog symbolizes – ancient wisdom. It all inter-connects.

The frog symbolizes:

Renewal, rebirth - Transformation, metamorphosis -Life mysteries and ancient wisdom.

The Egyptians believed that the soul lived on within the body and would therefore continue to need familiar things from everyday life. So, while its often assumed that the ancient Egyptians were obsessed with death since they did all they could to prepare for it, they actually loved life so much they did all they could to prolong it, convinced of an eternal existence based on an idealized version of earthly life. During another conversation with 'Edward', he told me that in this life I have chosen family which will offer me lessons that my soul needs to learn. He said that I would encounter emotional upheaval and that it would drain my energies, but to remember to transport myself to a place of love and support. He told me that I have inner integrity and will awaken vibrations in the universe. Looking back, I can see where I have needed support with emotional upheaval and some extremely challenging experiences. All have helped me to get to where I am today. He also told me that Mathew would have many wounds during this life, but that he has the ability to see past obstacles and will grow even more spiritually. He has chosen the obstacles to evolve and have the ability to see good in others. He also told me that we have shared many lifetimes together and are both part of a whole having the ability to see through each other's eyes. I know that I have shared other lifetimes with my eldest Son Christopher and my daughter Emma because of the strong bond of Love that we share. I recognise that we are all 'soul-mates.' Edward told us that Emma' s totem animal is the rabbit. If you have the *rabbit totem* in your life, it just means that you have no problem expressing happiness and affection when it comes to people you love. *This is so true of her nature.* My eldest son Christopher's totem animal is the Wolf. *The wolf* symbolises commitment and love of family and loyalty. Again, *this is very true of his nature.* I know that the deep-seated Love that we all share will carry us through many more incarnations and that *we will always be a 'soul-family'*. When Christopher was a passenger in a fatality car crash, he was in a critical state. The hospital called us at 2.00 am, one Sunday morning to say that Christopher was in surgery which would likely take up to eight hours or so, and as we had a four-hour journey to reach the hospital where he was, they advised us to get some sleep before we travelled. I struggled to go to sleep as I was agitated and worried, but I was in that state of '*in-between*', when Christopher's face loomed close to mine, as if he were actually in the room with me. I heard him say, "*I have come to you as you can't come to me*" I knew then that he had '*astral travelled*' to let me have the message. His spirit had actually left his body to project himself to me. When the soul astral travels, the human consciousness breaks free from the restraints of the body and is able to travel, to other locations. Some people are able to induce out of body experiences. They learn how to explore the subtle realms of existence and other dimensions. Throughout this life, I have been tested in many ways and have always sent my thanks to my guides and the universe for the help and support that they are able to give. As a family we have all been tested many times, but we all share the knowledge that there is a purpose to the experiences that we have shared. As you know, my mother left us a wonderful legacy of spiritual knowledge. She was the person that guided me and helped me to see the importance of spiritual well-being.

- She taught me how to forgive
- To see the positive in a situation.
- To see the good in others
- To love others
- To be true to myself
- To be humble
- To be grateful
- To be compassionate

- To be kind (always)

She shared visions, truth, awareness, the purpose and values of life, but most of all how to love and be compassionate. She explained why we go through struggles and suffering, and also talked about moral values. I learned about spiritual values and life lessons and in turn I have been able to pass this down to my family. My daughter Emma helps her girls to understand about life experiences and what happens to our loved ones when we pass. I loved her explanation of how we travel up the different planes of learning. She likened it to a video game where if you complete the task then you get to move up a level. If you aren't able to manage the task, then you either go back down a level or have to begin again. I think that this is a great explanation as it is true that if we do not complete the tasks that we have chosen to learn when returning to earth, then we do have the choice to return and begin again (in a different body) However, if we complete the tasks then we move up to a higher spiritual dimension or frequency. Emma feels the presence of her Nan (*my mother*) and Bob, her *uncle* that she looked upon as a grandfather figure. When she is in need of upliftment and support, she will speak to her Nan, and she will feel my mother's hand on her brow. Instantly she feels calm and falls into a restful sleep. She saw my mother (her

Nan) right after she had passed. I was saying goodnight to Emma, and she looked past me and said that Nan was standing right behind me with her hands on my shoulders as if she were real! She also has many fond memories of Bob, and the one memory that is prominent is Christmas times with him. They would do the dishes together and have a laugh. So naturally, when Bob is around, she will feel his energy while she is doing her dishes. This is how they connect with us. My youngest grand-daughter Florence, (age five) wasn't born when Bob passed away. However, she has heard Emma mention him. One day, she asked where 'Bob' was, as she felt that he was holding her hand. She said she didn't want him to leave. Bob would bring happy, loving energies with him as that was the kind of man that he was when on the earth plane. When my niece (Joanne) was a child, she would come to the house and play with Christopher in his room. One day she came running out and asked me who the man was that was kneeling on the floor playing with Christopher's toys. There was only Christopher in the room at that time, and so Joanne was seeing the spirit of a man that wanted to be in their company. This may have been Christopher's grandfather! **Whether you believe in spirits of the deceased inhabiting the earth or not, you've probably had at least one supernatural type of encounter or experience in** your life. Each of us have access to an immense trove of information by opening our minds to become channels that receive higher teachings from the higher realms. Many people have experiences that they can't explain, and children are no exception. Children have an innocence that allows them to see spirit without any filters. Children accept what they see. Also, they are more connected to spirit as they have only recently left the spirit world. It is said that usually until around the age of 5 they still have their innocence of the world. Some children are born with a stronger connection to spirit, an empathic child can pick up on energy easier. Children aged 5 and under are already sensitive to spirit energy so this just makes it even more amplified. This means that they may be able to physically see or hear them. If your child is waking up and feeling frightened, comfort them and let them know you are there keeping them safe. Animals appear to be highly sensitive to spirits. Pets often perk alert when a spirit is present. You may notice your dog whining for no apparent reason. Your dog may suddenly come to attention with ears perked up and tail wagging as though happily greeting your loved one. Some cats and dogs might respond in fear by hissing or barking while looking in a specific direction, yet you can't see anything. These are a few of the reactions that people have noticed in their furry companions while, at the same time, they have sensed the presence of their loved one.

More about spiritual dimensions

Each dimension of reality has a different set of laws that govern what generally can and cannot be done by an individual soul or consciousness that is in that dimension. Lower and higher (dimensions) refer to rates of vibration or frequency and are not considered "better" or "worse". They form a gradual transition from one to the next. All dimensions exist at the same "*time*" and occupy the same "*space*". They are just occurring at different *vibrations or frequencies of energy.* In spirit form, our soul has a presence in all dimensions at all times. Which dimension *(or reality)* we are consciously in at any moment is a matter of where we focus our attention. Therefore, once you are established in one dimension, then you have full and easy access to the dimensions below where you are, but only limited access to those above. Overall, *lower dimensions* are *dense, heavy and rigid* and here we are still individual. We feel **a connection to the earth plane and there is still** learning to be done. There are still negative and positive elements on the lower planes. You will still have the same characteristics that you had while inhabiting a solid earth body. You won't have a solid body, like on earth, but you return to pure energy. **In** life we use a physical body to experience lessons we have chosen. While in the physical body we become accustomed to its appearance day after day, through our senses, physically, mentally, and emotionally and we use devices such as mirrors which reflex our image. We believe and accept this body/image to be us and are constantly reminded of its appearance through others, our health, aches and pains keeps us locked into our beliefs. We are a spiritual being having a human existence. In spirit, we still accept our last physical body/image and believe it to be us, along with our ingrained thoughts and expectations; we still create our reality. And as there isn't the constrictions of physical weight, time, space*(distance)* we can simply travel and be there instantly; through using our thoughts. If we reviewed a past-life, we would be able to perceive our appearance in the same manner as we see ourselves now, through our consciousness and memories of that lifetime; as a male, female and being able to have full description of our daily life and accompanying emotions, thoughts feelings and knowing decisions we have made at that time. We still have a mental picture of ourselves, as we do when we pass-on from this lifetime. As a spirit we can show ourselves to be how our loved ones remember us. Our soul is a vehicle of light that contains intelligence and love. It is luminous and bright and most have a slight tint of golden light. I'm not talking about a person's aura or astral body, but the core essence. The aura can have a wide spectrum of colours, and the astral body can appear like the physical body, but the soul is different from either. The form the individual soul takes can vary from a sphere of light to a modified human form with curtains of shimmering light around it. The astral plane created the world and all the material things and beings that we can see, touch, and feel. This is where all creation comes from— creative ideas, divine creation, laws of nature. Therefore, the astral dimension is the blueprint of the physical world, but think of it in terms of *energy, frequency and vibration.* When we reach the astral plane, we become free from the limitations of the physical world. We become *light, energy, and vibration.* We are essentially the same as we were in life. We have all of our memories, the same beliefs and attitudes toward things, and may even manifest the same surroundings that we had on earth. This is why some people who have died aren't even aware that they are in the spiritual world and may try to deny it if they are told so by an angel. When the soul leaves the body and enters the spiritual world, it will meet friends or relatives who crossed over before. Spouses will be reunited, although not necessarily forever. The spiritual world is a place where a person's *inner nature* becomes the whole of their being. If two people were truly of one mind on earth, they will live together as spouses in *heaven* too. However, if they were not happily married, or if their personalities are fundamentally different, they will eventually part ways. Those who did not find love on earth, will eventually find their perfect match in *heaven*—no one is ever alone unless they wish to be. Friends and relatives become the new arrival's guide to the spiritual world, and with the help of good spirits, the person's true inner nature will gradually be revealed. This first state might last anywhere from a few hours to a year or more, depending on how long it takes for a person's outer nature (*what they outwardly say and do*) to harmonize with their inner nature (*what they truly feel and believe*). In the second state after death, the person becomes aware of the deeper parts of his or her inner nature. They start saying what they really think and act according to what they feel without worrying about appearances or making other people happy. They act according to their *inner values*—the way someone on earth might act when nobody else is watching or when they're sure they won't get caught. People who are truly good inside will be kind and generous to others, while people who are inherently evil will be openly selfish and cruel. While we can all be generous or selfish sometimes, inherently good spirits will reject the selfish thoughts and work to rid themselves of those impulses, while inherently evil spirits will justify their bad behaviour and thereby embrace it as part of themselves. At this point, *like is drawn to like*, so the sorting out begins. As I have already explained, no "judge" passes sentences of guilt or innocence—we seek out kindred spirits because that is where we feel at home. We have a life review, and it is then that we *judge ourselves* on our behaviour. We see where we have been loving and just but also where we have inflicted hurt on another person. This is where we will sit with our loved ones and higher beings to discuss what it is we need to '*put right*' by possibly returning to another life. This is where Karma comes into play.

It's important to note that all human beings arrive in the spiritual world as equals. Regardless of their religious background or their personal beliefs, nationality, gender, or race, all people have an equal chance to go to either the higher planes (*heaven*) or the lower planes (*hell*)

Stories from spirit

My mother told me a story to help me to understand the concept of "*As we sow… so we reap*". This is a story about a young schoolboy (Billy) and his older brother (Jack). Jack never had much love for his younger brother, Billy. Their parents passed to spirit when they were both young. Before passing their mother asked Jack to take care of Billy when she was gone. Jack loved his freedom and didn't spare much time for Billy. Billy loved Jack and couldn't do enough for him. He tried very hard to make Jack happy. Even though he was the younger, he would light a fire and prepare food for when Jack got home from work. Jack ignored Billy most of the time. Or would find fault with the things he did. He would often have his friend's round and send Billy to bed. Billy became very lonely. Eventually when he could stand the unhappiness no more, he left home. It was some while after that Jack began to miss Billy, and all the things that Billy had done for him. It was then Jack's turn to feel lonely. He decided to look for Billy and ask him to come home. However, he never got the chance as on his way home from work he was killed. Upon leaving his body, Jack found himself in a situation, the same as being on Earth. He found that he was living in a row of terraced houses. After being here for a while he could stand the loneliness no longer and so he walked the length of the houses hoping that there would be someone that would talk to him. Those that Jack saw would ignore him or growl in answer. Jack offered to do small tasks. Many refused his offer, while others found fault in everything he tried to do. He was utterly lonely and dejected. After a time, he began to realise that how he was being treated, was how he had treated Billy. He wanted to run away, but there was nowhere to run. It was then that he called out, "please God, help me". Upon doing this there was a knock on his door. Jack opened it to find a gentle faced man standing there. He said, "I heard your cry for help". This was Jacks spirit guide. Jack asked his guide to release him from his misery. The guide then said, "this is something you must do alone" "This will not be an easy task, but you must try to make friends with your neighbours". "You must offer help and friendship" "You will be hurt and rejected many times, but only then when you have earned their friendship and trust can I come again" "I will then be able to take you from here". There were many times that Jack wanted to give up, but he persevered, and the time did come when his guide retuned." "He said "now you have learned the meaning of as you sow, so you reap". He then took Jack to another plane where there was light and happiness. Everyone here worked together.

The guide said, "I will leave you here, and this is where you must learn to share all things". A man came up to Jack and asked, "Have you come from that awful place". "Yes" answered Jack. "I know what it is like", he said, "as I have been there" So you see that if you treat people badly, then you do not get a free pass to happiness when you pass over. We have to *re-pay* unkindness at some point. Another story shows how our guides can direct someone to be in the right place at the right time to help someone in need.

During our sleep state our spirit often meets with our loved ones that have passed to the spirit world. I believe that this is called half- way house.

The story is about two little street urchins named *Benny* and *Bully peg*. They were inseparable. They searched dustbins for food, and rubbish heaps for clothes. When they were cold and tired, they would find a corner of an old building to sleep. During the day they would offer to do tasks to earn a penny. If they were lucky, they would earn enough to buy a box of matches to sell for a little more money. What the children didn't realise upon waking that during their sleep state, they were taken to some big hall for a while where they could be happy and carefree. They were told that *God* loved them, and it was mankind that that caused them to live as they did on Earth. They were told that when it was their turn to pass to spirit that there would be a beautiful home waiting for them. Bully peg asked when it would be his turn. The guide told him that it would be his turn next. Bully peg jumped with joy, and said, "then I don't have to go back". "I am sorry", said the guide, "you must go back long enough to be released from your body". "Can Benny come too?" he asked. "Not just yet", answered the guide, "it is not his turn yet". "But how will he manage without me?" asked Bully peg. "You will see" answered the guide. "He will be taken care of". That night Benny and Bully peg slept under a pile of rubbish at the back of a warehouse. The next morning Benny woke first and went in search of food for them both. Upon his return he found workmen removing big heavy boxes which had fallen and crushed Bully peg. The ambulance took Bully peg' body away. Benny ran after it and sat on the hospital steps weeping for his friend. An orderly came out and explained that his little friend was dead. He gave Benny a sixpence. Bully Peg's spirit could not rest. He begged to be able to return to Earth to help Benny. His guide took him to where he could see Benny. Bully peg reached out to touch his friend, and he called his name. "He cannot feel you or hear you", said the guide. "Then let me return to Earth", pleaded Bully peg. "I don't believe in *god* anymore". "Come with me", said the guide "and watch what happens". He took Bully peg to where a group of soul's were discussing how they could best help Benny. So, Benny's guides orchestrated the meeting between Benny and a gentle old man. On the Earth plane, the chosen man suddenly wondered why he felt the urge to take a tram to the city. He followed his *instincts*, and upon alighting from the tram he saw a group of urchins all pushing to sell matches. A big lad pushed Benny and he fell, spilling all of the matches underneath a passing tram. Benny wept. The kind old man put his arm around Benny's shoulder to console him. "That was all I had, so now I won't be able to eat" wept Benny. The man took Benny for some food and asked him where he lived. "I live on the streets, and sleep wherever I can" replied Benny. The realisation came to the man, that the reason *he was meant* to catch the tram was so that he would meet Benny. He took Benny to live with him in his lovely home where Benny was very happy. Bully peg watched this and said, "Thank you" "Now I do believe in *God*" This story shows that the man and Benny were meant to find each other, and so they guides gave him the '*gentle push*' to be where he needed to be in order for them to find each other. This also shows that when we pass over, we can still see what goes on in the lives of the people we leave behind. We can watch their progress and often become guides ourselves in order to help. For souls' who are ready for the higher planes there is a third state, a time of instruction. It is a time for learning about *the heavenly realms,* and how to lead a life that allows one to experience it. At this point, the person is already in touch with the community in these other dimensions where he or she will ultimately live, but still has a lot to learn about that community—what it does, how the individual can contribute to it, how the community can fill the individual's needs, and so on. These realms that some might call heaven, is not a place but a collective entity made up of good people who perform an important use, much as we ourselves are made up of individual cells and atoms that are essential to the full functioning of our body. People ask if there is a 'hell'. Hell is *not a place.* but it is the *consciousness at the lowest level*. As I mentioned earlier, like attracts like and it is at this level where people that have committed sins against humanity and the evil minded live together. These souls live together in torment, lying and manipulating each hoping to dominate and gain power (just as they were on the earth plane). *This is their hell.* I would imagine that this is a very depressing place to be with so much darkness and negativity, and you could give this the name of '*hell*'. The soul here will have hard work to do before it may finally can ask to be helped. Once a soul asks for help, (*like Jack in the first story*) then the higher beings and the angels with do what they can to assist. Higher dimensions are described as being light, transparent, flexible, less complex, more broadly encompassing, having *higher frequency vibrations*, and an increasing sense of universal oneness. It is the soul's journey to reach the higher levels of existence, therefore returning to earth time after time to either balance Karma or to find perfection of the soul. You are permitted to spend as much time in the spirit world as you need to recover and review your previous lives. After time you will be encouraged towards taking on another life. If you choose to return for another physical experience this will be carefully orchestrated to find the path that you want to play out and to find the most suitable body and circumstances that will allow you to achieve your goals. I realise that I have already touched on this subject, but sometimes I feel it necessary to cover some of the information within different chapters. When you have chosen the theme that you want your next incarnation to be, you then create *contracts* with those in your soul group and soul clusters to perform specific functions for one another during your next life. This may be that you want to balance past life Karma.

Life is like a play

Life is like staging a play with supporting characters around us, who are also the main focus of their own story (play). Before you embark on your reincarnation process, you will go through a preparation class with other soul who will appear in your life. This is why when we meet someone for the first time on earth, you may feel like you have known them all of your life. So, we recognise people that are important to our journey, we can have that '*Deja vu moment*' or what we feel is a '*coincidence*' that draws us to each other. The last step is to meet with the council elders. These are the group of guides who oversee the wider organisation of the spirit world. They have the responsibility to understand what your goals are in the life that you are about to undertake and to make sure that you are aware of your duties and responsibilities. You will be given a final chance to make any amendments and you can even refuse to go forward if you don't then feel that this is the right thing for you to do. You will have chosen your parents (*it will all be agreed*) and as you separate your consciousness from the spirit world, you will enter the womb. You will pass through a tunnel similar to the one you pass though at death. For the first 2/3 months you are free to come and go, but beyond that point you make the bond more permanent between your new body. Once you have entered into the physical world, all of your planning will effectively go out of the window. You come into each incarnation with the state of amnesia to prevent you from '*cheating*' on your journey through life. You may get nudges from time to time sometime in the form of dreams but because you have 'free will' you may choose to ignore them. You may stray from your original 'plan' (as I described the train journey) You may decide to get on and off at different chosen stations, and therefore go '*off track*' but ultimately to you have to get back on to reach your final chosen destination. (Whether it be in this incarnation or another.) When it is time for you to return to the spirit world, in most cases there will be a smooth transition. Your body will detach and most describe the calling of the white light. Depending on your level of development, you may be met at this point by someone close to you that has already passed on, or a spirit guide. From here, you will be guided back to your '*soul group*' for your homecoming and to reunite with those from previous incarnations. Then, as I mentioned earlier, you will have your life review with the council of elders who were your last contact in the spirit world before you entered the physical. This is where you will be able to pinpoint exactly where your best efforts were made *or where you could improve next time*. The journey of the soul is infinite, and you choose whichever path you want to follow. In spirit there is only learning, and each experience is valued for what it brings to the narrative of your journey. There has to be a balance. '*Free-will*' is paramount and *you are always in control. "Love is the ultimate and the highest goal to which man can aspire.* "Which brings me to mention my eldest son, Christopher. As quoted above, *Love* is the ultimate and highest goal, and I feel that my eldest son has reached this point. The love of his family is paramount to anything else on earth. He is a spiritually evolved soul and seeks to put others before himself.

LOVE IN THE ULTIMATE GOAL

My family in this lifetime, including mother, father, brothers' sisters, nieces, nephews and my three children along with my grandchildren have all chosen loving pathways. My partner is a kind and loving man and my ex-husband, and I still share a loving bond. My son-in-law and two daughter-in laws also add to the loving relationships. As a family we have all gone through many times of stress and many challenges, BUT we have all pulled together and shown *LOVE* and support throughout. *The state of love is the highest frequency that we can reach for.* When we operate with love, we vibrate a signal which brings us into harmony and love is the core of all creation. We are all beings of vibration, and the frequency of love carries the harmonic wavelengths that represent the very essence and presence of life. Love is so natural a state that we have to be taught the opposite: to *not* love. Loving attitudes create loving outcomes. Love is the ultimate soul-food, the very substance of our heart. Without love we become lost, destabilized and UN-inspired. *We have to love ourselves as wells as others.* Love is unconditional. Our hearts create electro-magnetic waves that influence the world around us. *Everything is energy*, and everything is brought into being through the power of love. Love heals all wounds, and love is in forgiveness. I am a great believer in forgiveness. Sometimes it can be difficult to forgive someone for the hurt that they may have caused you but remember the *contract* that we talked about before we incarnate. *That very person is the one to give you the lesson that you need in order for your soul progression and healing.* It is the same with people that are challenging. We have chosen to accept those challenges as part of our process on the Earth plane. *It is 'how' we deal with these people/challenges that is important to our soul growth.* It is possible that we have chosen to balance Karma and so the challenge is a *lesson/exam* that we need to pass. Often, we can feel anger towards people that create challenges and if they hurt us, we can feel that we want to hurt them back. However, this is building *even more negative Karma,* which will ultimately have to be paid back. I think that once you can accept that *YOU* have chosen the *people/challenges* before you incarnate for the lessons that *YOU* need, you can look at the bigger picture and deal with the situation in a more positive way. We may have anger or a fire inside us that we have to let out. It is important to allow yourself to feel these emotions and not supress them, but just be mindful of the words that you say. Take a breath and if you can step away from the situation for a minute, do so. Believe me, I haven't always played by these rules and have experienced some battles within myself with negative outcomes. This is has been a learning experience for me, and yes, I will have added negative Karma to my slate. I am still learning to abide by the rules, but I can see the bigger picture of how life works, and I am finding more peace within and without. As I said earlier, I think that when we are feeling cross and want to respond in a negative or angry way – we should walk away from the situation, take a number of deep breaths before we respond. Think about what *YOU* are learning from the experience. If you don't deal with issues that are creating an imbalance in your life this time around, then you will have *to face the same issues in another incarnation until you learn to deal with each person/situation with a loving attitude*. As I said above- LOVE is the ultimate goal that we need to achieve in life. As you navigate a spiritual path, it is critical to understand that in every moment, you are either in a state of *love or* in a state of fear. When you are in a state of *fear*, you are in the brain's fight or flight system where survival is king. Higher reason and morality cannot play into the situation when this portion of the brain is in control. When you are in a state of *love*, you are in the most evolved portion of the human brain. Here, skills of higher reason are present along with the love-based states that support deep spiritual experiences. When you feel *angry, sad, anxious, unworthy, jealous, guilty or shameful*, you simply cannot experience yourself as the spiritual presence that you are. As a result, with each passing day, you become steeped in greater amounts of fear and separated from the spiritual experience you intuitively know is possible.

Healing within

Firstly, we need to get to know our unique physical body. Learn to listen to it, nourish it and keep it as healthy as we can. We also need to understand ourselves and what makes us tick by tapping into our own spiritual core and seeking answers. Life is simple… what *'we give out, we get back'* and what we think about ourselves becomes the truth for us. We are responsible for all that happens to us (*remember the contract*) Every *'thought that we think'*, *creates our future*. We create our experiences by *our 'thoughts and our feelings'*. The words that we speak have impact on our lives. We often blame others when things go wrong for us. We need to look within and see how we ourselves are creating negative outcomes. When we create peace, harmony and balance in our mind, we will find it in our lives. Our subconscious minds accept what we choose to believe. If we *always* have negative thoughts, then we will inevitably draw negative energies towards us, therefore we will experience negative outcomes. It is not until we begin to understand how the universe works that we can begin to understand how *we can change our thought patterns* and heal our lives.

Remember, if you can't change a situation, change how you feel about it. Some people are brought up with limiting and rigid ideas about life and how they should live it. When we are children, we learn by the actions and words of adults about what they see us to be. If for instance you have a negative father that always puts you down and says that you are useless, told enough times, you will begin to believe this of yourself, and in turn can become a very negative person. We can carry this throughout our adult lives. As I stated previously, I was fortunate to have a loving family. We had fun with our aunts, uncles and cousins and this was carried through to my adult life. My siblings and I were hugged and kissed and cared for in the best way that our parents new how. We had music and laughter. We didn't have money to waste, but we were fed and clothed, and were kept warm during the winter months. My memories of my childhood are happy ones. I am grateful for the family that I have, and also for my very dear friends. Sadly, there are many who haven't had such luxuries of love and cuddles. This is not necessarily the parent's fault, as maybe *their* parents didn't know how to love either. We do choose to be with the *parents/families* that we *need* to be with for the *lessons that we need* in this lifetime. So, when we look at life as *our plan*, it puts a whole new perspective on why we have challenges to face.

The most powerful tool we have for transforming our lives is our brain. It controls not only our state of health and healing, but the behaviours that lead to our successes and failures as well. It is important to know that we can influence what is happening in our brain and all of the physiological systems connected to it. We can think positive thoughts, we can think realistic thoughts and we can think negative thoughts. Some thoughts are fleeting and forgotten whereas others stay rooted and it's the ones that stay rooted are the ones that essentially define us. Just as our physical state depends on what we feed to our bodies; our mental state depends on the quality of information we feed to our brain. There's nothing new in the concept that *'we are what we think'*. We have two minds. The conscious, logical thinking mind and the subconscious creative, protective mind. We have been taught that our conscious mind is in control, but it couldn't be farther from the truth. Our subconscious mind is running the show and it has decided seconds before the conscious mind is even aware there is a decision to be made. How often have you said to yourself, "I am in two minds about this"? Words that we speak have an impact on our thoughts and what we believe. If a patient's survival rate can be affected simply by the means by which the doctor delivers the prognosis, it is fact we are affected by thoughts. If a person can be told that a pill will cure them, the placebo effect definitely demonstrates the power of thought. So why do we, as humans, continue to struggle? Why have we not chosen to change our life experiences? The answer is simply, we have never been told we could. Schools teach us to conform. Society frowns upon those who are different. We spend our lives trying to fit into a box that is designed for only one. Every illness has its roots in the soul. It is only when our bodies develop disease that we tend to take notice. So then, *your thoughts and values determine the way you see yourself and the world around you.* Thoughts and beliefs that are grounded in pessimism can negatively impact your *feelings, emotions, and mental health.* □ These harmful perceptions are common issues that can contribute to the symptoms of mood and *anxiety disorders.* And so, reiterating what I have already said, *your belief system is made up of your personal views, attitudes, and values.* Your beliefs are always with you, shaping the way in which you see yourself and the world around you. Self-defeating beliefs can set you up for failure and dissatisfaction and disharmony within, *which can also create illness.* I believe illness can be traced back to the soul level. If we don't deal with it then, it trickles down to the emotional level, then the mental and eventually it gets our attention when it gets to the physical level. People go through traumas and have behaviours they don't understand. They have addictions that they don't know how or why they got them. For me, it's about going back and letting the soul say what the real problem is and then letting go of any negative thoughts or beliefs, maybe even guilt of their behaviour, (*from possible past incarnations*). So, as I have explained, before we incarnate, we go through the process of looking where our soul could grow and the experiences necessary for our soul's growth. Past-life karma is looked at and evaluated on many levels. Your soul wants to experience many different scenarios with families, economic conditions from poor to rich or vice versa, social status, spiritual and individuals' beliefs, and whatever illness you may have that will create experiences that your soul needs for development. Your soul goes through many lifetimes in the hope of spiritual and soul growth. Some people think of their 'challenges' as nothing more than meaningless suffering. If they could realise that they had *planned these challenges*, they would see them as rich with purpose. That knowledge can greatly ease their suffering. So, understanding *why they had planned them*, they can consciously learn the lessons offered. Feelings of fear, anger, resentment, blame, and self-pity can be replaced by a focus on growth. If you continue with negative thoughts and focus on nothing else, this is where you will stay, stuck on a negative roller coaster. Try to accept and be grateful for the challenges that are presented to you. In the past I had also felt victimized by the universe and blamed others for 'bad' things that happened to me, until I had the knowledge of pre-birth planning. It was understanding '*why*' we choose to take on challenges that it gave me a different perspective on life. This is why I want to share my knowledge with others, so that people can understand that life and indeed suffering is not pointless. Physical life is temporary and the pain and adversity you face as a physical being is but a moment in your existence. Why do people choose to enter a life that is filled with pain and torment? Because from the perspective of the ether, any pain or adversity is but a blip of discomfort in the grand scheme of things. It's like asking if you are willing to suffer a paper cut in order to gain vast wisdom and knowledge and tremendous personal growth. As I keep saying: when we incarnate, we forget and so it can be extremely difficult to understand why horrible things happen to you and even more disconcerting to think '*you chose for it to happen*!' This is why I feel it is so important to remember where we came from. When you remember that *this life is temporary and that your goal is growth,* it can make even the most horrible conditions bearable. When you choose your parents and your life situation you are giving yourself an opportunity. What you do with that opportunity is entirely up to you (*free will*). Don't waste any of the life you've chosen. Learn from every experience. *That is why we are here.* So then, over many lifetimes, we accumulate many give-and-take accounts that are a direct result of our deeds and actions. The accounts may be positive or negative depending on the positive or negative nature of our actions. A large part of our lives is destined (*the train journey*) and a smaller portion of our lives are governed by our own '*freewill*'. All major events in our life are by and large destined. These events include our birth, the family we are born into, the person (or persons) we marry, the children we have, serious illnesses and the time of our death. (*Given we have a choice of 5 different exit points*). The happiness and pain that we *give and receive* from loved ones and acquaintances are by and large simply a case of prior *give-and-take* accounts directing the way relationships unravel and play out. In our lifetime, while we do complete our give-and-take account and destiny earmarked for this particular lifetime of ours, we also end up creating more accounts by using our wilful action. This in turn finally adds up to our overall give-and-take account known as the accumulated account or Karma. As a result, we choose to be born again after death to settle further give-and-take accounts (karma) I know that I have hit on the same subject of birth/death including Karmic accounts a few times, but I want to impress upon readers the importance of knowing that *life has a purpose and that we all have life goals*. First begin to understand that all the change that you are seeking in your life first begins with you. When you *Change the inside, the outside falls into place.* The sooner you learn this, the sooner you accept. Be grateful for your life and the lessons it gives you because these are the lessons that you soul has asked to learn in order to balance your karmic debts and to grow spiritually. The reality is that every day we are faced with new challenges, some bigger and more catastrophic than others. In spite of the emotional wreckage, we might find ourselves in, we must look inward to ignite the fortitude that allows us to pick ourselves back up and carry on. Do not compare your journey in this life to someone else's life. Often people will say "It's not fair that he/she has, this and that or either "It's not fair that this person gets away with this /that". You have to accept that '*We are all on a different journey'*. We are each learning from previous incarnations and indeed each other. Remember, every single person comes into our lives to teach us something, as we theirs. Look in the mirror and ask yourself, what self- limiting beliefs am I holding on to. What is holding me back from being happy. Your beliefs, your ideals, your habits, the way you speak to and of yourself, the extent of your self-acceptance, your subconscious behavioural and thought patterns… All these things, if not evaluated and upgraded, will sabotage your progress in life.

About the 'self'

There's self-esteem, self-compassion, self-acceptance, self-respect, self-confidence, self-love, self-care, and so on. There are so many words to describe how we feel about ourselves, how we think about ourselves, and how we act toward ourselves. We need to re-think our values about ourselves and change negative thought patterns. It doesn't matter if your beliefs are different from others. What people respond to is honesty and how the energy feels. You don't need to convince anybody of who you are. Just believe in yourself.

Try the following:

recognise your strengths and positives feel able to try new or difficult things show kindness towards yourself move past mistakes without blaming yourself unfairly take the time you need for yourself

believe you matter and are good enough
believe you deserve happiness

When I have conducted either an EFT therapy session or counselling, it has surprised me how many have cried when I have told them that they deserve to be happy. It uncovers the fact that so many people have negative *self-perceptions* that live in the conscious and subconscious. Deep rooted past experiences, including negative comments by others, negative values and beliefs of family and friends. The things that affect our self-esteem differ for everyone. Your self-esteem might change suddenly, - or you might have had low self-esteem for a while– which might make it hard to recognise how you feel and make changes. Difficult or stressful life experiences can often be a factor, such as:

being bullied or abused
experiencing prejudice, discrimination or stigma
losing your job or difficulty finding employment
problems at work_or while
ongoing stress
physical health problems
mental health problems
relationship problems, separation or divorce
worries about your appearance and body image
problems with money

Whatever has affected your self-esteem, it's important to remember that you have *the right to feel good about who you are*. It might feel as if changing things will be difficult, but there are lots of things you can try to improve things little by little. Try to learn more about yourself – for example *what makes you happy and what you value in life*. I would suggest keeping a journal. *Let yourself have feelings*. It's important to remember that you're a human being who can experience a wide range of emotions.

Try to challenge unkind thoughts about yourself. You might automatically put yourself down. Try to remember that you chose your body before you incarnated, for the reasons that you needed to learn lessons from and to evolve. Avoid comparing yourself to others. Try to remember that what other people choose to have in their lives is what they need for *their journey*. Look directly into a mirror and purposely say positive things to yourself. It might feel really strange at first, but you'll feel more comfortable the more you do it. Celebrate your successes. No matter how small they may seem, take time to praise yourself and notice what you did the best that you could. well. Accept compliments. You could make a note of them to look over when you're feeling low or doubting yourself. We *ALL* have something to offer, it is just realising what it is and *accepting it. Try not to focus on the negative.* If someone says something unhelpful or unkind, you might find you focus on that and ignore anything positive. You do not have to accept what others say. Do not give others the power to hurt or upset you. Write a list of things you like about yourself. For example, you could include character traits, skills or experience, beliefs or causes that matter to you or things you enjoy doing. The main thing here is to find the *positives and focus on them.* Try starting your speech by eliminating the negative phrases, such as "*I can't*",

"*I always give up*". Try saying instead, "*I will try to do the best that I can*" or "maybe *today I did not accomplish what I wanted to, but I will make a list and I will accomplish my tasks in my own way*". *Always find the positive* phrase rather than the negative. It is something we have to think about to begin with. If we have had years of negative comments, then to eliminate these straight off would be a challenge. It is far better to record the positive events of your day in your journal, no matter how small. If you are still having difficulty, call upon your angels and guides. They are there to help you when you are in need. If you don't believe me, '*just try it*' you will then realise that there is help for you. As you now know, your spirit team can *assist to make the right choices,* they cannot 'fix' your problems because these challenges are what you have chosen for your soul growth. The reason that I keep going over things that I have already talked about throughout this book is because, I want things to 'sink in'. I want people to understand that you don't need to fight against life but learn how to live through it.

Everything happens for a reason and that reason leads you to another destiny. Accept the fact that life throws you curve balls every now and then to teach you something, to push you to grow, and to encourage you to change. Use this as a drive to make successfully change yourself for the better.

A soulful life is one of thoughtfulness, care, and engaging in the present in everything you do. You give attention to the things that matter most. That means being in the moment, as much as possible, each and every day. When you do find yourself caught up in a whirlwind of stress, or mindlessly scanning your smartphone, take a deep breath and come back to the present moment. Your body is a vehicle for the soul, so take care of your body. To be healthy and remain healthy, it is helpful to engage in regular exercise. Just as I was checking this chapter, I felt I wanted to add something more about thoughtfulness. Thoughtfulness is also about letting other people feel their emotions and not trying to orchestrate happenings. We can sometimes try to manipulate others into a way of thinking that we want, so that the plan *we* want to take place happens the way *we* want it to. Admitting that you have tried to manipulate a situation is coming to terms with the fact that this is not what we are meant to do. This is the first step to self-knowledge and improvement. When we realise that things will fall into place when the time is right, we can stop trying to manipulate the situation, and *just let it be!* Not everything has to be in our control. It is best to acknowledge other people's boundaries and personal space and to be respectful during disagreements.

Ways in which our guides can contact us

A helper guide is a type of consciousness that aims to assist, support, help, guide, and inspire us. By helping us, they are also helping themselves to progress spiritually. *We are all evolving whether on the Earth plane or in spirit.* You can communicate with your helpers or your guardian angel by being peaceful, it helps to meditate if you are able. Just talk to them, this can be inside your head, share your problem with them and ask for their guidance. *Always show your gratitude* by thanking them first. Pay close attention to your thoughts and any inspiration, new ideas that pop into your head. Write down in your journal, ideas and thoughts that come to you. You will be surprised at how they will connect and communicate with you.

Intuition: They try to send ideas to us via intuition. They inspire us by providing sudden, unique ideas or different perspectives. Pay attention to your *thoughts* and *intuitions*, it can often be your inspiration from your guide. Intuition can at come at any time. It can be when you're thinking about your problems while taking a shower, outside gardening, walking or watching TV. Anytime is a good time for the helpers and angels to communicate with you. You may have a feather float into your hand, or right in front of you. This will be your angel telling you that they are there. They are not actual angel feathers, (*as angels don't have feathers – they are shards of light that take on the appearance of wings*), but they are feathers from birds. The angels will blow them into our pathway to get our attention. I will explain more about angels in another chapter.

White feathers:

These are the most common and often considered the symbol for purity, which is very much aligned with the meaning of angels. White feathers can also be a sign from the angels that your loved ones in the spirit realms are well and have successfully crossed over. Especially if the feather floats out of nowhere and gently lands in front you. It is often the person you are thinking of at that time. **White feathers often appear in your life when your spiritual desires and** requests are being answered. They often show up in your life as a way to provide encouragement and let you know that there the universal flow of energy is working in your favour. There was a point in my life when I was dealing with a crisis. I felt sick with worry and kept praying that the outcome would be good for the person concerned and all that were involved. My partner and I were sitting on a bench in Cornwall quietly listening to the gulls and watching the ships come and go. I closed my eyes and sent my thoughts to my spirit team and asked for a sign that all would be well. My answer was immediate. As I opened my eyes, a beautiful curled white feather floated towards me. I held out my hand, and it floated into the palm of my hand! How much proof could one ask for? I knew then that my thoughts had been heard. Incidentally, the outcome was the best that we could hope for. The feather was to let me know that my thoughts had been heard and the feather gave me some peace of mind.

White: is also a symbol of faith and protection, and when you find white feathers in peculiar locations the message is especially significant. This is often just to reassure you that your angels are around you, working with you, and answering your prayers. I will go into more detail on feathers and the colour interpretations later.

Dreams:

Your helpers and guardian angels often visit you in your sleep state. They communicate ideas to us so that we can reflect before making decisions. When you have a dream that is more "*real*" or more logical, make a note and meditate over the results or contents of the dream. It might be your guardian angel trying to tell you something. Some dreams are a mash up of things that you have done, said and maybe stressed over in your mind, but how you will realise that a dream has meaning, will be if the memory of it *doesn't fade* for a while and you can still remember the finer points about it. You may want to 'look up' spiritual dream meanings as we can often misread into what the dream means.

For example: Dreams about dying.

If you dream about yourself dying, it could mean that you are in a major life transition. It may mean that you are in a relationship or job that is coming to an end or even something that you are wanting to escape from. All dream meanings are symbolic, and you need to decipher them correctly in order to find the message within. The problem with death dreams is that they're often so graphic, or they feature people you know and love which is emotionally devastating. It can be so hard to tear yourself away from the emotional impact of seeing someone you love die in a dream and to focus on the fact that the dream is about *YOU – not about physical death*, but about the death of old ways within you. Difficult, but it must be done if you are going to discover the huge personal rewards of understanding your dreams of death. Worse still, of course, are those terrifying dreams where you might kill someone. Again, you must focus on removing yourself from the emotional impact of the dream so that you can consider its symbolism and recognise its meaning and application to your life. The reason that they are often so graphic, *is to get your attention.*

People in your dreams symbolize something about you.

Just as many of your dreams feature people you know who are still living, or who you knew in the past, they can also feature people who have passed on. A deceased relative may simply be featured in a dream to symbolise something about you in the same way as anyone else may feature in your dream to symbolise something about you. *Your dreaming brain picked them up to suit the character part in your dream.* They may symbolise an aspect of your personality, or a belief you share, or a conflict that remains unresolved. How do we know then when our loved ones are visiting us in our dream state?

These are known as *visitation dreams* and can provide great comfort. It is actually easier for spiritual entities of all kinds (e.g., deceased loved ones, guides, angels) to communicate with us while we are sleeping. Why? Because when sleeping, we are in that "*in between place*" between our Earthly reality and "*the other side of the veil*" (*the spiritual world*). During this time, our rational mind and our ego are not engaged. Things can happen in our dream world that we would normally stop or discount while awake.

For example: when someone who has died comes to visit us in our dreams, we aren't as likely to have the "*rational thought*" that this person is actually dead and shouldn't be in our dream. When they appear, we accept that person's presence without argument. *Think of your dream as a play or a movie.* Your subconscious mind is the director that must select who will play the different roles. For example, that role might need someone who is a businessman, so your beloved Grandfather (Harry) is selected because he was a successful businessman. Or perhaps the role requires a loving mother figure; then perhaps your mother (Flora) is chosen because she was a very loving presence in your life when you were a child. Based on all the people you have known during your lifetime (even those you may not consciously remember and possibly even people from past lives), the director selects the best actor for that part. Sometimes the actor who is selected is alive, sometimes the actor has passed. But the actor is simply *"the best person for the job"* because he or she fits the requirements you need for that dream. The most important characteristic of a true visitation dream is that it *feels "real."* It will also be *very vivid*. If you have to ask whether the visitation dream was really a visitation dream, then it probably was NOT a visitation dream. They are so real and vivid that you won't have to ask this question. When you **do** have a visitation dream you will feel it in your heart or gut, and you will *"know"* it was real. Because they are so real and so vivid, you will remember visitation dreams very clearly for days, months, years, and probably for your entire lifetime! I had a dream quite a few years ago that I remember *vividly* to this day. I was standing by the ocean and the sea was rushing to the shore bringing all of my loved ones to me on the crest of the waves. The sea rushing to shore indicates that my life and love are full of energy. I remember clearly a sense of overwhelming happiness. I know that the dream will live with me forever, and I can recall the happiness it brought me when I bring it to mind. Whether or not people speak to you verbally in the dream, they will communicate very clearly. When they do communicate (*either* *verbally or non-verbally*), it isn't because they want to engage in idle "chit-chat." It isn't easy for deceased loves ones to enter a dream. They come with a purpose, and they will convey the message and then be gone. Most often, their messages fall into the category of *"reassurance."* They come to let you know that they are fine and that they want you to be happy. Occasionally, they will come with a warning. However, when giving a warning, they will give you loving support and you will feel reassured by their presence. After a *visitation dream*, when you wake up, you will often be filled with a *sense of peace and love.* Before going to sleep, you can ask for a visitation dream. Spend time thinking about the deceased loved one and ask him or her to come visit you in your dream state. You may also want to ask your guides or other spiritual helpers to assist this person to come to you clearly. However, please don't become discouraged if the person doesn't come to you. They want to, but there are many reasons why a deceased loved one may not show up when requested.

For example: the soul may be relatively new at entering dreams and may not know how to do it (yet). Or your guides know that you want to know something that your deceased loved one can't tell you because you need to find the answer for yourself. But there's no harm in asking for him or her to come visit with you. When visitation dreams do occur, be sure to thank your deceased loved one for coming and send them *love and gratitude* for taking the time to visit with you. I will list some spiritual insight dreams that have impacted my life in a separate chapter.

Be thankful: Before you go to sleep make a mental note of all the things that you are thankful for today. This is a great way to shift into a positive mindset and get a good night sleep.

May the light of a thousand stars shine upon you

May the Love of a thousand angels surround you

May the troubles of the day be behind you

May the happiest of dreams find y

Opening up

As I have explained, I was introduced to a spiritual way of life from a youngish age. I searched for my own enlightenment, inspiration and guidance as I got older. I sat in a development circle with a group of ladies that also wanted to progress and improve their medium- ship/psychic abilities. We were guided and watched over by a lady by the name of Celia, who was our mentor and gate keeper. She would protect the circle. When we decide to connect with others with similar goals and learn to cooperate as a team, the rewards to the group, as well as each individual, are amazing. Each person has important things to contribute. When one person supports the other the love flows back and forth. Our collective energies combined helped to raise the vibrations to enable us to connect with spirit. Development takes time, patience and trust. In time you reach the point where you have the ability to channel messages from the spirit world and offer psychic readings. I have mentioned the types of psychic abilities that we channel through earlier in the book. I found that I was able to '*feel*' the presence of spirit, *see images and 'hear'* in my head the messages that were being channelled. I can *sense* things about people when they come to me for a reading such as their emotional sadness and I am able to link with the other side to give people the '*proof*' that they need that their loved ones are still around. Channelling is a very different state of mind when you bring channel through you. A good thing to do when you get a message is to write it down as soon afterwards as you are able to. It's aways good to go back to them at a later date and applying it to your life to see how the message may have helped you. If you get a message that you can't identify with, then don't focus too much on it. It takes time for us to properly connect with our guides and get accuracy. We are paired with the guides that can help us the most. They are wonderful at helping us out and guiding us in healing and growth. Our circle was a '*closed*' circle, which means the same five ladies would sit at the same time in the same place every week. No-one else was allowed to join because we formed a trust in each other and learned how to ground ourselves and merge and channel our energies. We asked only for truth, love and light to enter our circle. *We created a sacred space.* We would meditate to open up our heart space and run energy through our Chakra points.

We learned how to raise our collective energy vibrations to help our guides and loved ones to meet us half-way. It is important to be grounded and to ask for protection, love and light at all times as negative energies hang around and look for an opportunity to enter your space. Grounding is basically balancing out the spiritual and physical energy in your body, by connecting yourself with the earth.

Visualisation and connecting: To be grounded gives your energy a point of steadiness and you will feel clear, centred, strong and focused. Sit with your feet flat on the floor, and back straight. Visualise the soles of your feet being drawn into the Earth, like the roots of a tree. Keep going until the roots are deep into the

Earth. Take a slow deep breath in, hold it for the count of 8 and then slowly exhale. Listen to your breathing. Do this a few times until you feel relaxed and centred. Your breathing will regulate itself to a slower pace. Then visualise a bright white light being pulled from the centre of your head reaching far into the sky. Feel safe and connected. By now you will have heightened your energy/ vibrations, thus making it easier for your guides to connect with you. You can now invite your guides to join you. You could say *"Welcome friends and spirit guides, please join us with love and light"*. *"Let me know that you are with me"*.

I also ask that only love and light enter my space. You can say this telepathically. Relax, don't try to force anything and be open-minded. Once your guides feel that you are ready, they will give you impressions, feelings and visions. The visions come from the *"third eye"*. The third eye chakra is considered to be the sixth chakra in the body. This chakra *(energy wheel)* is located in the centre of your forehead, parallel to the middle of your eyebrows. This is the link to *perception, awareness, and spiritual communication.* Speak to your guide as a friend and ask what information they have for you. As you sit with your guide in your space, you may sense some thoughts being projected into your mind. Let the guide download into your mind any feelings, thoughts, or symbols. Sit with your guide and listen to his or her teaching and philosophy. Each time you meet with your guide the *connection/bond* will become stronger, and eventually you will just '*know*' when he/she is with you. You can ask for a name so that when you want to connect you will be able to call them by the given name. When you are ready to close, bless your guide and give thanks for their service and advice. You will have begun with a meditation, so on closing take some deep breaths.

Become aware of your feet, then your legs, and upwards to your head slowly bringing the light back into your body. Inhale and exhale a few more times. When I connect with my spirit team, I concentrate on my breath, thus slowing it down, and then as described I will ground myself. I clear my mind and I can feel my vibrations lightening. It feels like I am floating up and up, getting lighter and lighter. I feel that I am spiralling upwards. It is almost a feeling of being out of my body, because I become so peaceful and relaxed. Sometimes I will play 'new age' or 'healing' music to help me connect and raise my vibrations. The *visualization* method may be easier for you if you're a visual person and prefer to work with the chakras. (I will go into more detail about chakras in a later chapter) but basically a chakra means "wheel" and refers to energy points in your body. They are spinning disks of energy that should stay "open" and aligned, as they correspond to bundles of nerves, major organs, and areas of our energetic body that affect our emotional and physical well-being.

Visualisation using the chakras

Begin with sitting comfortably, closing your eyes. Start with the *root chakra*, (this is at the base of your spine) visualizing a bright, *vibrant red colour*. You can just visualise it as a flower if it is easier) As you visualize this colour, imagine that it's activating the chakra and *opening it*. After you feel that the chakra is activated, move the energy from the root chakra upwards to the *sacral chakra*. (Located below the navel) Now visualize this chakra as a *brilliant orange colour*. Once you feel the sacral chakra is open and activated, move the energy from the sacral chakra upward to the *solar plexus*. This is located below the chest towards your middle. Repeat the same method as earlier with the root chakra and sacral chakra, but this time the solar plexus chakra is a *vibrant, bright yellow colour*. Visualize the yellow colour to activate the solar plexus chakra. After you feel the chakra is open and activated, move the energy from the chakra up towards the *heart chakra*. This is located in the centre of the chest. Activate the *heart chakra* by visualizing a *bright, vibrant green (or pink)* colour. Once you feel this chakra is open and activated, move the energy from the heart chakra to the throat chakra. Located within the *throat*. Visualise this as a *bright blue*. Activate this and then move up to the centre of your forehead where the *third eye chakra* is located. Visualize this with a *deep purple/indigo* colour. After this one is activated, move up to the top of your head where the *crown chakra* is located. Visualise this as either a *violet or bright white light* and activate this. Make the colours your focal point to help with the visualisation. Once you have done this you will have reached a state of calm and at oneness. You can either do this to connect with your spirit team, or just for well-being. In the next chapter I will explain about health problems that can occur if your energy centres (chakras) are blocked.

Chakras and well-being

This chapter highlights the problems that can occur if your chakras are blocked

ROOT CHAKRA: *Base of Spine – colour Red – physical identity, stability and grounding*

A blocked root chakra can manifest as physical issues like arthritis, constipation, and bladder or colon problems, or emotionally through feeling insecure about finances or our basic needs and well-being. When it's in alignment and open, we will feel grounded and secure, both physically and emotionally.

SACRAL CHAKRA: *Just below belly button – orange – sexuality, pleasure, creativity*

Issues with this chakra can be seen via problems with the associated organs, like urinary tract infections, lower back pain, and impotency. Emotionally, this chakra is connected to our feelings of self-worth, and even more specifically, our self-worth around pleasure, sexuality, and creativity.

SOLAR PLEXUS CHAKRA: *upper abdomen – stomach – yellow -Self-esteem, confidence. This is where we get our 'gut instinct'*

Blockages in the third chakra are often experienced through digestive issues like ulcers, heartburn, eating disorders, and indigestion. It's the chakra of our personal power. This means it's related to our self-esteem and self-confidence.

HEART CHAKRA: *Centre of the chest – Green – Love and compassion*

Blocks in our heart chakra can manifest in our physical health through heart problems, asthma, and weight issues. But blocks are often seen even more clearly through people's actions.

People with heart chakra blocks often put others first, to their own detriment. It's the middle of the seven chakras, so it bridges the gap between our upper and lower chakras, and it also represents our ability to love and connect to others. When out of alignment, it can make us feel lonely, insecure, and isolated.

THROAT CHAKRA: *Centre throat – Blue – Communication*

As one would expect, this chakra is connected to our ability to communicate verbally. Voice and throat problems as well as any problems with everything surrounding that area, such as the teeth, gums, and mouth, can indicate a blockage. Blocks or misalignment can also be seen through dominating conversations, gossiping, speaking without thinking, and having trouble speaking your mind. When in alignment, you will speak and listen with compassion and feel confident when you speak because you know you are being true to yourself with your words.

THIRD EYE CHAKRA: *Between the eyes – Indigo – Imagination and Intuition*

Since this chakra is physically located on the head, blockages can manifest as headaches, issues with sight or concentration, and hearing problems. People who have trouble listening to reality (who seem to "know it all") or who are not in touch with their intuition may also have a block. When open and in alignment, it's thought that people will follow their intuition and be able to see the big picture. This is also where we can 'see' spiritual images.

CROWN CHAKRA: *The top of the head – Violet or white – Awareness and Intelligence*

The crown chakra is linked to every other chakra (and therefore every organ in this system), and so it affects not just all of those organs, but also our brain and nervous system. It is considered the chakra of enlightenment and represents our connection to our life's purpose and spirituality. Those with a blocked crown chakra may seem narrow-minded, sceptical, or stubborn. When this chakra is open, it is thought to help keep all the other chakras open and to bring the person bliss and enlightenment. As these are all *energetic centres of the body* that correspond to feelings, one of them probably resonated with you as you were reading. A different one may resonate with you tomorrow. It's likely that one resonates with you more than any others as a continuous problem, a chakra where you often deal with blocks. Other blockages may pop up every now and then. In the chakra system, these patterns have specific terms and there are recommended treatments.

So then… Chakras are energy or vortexes if you like. Everything is energy within its own vibrational frequency. The body is a human energy field that extends beyond the physical body. When we feel '*off balance*' or '*out of sorts*' usually it is due to one or another of the chakras being blocked. To restore balance, you can either do the breathing meditation as described above or seek out a Reiki practitioner. Yoga is also affective. Healing and EFT can also be beneficial. More on the healing methods in another chapter. (Check the index in the back of the book)

Just to note: Everyone can benefit from chakra balancing. You don't need to be suffering from an illness to have your chakras balanced, realigned, or healed. People who want to alleviate their stress can benefit from it. Chakra balancing is particularly helpful to those experiencing physical, or emotional instability. It will help people who feel disconnected or out of touch with themselves and other people. When your chakras are balanced you will be able to release any emotional energy, negative emotions or blocked belief patterns. This is where EFT can also help as we work with blocked emotions. I think sometimes we need to step back and look at what emotional baggage we need to clear out. Look at things that you no longer resonate with, or what doesn't serve you anymore. Sit back and reflect and look within. Listen to what your higher self is telling you for mental clarity. I have written and will include a whole chapter on reflection which I will include towards the end of the book.

HEALING THERAPIES

Aromatherapy: is a healing method. It is a holistic healing treatment that uses natural plant extracts to promote health and well-being. Sometimes it's called essential oil therapy. Essential Oils have clinical research supporting claims that they may increase energy and relieve fatigue. These aromatic oils are administered to improve the health of the body, mind, and spirit. they enhance both physical and emotional health. If you need improvement in health problems from anxiety to poor sleep, you may want to consider aromatherapy. In this kind of treatment, you can breathe in the essential oils through your nose or by putting them on your skin. Some people put the oils on their skin when they get a massage or take a bath. It is always important to read the bottles before use or try a tiny drop on the skin first as some can cause irritation. You may want to contact a qualified therapist.

Indian head massage stimulates the nerves from the head area. This helps you to relax which, in turn, improves mental and physical health.

Reflexology: is the application of pressure to areas on the feet. The theory behind reflexology is that areas of the foot correspond to organs and systems of the body. Pressure applied to the foot is believed to bring relaxation and healing to the corresponding area of the body.

Crystal healing: is a type of alternative therapy that involves using gemstones to bring balance to an individual's life and mind. Crystals are said to "have a stable and unchanging energy pattern, each with a unique frequency and energy field, or resonance" that gives them special properties. The healing benefits of crystals predominantly surround areas of mental wellbeing, including feelings of increased tranquillity, positivity and focus, as well as enhanced immunity and pain relief. Individual crystals are also known to have their own special energies that align to different areas of your life, with their shape and colour as well as their type, affecting their influence. A few of the most popular crystals include:

JADE: FOR HEALTH: *Properties: longevity, purity, fertility, wisdom, peace.*

CITRINE: prosperity, creativity, digestion, confidence.

ROSE QUARTZ: Love, relationships, friendship, fertility, recovery

TURQUOISE: protection, friendship, love, balance, wisdom, purification.

CLEAR QUARTZ: psychic abilities. healing, energy

AMETHYST: healing of mind, body and soul.

I have also recently found out that the diamond can help with strength.

After choosing your individual crystal you need to set your intention, which means, deciding upon what it is you want the crystal to aid or promote you in". In a meditative-like state, hold the crystal in your hand and then focus on your goal, silently repeating a mantra, such as "please help me see my soul purpose" if you are looking to overcome self-doubt. It is necessary to occasionally cleanse and charge your crystals too, as "much like a sponge, your crystals soak up the remanence of your emotion or day. To do so, you can either wash them through or nest them in sand or natural salts.

Colour Healing: Energy exists in all forms around us. As we know, light is made up of the colour spectrum, and light is also energy. When seeing light and colour, we are actually seeing different electromagnetic wavelengths of energy. These wavelengths vary and form part of the electromagnetic spectrum. Some colours have larger wavelengths than others. These different wavelengths will have different effects on the mind and body, and these effects form part of energy healing to balance our energy levels. Each colour falls into a specific frequency and vibration, which many believe contribute to specific properties that can be used to affect the energy and frequencies within our bodies. Colours are known to have an effect on people with brain disorders or people with emotional troubles. For example, the colour *blue* can have a *calming effect* which can then result in lower blood pressure, whereas the colour *red* might have the *opposite effect*. *Green* is another colour that may be used to *relax* people who are emotionally unbalanced. *Yellow*, on the other hand, may be used to help invigorate people who might be suffering from *depression*. A person's aura contains different layers of light which can be used for cleansing and balancing. Knowing the colours in your aura can help you better understand your spirit, and thus help you better understand how to heal. Additionally, the colours surrounding you can also have various effects.

White: represents purity and is considered to be a powerful colour in feng shui, a system of arranging your environment to create peace and harmony. The frequency of the colour white matches the *'crown chakra'* located at the top of the head. This is where our spiritual life exists and where we achieve unity with our "source. It has a wide range of healing properties. Its main function is to bring about harmony and balance within the body as quickly as possible.

Indigo: The healing properties of indigo are also for a range of mental problems. It is also used to assist in the treatment of headaches, memory problems, and nightmares. Energy imbalances affect our psychosocial well-being, and so Indigo is often used to treat these symptoms by changing these energy levels. This is the colour of the *'third-eye chakra'*. This is where we find intuition and the realisation of our abilities, talents and potentials. Indigo allows you to withdraw into your inner-self and to obtain peace, quiet, and freedom. It is also the source for intuition, clairvoyance, extrasensory perception. Indigo stimulates the sense organs such as the eyes and ears.

Blue: Often viewed as the 'cooling colour', helps treat inflammation and fever, as well as high blood pressure and it is also known for treating negative emotions and a general negative state of mind- negative energy. By achieving harmony and balance, we can replace our negative energy with more positive energy levels. Blue: represents the feelings of calmness or serenity. The *'throat chakra'* is blue and can be associated with empathy communication and honesty. It is a tranquillizing colour and calming energy and can help to calm strong emotions such as anger and aggression or anxiety.

For example: the colour blue is almost always associated with blue skies, which when we are children is a positive thing as it means playing outside and fun. It can also mean that there are no storms to come and so this is why blue reminds us of stability and calm.

Green: Green is known specifically for tackling hormonal imbalances, as it affects the growth hormone in the body. Green represents balance, harmony and security. This is the colour of the '*Heart Chakra*' which deals with our ability to both give and receive love for ourselves and others.

It is also useful for treating bacterial problems and infections as it works on the nervous system, and the immune system.

Yellow: The healing properties of yellow help strengthen the nervous system- affecting the brain and mind. It helps stimulate the brain and increase spiritual well-being. Yellow provides positive energy that promotes healthier psychosocial well-being and positive state of mind. You will find your *'solar plexus chakra'* in the pit of your stomach. This chakra deals with confidence as well as overall self-worth and self-esteem. The solar plexus is where we get our 'gut feeling'

Orange: Orange is a warm and brightening colour. It helps the body free itself from any constrictions and repressions of the mind. It is also known to help restore any imbalances from hormonal glands and is known to treat infertility problems for both males and females. Like yellow, it also provides positive energy to restore imbalances caused by negative energy. It represents emotions. When it is open, we are more alert and less susceptible to fatigue. Orange gives us the power to remove suppression and inhibitions. It allows us to create ideas and gain courage and strength. The *'sacral chakra'* is located just below the navel, right in the centre of your lower belly and in your back. This chakra is associated with the colour orange.

Red: Brings warmth and increases energy by stimulating the nervous system. It is therefore good for reducing fatigue and also prevents illness such as the common cold or flu. Many people find that red helps with physical energy. The *'root chakra'* is at the base of the spine and represents the feelings of insecurity and imbalance.

The study of colour therapy began hundreds of years ago in different forms all around the world. As seen in ancient Egyptian mythology, chromotherapy was used to treat illnesses by providing various minerals, crystals, dyes, and stones of different colours and shades. Since then, colour is known to play a major role in our daily lives, affecting our mood, state of mind and energy levels. We are often drawn to a particular colour without realising that we are balancing a certain energy within. We are drawn to certain colours depending on the mood we are feeling at the current time. Warm colours can evoke different emotions than cool colours and bright colours can create different feelings than muted colours. They all have a psychological effect upon us. They all have positive and negative affects upon us: How often do you feel the need to wear maybe a red scarf! Red is a dominant and bold colour. It communicates caution, excitement, and courage. Red can be used to encourage action, create urgency, or draw attention. Colours subconsciously communicate emotion or action in our everyday lives. For example, traffic lights and stop signs—we automatically know to stop, go, or take caution when we see the colours red, yellow, or green. So *blue* and *green* are soothing colours, while *red* is the *intense emotional* colour. When we feel confident, or even powerful we are drawn to red. Wearing *yellow* makes us feel *spontaneous and happy* as it is associated with sunshine. We can feel optimistic and cheerful. Orange is a colour of *stimulation and enthusiasm*. It's not as aggressive as red, but can catch attention, so it's good to wear in moderation.

Warm colours: Red, orange and yellow are next to each other on the wheel and are all warm colours. Warm colours often evoke feelings of happiness, optimism and energy. However, yellow, red and orange can also have an attention-grabbing effect and signal danger or make you act (think stop signs, hazard warnings and barrier tape). Red can also increase a person's appetite.

Cool colours: include green, blue, are usually calming and soothing but can also express sadness. Purple is often used to help spark creativity as it's a mixture of blue (calm) and red (intense). If a company wants to display health, beauty or security, they will incorporate these colours.

Reiki healing: works with the energy fields around the body and involves the transfer of universal energy from the practitioner's palms to the client. Where there has been physical injury or even emotional pain. In time, these energy blocks can cause illness. Energy healing helps the flow of energy to remove blocks in a similar way to acupuncture or acupressure. By improving the flow of energy this can enable relaxation, relieve pain, speed healing, and reduce other symptoms of illness. My friend, Marion who is a dear and trusted friend is a

Reiki master, and a reflexology therapist. With her permission I am including her email address in case you feel that Reiki or reflexology could help you.

marionsreiki@gmail.com

Also, my very dear niece, Joanne Frances is a holistic practitioner and some of her therapies include Reiki, Indian head massage reflexology, Aromatherapy and is a mindfulness and meditation instructor. Her email address is:

floradorcus@gmail.com

Reflexology: is based on the idea that different points on your feet, hands, face and ears are linked to other parts of your body through your nervous system. During a typical session, a reflexologist will use their hands to apply gentle pressure to these points. Reflexologists recommend this treatment to relieve tension, improve mood and help you to sleep.

Yoga: involves spiritual and physical practices designed to increase self-awareness, such as posture work, breathing exercises, meditation, sounds and visualisation. Studies show that yoga can be helpful in reducing symptoms of depression and anxiety.

Hypnotherapy: Hypnosis involves putting you in a state of deep relaxation to access subconscious beliefs, thoughts and memories which may affect the way you act.

Hypnotherapists use hypnosis to help you change unwanted thoughts and behaviours by using suggestion and increasing your self-awareness. You're always in full control under hypnosis, and your therapist will only use methods that you've agreed on and feel comfortable with.

Spiritual Healing: Healing is not of the body; *it is of the mind.* It is the state of true empathy. As Spirit pours through, you are guided to shine the light. We act as a channel for the healing energy to be directed to aid relaxation and emotional conditions. Life experiences can leave us feeling stressed, emotional and often distressed. They can leave us feeling overwhelmed and sometimes powerless to function at a healthy level. This is where spiritual healing can alleviate healing within. So, myself and other spiritual healers transfer our energies to the recipient. (Very similar to Reiki). It promotes self-healing by relaxing the body, releasing tensions and strengthening the body's own immune system. Healing is natural and non-invasive with the intention of bringing the recipient into a state of *balance and wellbeing* on all levels.

I have included the healing therapies in this book as I believe that spirituality and health-related behaviours play a significant role in psychological well-being. The health of the human mind and spirit can also promote psychological well-being.

Spirituality can provide a sense of hope to balance hopelessness linked to depression. There is this common human tendency to be stuck in the moment but reminiscing about a time in life that was happier or in which they were stronger can take people out of the moment. By meditating, or even taking a walk-in nature can help boost your immune system. When you are in deep meditation, your fight-or-flight response goes off and your rest-and-repair turns on. This allows your immune system to supercharge your whole body and is incredibly healing, whether you are under stress or have an actual illness or are trying to prevent illness or stress. Throughout this book I have tried to cover all aspects of health and happiness, from *finding you pathway* in this life, connecting with your guides and helpers, to 'self' help with achieving your goals. Your spiritual body and your physical body are intertwined. Research shows that the colours we choose to wear affect our moods. There are many healing therapies to help with well-being If well-being is the destination, think of wellness as a way of getting there. That is to say, wellness is action oriented. It's about the pursuit of health and happiness through healthy lifestyle habits, like mindfulness and regular physical activity.

Wellness is a practice that can lead to greater mental, emotional and physical health. The benefits of spiritual wellness include Having compassion, the capacity for love and forgiveness, joy and fulfilment. This is where I will highlight the importance of forgiveness. The first step to forgiveness, is, however, *all about you*, your health and your energy. When there is a need to forgive, the chances are that there are trapped emotions of anger, resentment, bitterness, heartache, guilt, blaming, frustration, jealousy, humiliation, betrayal, abandonment......the list goes on. It is these trapped emotions that are the problem – releasing these is where you will find the relief and energetic shift you seek. Step two to Forgiveness and Acceptance comes from Understanding. Understanding raises Awareness. Awareness puts everything into perspective. And I believe this awareness can be found at Soul Level and comes from understanding the Soul, its journey and its evolution.

Understanding the different stages of Soul Evolution shines a new light on, not just your life, but the world around you. A young soul may find the art of forgiveness more difficult that a more advanced soul. There are a number of different reasons why people may turn to spirituality, including, finding the purpose of life and its meaning. By exploring spirituality people find answers to questions they have about philosophical questions such as "*what is the meaning of life?*" and "*what purpose does my life serve?*" As mentioned in the healing information, spirituality can help us cope with stress, depression and anxiety. It can help us to restore hope and optimism, thus giving us a more hopeful outlook on life. Whether you are rediscovering a forgotten spiritual path, reinforcing your commitment to an already well-established one, or seeking a new source of spiritual fulfilment, exploring your spiritual side can help improve your well-being.

Each of us has meaning and we bring it to life. We first incarnate as infant souls and through a series of choices, lessons and experiences over the course of many lifetimes we evolve. We haven't always been nice people who some people don't like to hear but it makes perfect sense as we have been learning and growing from our experiences and choices along the way and that's what it's all about. There is no judgement here of yourself or others. You wouldn't judge a baby for not being able to feed itself and you wouldn't expect a toddler to be able to drive a car. Keeping this idea in mind will really help you understand some of the difficult people you encounter in life. I feel that I can relate to this because of how I feel today about ill treatment of others and cruelty in any form. It creates extremely strong emotions within me. I have said previously that I think that I was a troubled soul in my life as a Chinese soldier, or maybe conditioned to be not very kind, and this is something I need to find balance with today. In this life I have had people say that I am too nice!! Maybe I am overcompensating for the negative traits that I had back then. Also, this could be the reason that I have chosen to do service and help people in this life. When I first thought about myself as not being kind, I didn't want to accept it, because I am happy with being the kind caring soul that I feel that I am today. The thought of being unkind feels alien to me. However, we have to realise that we incarnate many times in all forms and different roles depending on what our Karma dictates. Karma is the memory of our soul which means that we carry debts from prior lives. Our current life is mostly determined by earlier lifetimes. What we don't finish then, we come back to finish now. Unpleasant situations are the consequence of lingering Karma. Karma places everyone into your life for a reason, that's why it's important to acknowledge the role of each person in your life. One of the most fascinating facts about karma is that it often causes us to reincarnate in a reversed manner. This means that your parent may have actually been your child in a former life. Then, before reincarnating in this lifetime, the souls agreed to take on the opposite act. Souls switch genders, too. Positions shift throughout lifetimes based on karmic need; whatever dynamic is needed to repair or heal karma will be manifested through changing roles in our cycle of lives on earth. The people you know now may have had a very different impact on your previous lives!

INFANT SOULS: Infant Souls deal with issues of survival and usually focus on fear. These souls flourish in simple environments close to nature. These souls have no concept of wrongdoing so without the loving guidance from older souls who can teach them right from wrong, they may react violently to perceived threats and commit anti-social and immoral acts. They are purely instinctive.

BABY SOULS: Baby Souls have a need for structure, and they tend to follow beliefs based on authority. They are typically moral and law-abiding citizens but suffer from rigid thinking. They sometimes have difficulty accepting others with different beliefs from their own.

YOUNG SOULS: Young souls set high standards of personal achievement. They are goal setters and goal getters. They recognise their personal power and are very assertive. Their experience of life is competitive, industrious, restless and independent. Winning is important to them and they want to leave an impact on society. They value their personal power but view it as something unique to them and tend to separate themselves this way. Young souls focus on being a free agent and are here to learn independence, self-advancement and personal achievement.

MATURE SOULS: Mature souls are emotional, and relationship orientated. Their focus is on their inner world and exploring self-awareness. Their experience of life is self-aware, emotionally dramatic and intense. They question everything, have a *growing understanding of self* and are literally soul searching. These souls are far happier when they share good, and they crave to live in a loving world.

OLD SOULS: Old souls seek the bigger picture and tend to be philosophical and spiritually minded. They focus on being part of all that is and are here to learn, among other things, wise counsel and *spiritual awareness.*

Soul definition: the soul is our humanity that makes us feel emotions. The spirit is our deeper connection with the highest realm. Our Soul is that part of us that observes quietly behind what we do, think, believe, and feel, existed before this human life and will continue to exist after our present physical transitions. For each of us, our Soul is where unconditional love resides. Soul ages and levels of consciousness are very different. You can be a mature soul, for example, stuck at a certain level of consciousness. *It's all about what you came here to experience.* This serves the purpose of raising your awareness so that you can, not only, better understand your 'self' and your present path but also better understand those around you. This, in itself, helps develop tolerance, forgiveness, acceptance and non-attachment. It also helps to not take things personally which, in my experience, opens the door to greater inner peace and happiness. The soul age stages relate to stages of the soul throughout all its incarnations.

LIFE GUIDES AND GUARDIAN ANGELS

Life Guides and Guardian Angels are with you from death to birth and chose to be with you specifically to help you achieve your life purpose. These guides offer us pure, unconditional love, and are high vibrational beings. They operate at a much higher frequency than us, so as to be in a position to impart their knowledge and wisdom when needed. They never leave our side, unlike other guides. If you've connected with your life guide or guardian angels before, you may know their name, if not, then ask) their appearance as well as more about their background as a spirit. Your life guide in particular is like the office manager of all of your spirit guides. They're pretty organised and make sure nothing is too chaotic at once.

DIVINE TIMING GUIDES

Divine timing guides hold the master plan or blueprint to your life. They allow your wishes, desires and plans to unfold at the right time. That doesn't mean you should get angry or annoyed at them for not giving you what you want though – they are always working to present the best and only the best opportunities to you at the right time depending on *what you are ready for, depending on what you have chosen to create your journey.* These are also the guides who oversee synchronicity, so if you've been seeing repeating consecutive numbers or patterns, you've got these guides to thank. Angel numbers are a repetitive sequence of three or four numbers that appear in seemingly random places. If you see repeated numbers over and over, such as 11:11 (as I kept seeing) then there is a message for you. Angel numbers 11:11 signifies that an energetic gateway has opened up for you, and this will rapidly manifest your thoughts into your reality. There is an opportunity opening up for you, and your thoughts are manifesting them into form at lightning speed.

Angel number 11:11 is an indicator of a new beginning. It's a harbinger of a *new opportunity in front of you*. Your prayers have been heard and it's the perfect moment to start a new chapter in your life. The universe sends you a message that angels are on your side. Guardian angels are choosing different ways to communicate with you and number 11:11 is definitely one of them. The presence of number 11:11 is a sign that guardian angels are close by, and they are trying to show you a direction. There are many reasons why this number is very special to me. Even today, my phone alerted me to what I thought was a txt message, and so I looked to see who was messaging me, the time was 11:11 *There was no message!* 11:11 angel number is one of the most powerful messages your guardian angels can send you. And while it has many different meanings depending on your situation, but another meaning is leading you towards creativity, motivation, innovation.

After I had seen these numbers a few times, I looked up the meaning in my Angel numbers book. I then felt inspired to write this book.

WARRIORS AND PROTECTOR GUIDES

Warrior or protector spirit guides act as your own personal bodyguards. Their mission is to protect you physically, mentally and spiritually, though often more the latter, protecting you against psychic and spiritual attacks. Warriors are incredibly enlightened beings who assess all of the spiritual guidance you receive and help you to filter out advice or guidance which may lead you astray from your higher purpose. These are the guides most likely to send you that awkward gut feeling '*something's not right*' instinct. These protectors may take a literal form of a warrior; a soldier or another being in the form of defence.

CREATIVE GUIDES

Creative guides are artistic geniuses. Helping to open up your imagination and creativity, creative guides encourage you to recognise and use your soul's talents, skills and abilities for the greater good. This doesn't just apply to artists, writers or traditional creative roles, they can help you to find creative solutions to almost anything. If you've been wanting to make a career out of your passion and artistic abilities, they're great for giving you practical ideas on how to do just that too.

GATEKEEPER GUIDES

These guides are incredibly important as they hold your Akashic records (*everything to have occurred in the past, present and potential future*) and act like a second bodyguard after the warriors. Gatekeepers offer psychic and physical protection to all spirit communicators. You can think of them like a bouncer at a club with a checklist, only allowing high vibrational, loving energy into your life. Celia would always call upon her gatekeeper to keep our circle safe from negative influences.

TEACHER GUIDES

As their name implies, teacher guides are here to teach you a lesson and guide you along your path. Teachers are typically very wise and practical. They might come to you in dreams, meditations or leave subtle signs around for you to pick up on. These guides are the ones who bring what we traditionally think of as 'good' and 'bad' experiences. The bad (negative) experiences are given to us to either *change our path, to re-assess our current situation, or to bring us a new perspective*. If we're not following the path that's best for us, (*the path we agreed upon*) these experiences will appear until we *'learn the lesson and change course'*. People often ask, "*why do the same things keep happening to m*e"! And "*why me*"? The reason for this is that if we keep following the wrong course, then the lesson will be given to us time after time, until we realise this and change the course.

HAPPY OR JOY GUIDES

Joy guides are like children, in a good way. They're incredibly imaginative, creative and happy. They also encourage you to find hobbies that bring you joy. If this guide had a motto, it would be 'laughter is the best medicine'. My son, Matthew has a guide called '*Whan chin*'. Once we had made connection with him, he brought so much laughter. He told us that he was a fat Chinese man with more than *one-chin*!!! When Matthew connects with him, he instantly gives him a 'boost' and lifts his spirits. He says, "He can't help but smile".

HEALING GUIDES

Healing guides help us to heal during stressful times, and connect us with our physical, emotional, mental and spiritual health. When I decided to channel my healing abilities, my father (*in this life*) who passed when I was only 14, connected with me and channelled healing energies through our connection. As I begin to channel, I feel the change in my hands. My father suffered with rheumatoid arthritis, and his hands in particular became very stiff and disfigured. When I connect with him and begin to channel the energies, my hands feel much larger and I feel a change in shape. This is one way he lets me know that it is him connecting with me. I feel his energy presence and his healing energy passes through me to the person that I am giving healing to. Healing is given to raise the vibration of the molecules in the body. By vibrating at a higher frequency, the body can better heal itself by bringing balance back into the energy centres within the body. This can improve the health and wellness of the mind, body, and spirit. *Energy/spiritual* healing brings relief, relaxation and can sometimes help unblock stuck energies. Our consciousness can be compared to a lens through which we view and perceive the world. As we raise our consciousness, we change the lens of our perceptions. The perceptions, beliefs, mindsets and values we hold right now are a result of the consciousness we are operating in. So, whenever we shift our conscious feelings and beliefs this reflects in our actions. Therefore, consciousness is an inner sense of awareness about ourselves and our surroundings.

We are living in a human consciousness, and that is just one small phase in an enormous range of consciousness. Our consciousness evolves during its journey and as it evolves it becomes greater and dimensionally different. An individual soul is a tiny particle of spiritual energy. When consciousness is identified with the physical body, we have ego (*impulses, feelings and physical sensations*) When consciousness identifies with the subtle level, we have a soul, an extra-individual sense of "*self*" that goes beyond the usual conventional level. While consciousness develops even further and identifies with non-dual reality, we have a spirit.

Love, unending forgivingness, compassion, harmony, peace, and joy reside. Our Soul is a little piece of the 'the all' here to experience this life and its lessons. We are, indeed, Spiritual Beings having a human experience.

SPIRIT ANIMAL GUIDES: A spirit animal reflects you. They represent typical traits that are personified by a specific creature.

There will be something familiar about your animal, and they're there to teach and guide you in a direction that supports you. When a particular spirit animal stays with you for many years or even throughout your life it is termed a *power* or *totem* animal. Whichever spirit animal serves that purpose will depend on numerous factors, including the timing and direction of your life, specific occurrences that manifest, which phase of life you're currently in, and which tasks you are responsible for completing. Consider the physical characteristics of the animal as these will give you clues as to what the message is. The characteristics become a metaphor for the spiritual message.

HELPER GUIDES: Helper guides are there to assist you on *something specific*. They are free spirits who are quick to move on once they've helped with your situation or project.

ANCESTOR GUIDES: If someone in your family has passed over, it's common for them to want to guide and help younger members in their family. Ancestor guides could be an ancestor from a few generations ago.

And then of cause there are the Archangels, Elementals, Ascended Masters, Saints and Star Beings, although you may not know you are working directly with these beings.

Just to remind you: There are many factors that determine who you get on your spirit team.

These factors are: Your energetic blueprint (this is your state of being, your energy, the creator within, which creates circumstances) Your ascension level and soul age and Pre-incarnation agreements.

YOUR ENERGETIC BLUEPRINT

Your energetic blueprint is like your soul's DNA, it's what makes you identifiable to the spirit world. DNA molecules are the building blocks of the living world of our 3rd dimension. It accounts for our appearance, choices and everything related to materialistic world. But *our soul is a form of pure consciousness. Our soul is pure energy and the real 'you' that is nonphysical.* The soul is Love, goodness, peace and light consciousness. It is our emotion, the source of feeling. Everything that exists is a vibration of energy. As this book is about spiritual enlightenment, and also the importance of well-being, I will begin the next chapter discussing Negative Energy. Negative energy is known to have harmful effects on our lives. Your home should feel peaceful. For a healthy balance, it is imperative to find peace within ourselves. Negative emotions can cause stress which in turn impacts your health. Stress can destroy your body's hormone balance, impair the immune system, and drain your positive brain chemicals. Negative energy in the form of poorly expressed anger can cause dysfunction of the heart and digestive system.

NEGATIVITY V POSITIVITY

Criticism: As human beings we all tend to criticise. We can all be judgemental. Some people don't think twice before criticizing someone else if their ideas are different from their own. As spiritual beings we should recognise that everyone is on their own individual pathway, and that we have *all chosen the pathway that is necessary for our soul growth.* What is 'right' for one person, is not necessarily the 'right' path for another. Each one of us is entitled to our own beliefs and is entitled to express their emotions. When we criticise, we are creating negative energy. When you throw negative energy at another human being, you are hurting him or her, whether you realize it or not. You have the ability to interfere with another's self-esteem and self-worth, which changes how they perceive the world around them. At the same time, for yourself. *What you put out is what you get back*. Would you want someone to do or say something to hurt you? Of course not! Be nice. Be mature. Let's not forget the Golden Rule. *Everyone makes mistakes*. Mistakes are necessary tools of wisdom and growth. If you truly feel that someone is wrong, then don't give them any energy! *Focusing your attention on them only gives them more power over your feelings*. It is important however to look within and take ownership of anything you may have done to trigger someone else's anger. It's often difficult to admit that you have done wrong, as we tend to put our focus on the person that is or has hurt us. It is all cause and effect. The relationship between two things when one thing makes it happen, is cause and effect.

Psychology: What we have experienced through each of our lives, is what shapes us. All thoughts and deeds have carved our character. There will be aspects about you in previous incarnations that you have needed to change or perfect and so you will have chosen different scenarios to perfect the soul. So, when you make derogatory statements about others, you are disliking what was once a part of yourself! The ego is at work here, and whenever the ego takes over you can rest assured it is not going to be a positive experience. The ego only looks out for number one. It is self-centred, not self-interest. Big difference! Respect yourself by respecting others.

Unless the other person is upsetting your life, then leave be.

Everyone has to make their own mistakes. It is their 'life choice' and not yours. We all can think that we are right and that we know what others should or should not do or think. *Anger begets anger. Violence begets violence,* and that is why there is so much pain in the world. However, we should never be accepting of behaviour that blatantly harms another human being, either. Negative emotions stop us from thinking and behaving rationally and seeing situations in their true perspective. When this occurs, we tend to see only what *we want to see* and remember only *what we want to remember.* This only prolongs the anger or grief and prevents us from enjoying life. The longer this goes on, the more set the problem becomes. Dealing with negative emotions inappropriately can also be harmful – for example, expressing anger with violence.

Jealousy: Jealousy is another destructive negative emotion and can stand in the way of living your life as a secure and fulfilled individual. Though it's a natural emotion, you can learn to control the negative aspects of jealousy and envy. Who could possibly enjoy the terrible gnawing feeling in their gut as a loved one flirts with another suitor, or a colleague appears to be in line to take your job, or a friend starts spending less time with you because he's hanging out with another friend? In fact, researchers believe there's more to jealousy and envy than just a lack of control over one's emotions. They theorize that these feelings are rooted deep in the evolution of the human species, and as such, form a fundamental part of human nature. Understanding and overcoming your jealousy and envy can be a way of better understanding yourself and what drives you, and ultimately can make you a healthier, more well-rounded person. Jealousy involves a perceived or actual rivalry in which two people are vying for an object of longing — a love interest, a promotion at work, or a good friend for example. The jealous person feels a sense of betrayal and also a sense of potential loss, because his rival stands to gain something he will lose.

Envy: Involves looking with longing at someone whose circumstances appear better than your own. Or you just wish you had what the other person has. The person experiencing envy has an intense sense of deprivation and ruminates over the unfairness of his situation. Comparing yourself to others makes you unhappy. This is turn can cause bitterness which is extremely unhealthy. To overcome envy, you need to shift your focus and be *grateful for what you have in life*. Again, I will reiterate that we come into this life with *what we need and the lessons we need to learn from what we have chosen.* There is more to life than just living. In life, there is a higher purpose, and that is to obtain the real answer to, 'Who am I?' 'What have I come here to experience'. Some people will always have more because that is their chosen pathway.

Self-esteem: Is at the root of both emotions. A person reacts with jealousy when his/her self-esteem is threatened by a potential loss of something or someone he/she holds dear, and with envy when his/her self-worth is threatened by comparing his situation with that of someone enjoying better circumstances.

Romantic partners - may feel threatened or frightened by a person's jealousy — and with good reason, since jealousy is often cited as a reason for abuse of partners or spouses. A jealous person may end up losing the person he/she loves through uncontrolled jealousy, as his/her significant other reacts to his possessiveness by pulling away.

Colleagues at work - can develop a lot of ill will toward a person who is envious of their success or jealous of their relative advancement. He/she tends to spread negative gossip about the person toward whom he/she feels jealousy or envy, in an attempt to "take them down a peg." A jealous or envious person also may become boastful, trying to inflate himself to mask his insecurity. Overcoming jealousy and envy means involves a lot of self-awareness. When feeling these emotions, you should: **Take a step back,** start by understanding that these are normal and natural emotions, hard-wired into our being. Acknowledge that you are feeling jealous or envious. It is ok for you to feel this way, but also understand that this is ultimately your problem, not anyone else's, as it is your own threatened self-esteem that's prompting the emotions.

Overcoming jealousy is up to you.

First and foremost: Figure out the reason for your jealousy or envy. Is it another suitor threatening your relationship with your lover? Is it a work competitor about to best you for a coveted promotion? Keep in mind that just these things may not be real; they may just be something you've perceived. Ask yourself 'why do I feel threatened'? Be truthful with yourself. Jealousy is often overwhelming. We can all be jealous from time to time, but extreme jealousy can interfere with your daily life. Envy and jealousy often come hand in hand. Jealousy is commonly used interchangeably with envy, but the two are distinct emotions, and each word has a different definition. While jealousy can be described as a **fear** that another person may take something that is yours or something you consider to be yours, envy is the desire for something that belongs to someone else. However, both jealousy and envy can cause feelings of insecurity. Envy is more likely to cause feelings of sadness and a desire to change. Meanwhile, jealousy is more likely to provoke anger and resentment. Sometimes jealousy and envy occur together. When someone feels jealous, they may also envy the person who is causing them to feel jealous in the first place. When jealous feelings are long-lasting, pervasive, or severe, it may indicate that the cause is an underlying mental health issue. Some mental health issues and symptoms associated with jealousy include:

Schizophrenia-paranoia-Psychosis-Attachment Issues-Anxiety- personality disorders.

Be aware of the potential negative actions your jealousy or envy could inspire.

Resist the urge to control or stalk your romantic partner, "trash-talk" your rival, or become sullen and bitter over the unfairness of it all. These are all tempting options in the throes of jealousy but could ultimately cost you the object of your desire. They are *negative, destructive* patterns, and can take toll on your health.

Take positive action to solve the source of your jealousy or envy.

Communicate your jealousy to your partner, so he/she knows where you're coming from and can tell you if your feelings are groundless. At work, figure out what the person you envy is doing to enjoy his/her success, and try to emulate or even improve upon those actions. In both cases, you are removing the need for jealousy or envy by improving yourself. As I have said, jealousy and envy are incredibly strong emotions, and aren't easily dealt with. But by tackling these feelings with open communication and a desire to improve and better yourself, you can use them to spur you on to success, rather than keep you in bitterness. Jealousy can lead to possessiveness, unfounded suspicion and resentment. It can prevent us from enjoying what we do have by shifting our focus to what we lack. In romantic relationships, uncontrolled jealousy can turn into full blown anger or physical violence. At work, we may see a co-worker's success as our failure and shut them out. These emotions are unhealthy and not good for the soul. Emotional pain is pain or hurt that originates from non-physical sources.

Sometimes this emotional distress is the result of the actions of others. Other times, it might be the result of regret, grief, or loss. In other cases, it might be the result of an underlying mental health condition such as depression or anxiety. No matter what the cause, this psychological pain can be intense and significantly affect many different areas of your life. While it is often dismissed as being less serious than physical pain, it is important that emotional pain is taken seriously. There are a number of common feelings that are associated with emotional pain that can have an impact on both your physical and mental health. **Also Known As**: Psychic pain, spiritual pain, emotional suffering, psychological pain, soul pain, or mental pain.

The E.F.T therapy that I practice can help greatly with deep rooted suffering. As listed in the healing chapter, there are so many self-help therapies and trained therapist that can offer help.

Everything is energy and that's all there is to it. Match the frequency of the reality you want, and you cannot help but get that reality. It can be no other way. This is not philosophy. This is physics. Albert Einstein.

Symptoms of emotional pain can include feelings of:

Deep sorrow- sadness or depression
Grief -Intense distress -Loneliness –
negative emotions-Panic-Rage-Shame-
Worthlessness

In some cases, feelings of emotional pain may lead to physical symptoms that do not have an identifiable physical cause. When these thoughts, feelings, or behaviours that are connected to somatic symptoms result in significant distress or interruption in a person's ability to function, they may be diagnosed with a somatic symptom disorder. There are a number of different emotions that can lead to psychological pain. Everyone may experience these feelings from time to time, but when such feelings are intense and persistent, they can interfere with a person's ability to function and perform normal daily activities.

Sadness - is a natural emotion that is associated with loss and disappointment. However, if it doesn't fade with time, it might point to a treatable condition, depression, that can impact your whole body.

Anger - is a basic human emotion. It releases adrenaline, which increases muscle tension and speeds up breathing.

This is the "fight" part of the 'fight/flight/freeze' response. If it's not adequately managed, this response can lead to long-term physical consequences. Anger is an emotion that many people repress because they don't want to express it, or maybe they don't know how to express it healthily. We all feel anger at different times, to varying degrees, as it is an emotion that is a natural human experience. Sometimes there are valid reasons to get cross, like feeling hurt by something someone said or did or experiencing frustration over a situation at work or home. But uncontrolled anger can be problematic for your personal relationships and for your health. Feelings of anger can arise in many different contexts and often for underlying reasons that we have yet to understand. Maybe we are burying past emotions and experiences, and one little trigger will result in an angry outburst. Experiencing unfair treatment, hearing criticism, or simply not getting what you want are but a few of the potential triggers. The experience of anger can range from mild irritation to frustration, all the way up to seething rage. Recognizing your anger and addressing the underlying triggers are the first steps to working through your anger and resolving any negative feelings and thoughts associated with the anger. This may mean *writing down our thoughts*, setting boundaries and limits before becoming angry, recognizing any unresolved conflict or underlying ideas, forming a plan, talking to friends and family about our emotions, or seeking one of the may therapies. Expressing our anger at another person is not constructive. Expressing our anger while angry makes us angrier and can make the other person hurt and afraid, so they get angrier, and this does not help anyone. Try to identify warning signs that you are starting to get annoyed about and when you recognise these signs, *step away from the situation if you are able to.* Try not to dwell and keep rehashing the incident that made you mad. If you can step back and just focus on your breathing, taking slow controlled breaths, you may be able to control an outburst.

Anxiety: Anxiety is a type of fear. Even if you are not conscious of it. This can sometimes express itself as anger, if you stuff your emotions under the carpet. You need to *recognise where the feelings are stemming from,* and what emotions they cause you to feel. Maybe you are trying to control something that you have no control over. You may be producing an imaginary feeling of loss. A person suffering from anxiety may take a normal thought and make it the worst scenario that it could possibly produce by over thinking the situation. The thing that they are worrying about may never happen, but even if it did happen the imaginary situation is worse. The mind often creates fearful thoughts, and they can be worse than what is actually happening.

So then, the threatening presence is your thoughts. So then, if you can recognise these destructive thoughts, you can choose to step away from them. When you can realise that your thoughts are making you feel a certain way, and that the problem is not such a big issue, you can recognise that your mind is creating the problem. Again, my advice would be to use the breathing technique to slow down your rapid breathing. As you slow down, you're breathing you will feel your energy field widening and your breathing slowing taking you to a calmer place. Nature provides us with the instinctive 'fight or flight' response to external threats, but when the physiology is out of balance this response gets triggered too often and for the wrong reasons. The secret lies in dissolving the stresses and strains in the nervous system which have accumulated over time. This then allows the mind to be free from worries, anxieties or fears. By naturally allowing any negative emotions like fear and anxiety to dissolve, life becomes more fulfilling, and the body enjoys better health.

Anger amongst Siblings

Some people are fortunate to have loving, supportive relationships with their siblings, but occasional feelings of anger and hate can be present even in the closest of sibling relationships. Hatred or dislike for a sibling can set in at any age, in childhood or adulthood. It can intensify over time or dissipate as the years pass. Many siblings find it difficult to get along and cannot spend time together without arguing or fighting with each other. Either you or your sibling may feel that your parents favoured one of you over the other, which can lead to rivalry and hatred between the two of you. This may cause jealousy. It is not unusual for siblings to be compared to each other, either by others *or by themselves*. As you and your sibling grow, your personalities, tastes, habits, and needs may evolve and it may be difficult to see eye to eye, causing you to drift apart. Disapproval of each other's choices can lead to arguments. You may be dealing with stressful issues, and you can often take out your anger on your sibling. If you commit yourself to being deeply grateful for what's *good in your life*, and remind yourself of it daily, you'll be far less vulnerable to comparison and envy. If someone or something triggers that ugly feeling of negative comparison, stop and remind yourself of what's good in your life, right now. There is so much. No two human beings are the same so there is *no reason for you to compare yourself* with another person. Your insecurities will begin when you start comparing yourself with others because all you might see are shortcomings – if at all there are any. Your mind might trick you into believing that others are richer, smarter, more successful, or more beautiful than you. We often tend to compare ourselves to others. *We are all unique and have different talents.* We need to appreciate and love our uniqueness. We need to stop focussing on other people. What talents they may have does not make them any better than you, just different. You create a battle within when you spend an unnecessary amount of your time and energy. Recognise your own talents and focus more on your positive attributes. Learn to appreciate your own achievements.

Working with intentions

Create some intentions for yourself. Keep a day-to-day journal and write down your thoughts and feelings. After a time when you read it back, you will notice a pattern of your thoughts. Journaling is possibly one of the most simple but profound tools out there for enhancing your well-being on every level (mental, emotional, physical, and spiritual). I kept a spiritual journal when I was developing spiritually so that I could record my process, but it is also good to keep a record of the things that keep popping up and bothering you. When you read your journal back in maybe a few weeks, months times, you may see similarities about the things that may have upset you. So, you may have written that your sibling has upset you because of a certain action. When these similarities keep popping up throughout your journal, you will be able to recognise the triggers and maybe then you can find a way to change that pattern of behaviour.

Of cause there is writing for better health.

Journaling does more than just help you record your memories or find self-expression. It's good for your health. It can help reduce stress, which can be damaging to your physical, mental and emotional health. As I noted above, writing about stressful experiences can help you recognise and manage them in a healthy way. Just 20 mins a day writing can help you unwind and de-stress. Journaling evokes mindfulness and helps writers remain present while keeping perspective. It can improve your mood and give you a greater sense of well-being and happiness. I have found a love for writing, even though I am actually typing. I love putting my thoughts down and keeping information available for me to access when I feel the need.

Writing a Spiritual Journal

Writing a spiritual journal is different than keeping a regular journal. In fact, the slight change of intention in how you record your entries could completely change your state of mind, manifest new goals, and create a deeper sense of emotional well-being. A spiritual journal is a key for learning to open yourself up a little more, to integrate a little more deeply into your worldly pursuits, and to feeling that breath of quiet revelation that only comes as a result of flowing intuition. When you are engaging in a spiritual practice of any kind, it is really helpful to document that practice. I have found that in order to "not lose anything," I have to write down my experiences, weather they are meaningful dreams, messages from music, finding feathers or messages from meditation. Trying to keep everything in our heads is a sure way to lose some of the critically important details or insights we gain as part of our spiritual practices. Our mind -memories do not always recall things accurately, and this can change the perspective of something important that is attached to a certain time or place. By keeping a journal, you are able to follow your progress and the changes that happen as you progress. Journaling can also help to control your symptoms and improve your mood by helping you to prioritize problems fears and concerns. Tracking these from day to day can help you to recognise triggers and learn a better way of controlling them. It is a great way to keep a record of your personal thoughts, feelings and insights. It can also stop the constant trying to remember stuff that is important, that you keep turning over and over in your head. This can cause stress and anxiety.

Once you write things down, it takes it from your busy mind. Writing down your feelings about a difficult situation can help you to understand it better. It allows you to form new perceptions about events. I enjoy it because I like to reflect upon memories.

FEARS AND PHOBIAS

A phobia is an uncontrollable, irrational, and lasting fear of a certain object, situation, or activity. This fear can be so overwhelming that a person may go to great lengths to avoid the source of this fear. One response can be a panic attack. This is a sudden, intense fear. People with a specific phobia know that their fear is extreme, but they can't overcome it. I had an *intense* fear of frogs. I could not even touch a page in a book where I knew that there was a photograph of one. I was always scared that one would '*jump out*' at me from somewhere. It made me feel sick and anxious. I carried this fear with me from the age of 5 until I discovered EFT. *Emotion freedom technique*. Which is an emotional freedom therapy.

EFT tapping - is a powerful and simple way to manage your fears. Tapping helps you get to the **root** of these fears in the first place, and by learning where and how they originated, you can eliminate them once and for all. Phobias cripple the lives of many people. Phobic people experience unreasonable and excessive levels of fear. Phobias happen when an object or situation—or just the thought of it—escalates anxiety to the point of panic.

I had a session with an EFT (Emotional Freedom Technique) practitioner to help me with my fear of Frogs. He asked me to take a photograph of one with me as he couldn't produce one at his home. (Thankfully, I thought at this point). I couldn't even touch a picture and so my partner cut one out of a book and put it in an envelope. We went through the 'tapping' process a few times, and step by step, I managed to open the envelope, then the next step I was able to unfold the paper with the pictures. After more rounds of tapping, I was able to look at the picture of the frog. There were various poses of the frog, and I was able to look at them all, except for the one that looked *like it was going to jump.* This is when I had another negative reaction.

Tapping – helps you access your body's energy and send signals to the part of the brain that controls stress. By stimulating the meridian points through E.F.T it reduces the stress or negative emotion you feel from your issue, ultimately restoring balance to your disrupted energy. We then 'tapped' for **why** this particular photograph upset me. My memory recalled the time when I was five. My family had moved to a new house. My father was in the greenhouse which was overgrown with weeds and damp. Just as I was about to enter, a *frog 'jumped' out* and narrowly missed landing on me. The shock parallelised me with fear, and the 'tapping' took me back to this memory. By the time we finished the 'tapping' session, I was able to touch the photograph of the frog that I wasn't able to before. I no longer have the emotional charge when I see frogs on the TV (that I used to) I can't say that I like them, but I no longer have that powerful fear. I was so impressed with the therapy, that I travelled to Cornwall and completed a three-day course to complete a Diploma in EFT counselling and therefore became an EFT practitioner myself. I have been able to help other people with fears and phobias with this therapy.

There are so many ways to self-help problems within your life. It is often as easy as changing thought patterns. So often we put off making changes because we assume that it won't make a difference anyway. This is limited negative beliefs that we can address if we are not in a 'happy place'. As I mentioned earlier in the book, we grow up with certain beliefs that give us limiting ideas about ourselves. We can fear change. We can even deny that we need to change. For every experience we go through and every pattern that we repeat, there is a need within us to so. We need to be *willing to change* for change to happen. It is important to note that *we cannot change other people*, we can only change ourselves. So many things bother us— people, mostly. But pretty much everything has the power to upset our basic sense of well-being. Our tendency, when things bother us, is to blame the *other person or situation* for getting it wrong and thus causing our suffering. Once we have identified what we consider the cause of our disturbance, we usually set out to try and fix it. We often attempt to *change the other person's behaviour* or the situation into something we consider *right*, or at least something that will not bother us. There is no doubt that people and situations can be the cause of our discontent. If someone was to 'punch' you, then you will feel the pain. If someone speaks unkindly, then you feel the hurt, but we can try to change a situation that we don't like or that makes us unhappy. We need to try to change what's not working, where we can. When we cannot change the cause of our suffering, many of us continue to blame the other person or situation. This may provide us with some relief, at least for a while. But what happens when trying to change the *other* has failed and continuing to blame is not actually making us feel better either? *Where do we go when we have run out of moves?* Freedom from the whole *blaming/fixing cycle*, ironically, comes from moving our attention away from the other person/problem that is to blame/fix, and turning that attention onto *ourselves*. When you hear that it's time to look into yourself, you may assume (as most people do) that someone is telling you to discover how you are *also* to blame for the suffering you are experiencing. To turn your attention into yourself is to ask the question: What does this situation or person's behaviour trigger in me? What pain is generated in me when I am confronted with this behaviour. It is so much easier to put the blame on someone else. We can't control anyone else's behaviour, and we can't make another person want to or be able to change *nor are we assuming responsibility for having caused it.* Getting curious about what is happening inside us in a particular situation, naming it, understanding it, compassion to it—this is the surest path to freeing oneself from the cycle of blame and the need to change what we don't like. Ultimately, *self-awareness* is the most powerful and profound antidote to suffering. The relationship you have with yourself is highly influenced by the adults that were around you as a child. The way they reacted to us, the words that they used is the way we react to ourselves now. By making changes within ourselves is the *only way* to change another person's patterns towards you. Blaming is of *no use* and just makes us feel even more negative towards a person or situation.

NEGATIVE BELIEFS AND MANIFESTATIONS

By our negative beliefs we can create illness within our body. As with everything else, our body is a mirror our inner thoughts. We can create disease with '*dis-ease*' of the mind and spirit. Hence the saying, '*as within, so without*'. This expression is considered to be a universal truth or law which shows us that the outside world reflects our inner world. What we feel and what we believe tend to manifest in our lives. For this reason, it is very important to raise our awareness regarding this universal truth and to understand how it applies to our lives. So, when you have had periods in your life where negative things *keep happening* to you and it feels like you never get a break from the problems and challenges that keep weighing you down? Stop and think about this, remembering that your outer world reflects what you think, believe and are feeling inside.

It is said that the:

The HEAD represents us and how we are usually recognised. If something is wrong with the head, then this can mean that we feel that something is wrong with us.

The EARS, represents the capacity to hear. Problems with the ears can mean that you don't want to hear something that might upset you. If a parent forbids a child's expression of anger, and the child's ability to change things they can develop earache.

The EYES, represents the capacity to see. If you have problems with the eyes, it could mean that there is something you do not want to see.

The THROAT, represents the ability to speak up for ourselves. There are so many reasons why we have problems with this area. This is the fifth chakra, the energy centre of the throat.

If we feel inadequate to speak up for ourselves, we can get laryngitis. The throat is where we express ourselves.

The BACK is our support system. Problems with the back can often mean that we feel we are not being supported.

The HEART naturally represents love, while our blood represents joy. Our hearts lovingly pump joy throughout our bodies. When we deny ourselves love and joy, our blood gets sluggish which results in heart problems.

An excellent book to read on this subject is by Louise L Hay. It is called *'You can heal your life'* So many of her teachings are invaluable and teach us to look within ourselves to see what may be creating 'dis-ease' within our bodies and how we can help by changing thought patterns. This then brings me to having faith. *Faith is a high frequency.* If you have faith, you can make many changes to your life. One of the fundamental teachings is that all of our experiences are the effects of laws we establish with our thoughts, acts and deeds. Our reality is a mirror of what is happening inside us. From fear of heights to fear of embarrassment, we have all got our fears. Some fears are what we have carried back from previous lifetimes that were not balanced at that time. From childhood experiences to past memories, a lot is being processed below the level of conscious awareness. Since we are not mindful of these happenings, our emotions can be quite irrational. It is only by getting some handle on our subconscious mind that we can hope to get rid of them. Here are some ways you can do that: First you need to acknowledge that there is a problem. You need to break the cycle of fear. I learned that fear is a pattern that your subconscious mind has learnt. It could be through a series of negative events or traumatic experiences. Whenever you are facing the fearful situation, the same emotions stir up and the process gets reinforced through repetition. Your goal is to break that cycle. You need to be fully aware of the negative feelings and try to replace them with positive ones. You may wish to get a therapist to uncover where the fear stems from. You may be emotionally overwhelmed. This can result in anxiety.

Anxiety (as mentioned in an earlier chapter) can sometimes manifest as a need to get everything just right. A tendency toward perfectionism often stems from underlying worries about making mistakes and experiencing criticism or rejection as a result. This can often be subconsciously holding on to past negative actions. Anxiety can involve vague feelings of danger or doom rather than specific fears. You might feel as if you need to prepare for the worst, even if you don't know what the "worst" actually is. Instead of looking toward the future with hope and optimism, you are thinking about everything that could go wrong, so you can create a backup plan, just in case.

Then there are panic attacks:

A panic attack involves intense but short-lived feelings of anxiety and fear that seemingly arise from nowhere, often without any specific cause. You might experience difficulty breathing- chest pain – feeling of doom – a sensation of losing control – a sense of detachment from your surroundings. Panic attacks usually happen without warning, so you won't have symptoms all the time. An anxiety attack can feel similar to a panic attack, but it generally won't involve detachment or fears of dying or losing control. There are so many reasons for either of these heightened emotions. Anxiety can also lead to depression which is a persistent sadness and low mood. Some of the symptoms as anxiety, and indeed depression can include: Difficulty concentrating or making decisions- pessimism or worries about the future – general uneasiness and distress- changes in sleep habits and appetite – fixation on negative thoughts. Depression and anxiety often go hand in hand with each other. If you live in chaos and fear, it is because there is chaos and fear within. If your life is calm and grounded, it is because you have found peace within. Ask yourself what requires healing within. *Most talked about is the law of attraction*. Like attracts like, and you get what you focus on. Not only that, but you have to believe what you're seeking is possible to obtain. It is similar to the law of vibration in this way; it's important to learn how to vibrate at a level that attracts what you're seeking. For example: If you want love but do not give love, you're sending the universe a message about your priorities. If you repeat an affirmation but don't believe what you're saying, it's useless. When we focus on what we want versus what we don't want, it will show up in our life, We, need to invite what *we want* into our lives. Every action is preceded by a thought, with thoughts themselves having the power to eventually manifest in our physical reality. What you put out there may not come back to you in that moment, but that vibration, that energy you put out there, has a ripple effect. If you're coming from a place of anger or resentment, if you put that energy out there, you'll eventually be affected as a result. If you are struggling with any of the above, either seek a therapist that will help you or you can reach out for help from the universe and higher energies. They are always ready to help where they are allowed to do so. They can inspire you on what choices to make.

Active listening:

I think that it is important to practice in 'active listening'. This is the process of creating space for another person to talk and fully engage in what they have to say. It requires us to be patient, receptive, open-minded, and non-judgemental. It requires us to not put words in other people's mouths. Rather than internally rehearsing what they might say next or drifting into judgement. Or even trying to 'fix' your problem without being asked to do so. By creating an environment for someone to feel safe enough to speak, and trust that they're being heard, you're showing them you care. You're showing them that you appreciate 'who they are' and what' they 'have to say. All too often people will say: "What did you say?" So many are distracted by their phones, either checking their emails while you are trying to converse with them. We are constantly bombarded with new information. The brain works very hard to process all of what is coming at us – from our phones, the Internet, our voice mails and any in-person discussions we may have. We live in a world where we can put our hands on basically any information we desire, at any time. So, we have we lost the art of slowing down, concentrating on what someone else is saying and reaching true understanding. We lose a great deal when we neglect to focus on another person. When we aren't giving our full attention and we have to ask someone to repeat themselves, we send a message to that other person that they just aren't that important to us. Listen and don't assume you know what they mean. How often do we want to move the conversation along, so we jump to conclusions and make assumptions about what someone else is saying? We hear a word we recognize, or a theme that makes sense to us, and we stop listening – assuming we know what's going on. Most of us have had the situation where we acted on something, assuming we knew what another person wanted. We were sure of ourselves and responded – only to find out we were wrong. I learned about other people's well-being when I took my counselling course. Plus, my mother instilled in us the importance of good manners. Listening is paramount as the person you are counselling needs to be heard. You don't 'but in' when a person is opening up to you, but you show patience and empathy. Active listening builds strong relationships and is an invaluable communication skill. It includes responses that demonstrate that you understand what the other person is trying to tell you about his or her experience. This is a communication technique that's very different from the passive or unfocused listening that we often adopt in everyday conversation. I feel that it is important that the listener makes a conscious effort to understand the speaker's entire message. There are some people that will 'jump in' and talk over you before you have finished talking. They will add what they have done which is similar, or what they know, and can then take over the conversation without hearing what you have to say. This is a narcissistic approach and what the other person is doing is taking power over the conversation. I have often found myself getting quite annoyed by people who do this. However, to turn thoughts around, I have had to re-think my values and try to understand what it is the other person needs from their behaviour. As I have realised that I am doing service this time around, then I am providing a service (of sorts) by being 'the listener' I have also come to the realisation that I was letting myself get judgemental, which I try very hard not to do. These people probably have other wonderful qualities about them. It maybe that the person who talks incessantly about themselves, have low self-esteem. These people will often take centre stage. They will keep talking about themselves so that others don't have the chance to voice an opinion. So, there may be an emotional discomfort within some people that needs healing. I have conclude that there are some people that need attention (maybe they have felt un-loved and insecure because of) this Some that need to validate their feelings and wanting you to accept them for who they are. Then there are those that need to fill the silence. Ultimately though, we're all human – flawed, fragile – and no matter the circumstances, we all need to find our true identity and find balance. Acknowledge and accept that you won't be everything to everyone. There are people that love you for who you are, and there are those that won't. The greatest adventure in life is finding out who you are and looking at the whole story. Be true to yourself about your individualism. Look at how people treat you and how you would like them to treat you. None of us are perfect whatsoever. We would not be living a human life if we were!

Perfectionism:

Perfectionism describes the belief that one is never quite good enough. For example, you may believe that any little mistake you make or imperfection you have, makes you a less worthy person. You may put off completing tasks, fearing that you will never be able to complete them as well as you would like to. People who hold the self-defeating belief of perfectionism often think that others will not accept them for who they truly are. Perfectionism can affect your entire belief system and is often revealed through your personal self-talk and thinking. For instance, "*should statements*" are a type of negative thinking pattern that is often associated with perfectionism. One example would be thinking that you "*should be able to control your anxiety.*" Perfectionism also often takes on the form of negative 'self-labelling', such as believing that you 'must be crazy' for having panic attacks. Such self-criticism only tears down your self-worth and can derail your attempts at coping with your condition. The mistaken belief of perfectionism can greatly impact one's relationships and decided to tell others about their panic disorder. For instance, perfectionism may make you believe that others would not accept your condition. Such beliefs can add to the feelings of loneliness and isolation that are so common for people with panic disorder. Most of us want to be liked by others. However, this desire can become self-defeating when our self-esteem is tied to the approval of others. A constant need for approval from others can leave us feeling hurt, anxious, or angry. The truth is that no matter who you are, not everyone is going to like you. Remember that you are a worthwhile person whether everyone agrees with or approves of you. Those who measure their worth by how much they are liked by others will easily become upset over any form of criticism or difference in opinion. Ironically, wanting constant approval by others can push people away. If you struggle with the need for approval, keep in mind that others may approve of you as a person and are only offering advice and other ideas to be helpful or to engage in conversation. Our belief system is always with us, shaping our opinions and attitudes about ourselves and the world around us. Sometimes we fall into self-defeating beliefs that negatively impact our lives. Changing our self-defeating belief system begins by recognizing its role in our lives. Once you have begun to identify your typical faulty beliefs, you will start to notice what situations seem to trigger you the most. This knowledge gives you the opportunity to change your belief system. Begin to test out your typical self-defeating thoughts by examining if there is much truth in your views.

For instance, do people reject you for your imperfections? Do most of your loved ones still care about you if you don't get promoted at work, reach your desired weight, or make a certain amount of money? Is someone offering you advice because they don't approve of you or is it because they care about your well-being? By continually confronting your mistaken beliefs, you can begin to develop new ones that are potentially more realistic and less anxiety-provoking. Anxiety can make you feel sad. When you stop focusing on the things that are do make you sad and start looking at the little things that make your life worth living, you slowly experience a shift in attitude. Your general outlook towards life changes, making you a happier person.

Gratitude:

Practising gratitude is as easy as saying thank you for life's blessings, and the sooner you start, the sooner you'll start reaping the benefits of gratitude—of which there are plenty, by the way. It can elevate stress for one. when you're in the thick of a stressful situation, if you are able to refocus your attention and energy on things that you are grateful for in the moment, you can calm both the mind and body, therefore reducing the physical and mental symptoms of stress. Gratitude is good for your psychological well-being, and also can have an effect on your physical health. Some people have more grateful dispositions than others. For some, gratitude just doesn't come as easy. Research suggests that these differences may be rooted in our brains, genes, and even our personalities. If you're having trouble feeling grateful, don't despair! There are things you can do to bring more gratitude into your life. Make a list of all the things and the people in your life that you are happy to have around you. Your personal values, perceptions, and attitudes make up your belief system. Self-defeating thoughts are any negative views you hold about yourself and the world around you. Also known as mistaken or faulty beliefs, these views impact your self-esteem the feelings you carry about your personal abilities, and your relationships with others. Maybe keep a daily gratitude journal. Even when you are faced with a challenge, it may be hard for you to accept, BUT challenges are sent our way if the form of experiences, some happy, some not so. Again, I want to bring focus back to the fact that we have chosen to have these - (for whatever reason we decided upon before incarnation) challenges, and so we really should be grateful for these tests because once we have dealt with them, we can move on and know that we have ticked off one of the challenges that we chose to be tested on. *Everything and everyone are in our lives for the reason that we need them to be there. (Even though as a human form we have forgotten)* I want to include a very important conversation that I had with my daughter, Emma. Nearly all of her married life, she has struggled with finances, juggling to balance what money she had. Whenever she thought she had caught up and was free from the worry of money, something would come to challenge her again. She said that she railed against the unfairness of it all and felt cross at times that each time she felt she was on the up, she would go back to struggling. This went on for some while and she used to get very negative about the situation. It wasn't until one day when she was talking to her father that she suddenly realised that she was actually living what she termed as '*her best life*'. They talked about money and also the fact that her father wanted her to do a college course to give her an easier future, and therefore be able to have more money and a bigger house. She told him, that *being a mother <u>was</u> the best job in the world.* She said that she may not have had a job that paid a lot of money, but she had been able to take her children to school and collect them from school *every day*. She has been able to take them to their clubs and parties and spend quality time with them, taking them to the beach and to the park. *Every minute that she has spent with them has been more precious than money.* Even though they live in a relatively small home, she realised that they had to spend time together and that *this too was a positive*. Once she realised that this was what was important and that she didn't need lots of money to make her life happy, she stopped thinking about how unfair things were and started to be *grateful* for what she did have. Since then, things have been better for her financially. Things just fell into place. Karl was offered a job with better pay, and little luxuries became available to them. She does not feel the need for more money than she has. Her family is more important, and as she said, "she is living her best life", I think this shows a great lesson in gratitude, and love. Focussing on just one thing that you are grateful for increases the energy of gratitude and brings joy and peace into your life.

Gratitude helps you to see what is there instead of what isn't.

Be thankful for the difficult times.:

- *During those times you grow.*
- *Be thankful for your limitations, because they give you the opportunities for improvement.*
- *Be thankful for each new challenge, because it will build your strength and character.*

- *Be thankful for your mistakes, they will teach you valuable lessons.*

Some people, and tests are challenging, but through each we have the opportunity to grow. Every person and every experience teach us how to Love, trust and forgive.

Remember that people who challenge you are bringing you the life-lessons needed for you growth.

"Ultimately, man should not ask what the meaning of his life is, but rather must recognize that it is he who is asked. In a word, each man is questioned by life; and he can only answer to life by answering for his own life; to life he can only respond by being responsible"

Viktor Frakl

I will relay a dream that shows the significance of challenges:

Someone close to me had said some hurtful things and I was feeling very 'out of sorts' and felt that I needed some space from this person and also peace. The incident was while I was in the middle of writing this book. I accepted that this person was bringing me a challenge that I had obviously chose pre-incarnation. Obviously, something that we both needed to balance.

The Dream:

The journey began on a bus journey. The person that had challenged me in real life was on the journey with me. There was a most beautiful sunset that stretched as far as the eye could see. I had given my camera to the 'other person' and because I wanted to capture the sunset, I tried to take a photograph with a pen!

The Sunset: *represents major changes and that one will gain spiritual enlightenment. It also indicates the end of a cycle or condition. It is a period of rest, contemplation and evaluation.*

As with most of my spiritual dreams, I never have my camera when I want to capture moments and so I try to use whatever I have. That being either my fingers, or a pen in this case.

Camera dreams: *Are all about new perspectives. They usually show up when the tried and tested isn't working and they are our subconscious way of letting us know that it is time to look at a situation, person, event or a way of thinking in a new light*

The next part of the dream was that I am climbing down a cliff that was made entirely of sand. This other person was with me, but I went ahead. I managed to slide down to a safe place and the other person slid down towards me and stopped in a curve in the sand, beside me.

This person was naked apart from a tattoo on the neck. The tattoo was a Native American necklace. I looked at this person and thought how beautiful she was.

Climbing down a cliff: *represents inner change, self-knowledge and amazing development occurring in your life. Bringing more serenity and quiet. It also means that you are entering a time when many improvements will happen. Sand suggests that you are thinking about your life, and that you will need to grasp the time to do what you wish in life.*

[As I said, after the disagreement I did feel that I needed some space and peace for myself.]

Seeing someone naked in a dream: *This often means that we need to change our perceptions of someone or something. It goes on to say: You are seeing this person for who they truly are. I had thought how beautiful she was in the dream, which is true of her nature even though the argument itself brought challenges.*

*The **tattoo:** represents a pledge of Love. So, you see, within this dream was very detailed* *message which was clear that I am finding change within. I have thought more about my life and that I want more inner peace.*

 It is also telling me to walk away from negativity and challenging experiences, but it was also showing me the love that the two of us share in this life.

I feel that the fact that the tattoo was of a Native American necklace resonates with part of my soul energy. The fact that part of my soul journey was in Dakota and also that my guide is a North American Indian. (And again, part of his soul energy)

Dreams touch on every level in our life. They may let us glimpse the future, or give suggestions for healing, or even share insights into our relationships. Above all they can and will steer us more directly to our true self. I have included a chapter about different types of dreams that will come later.

To re-cap on reincarnation: Life and Death

As you are now aware, when you choose to incarnate back to Earth, *it will be your Spirit with all the memories of all the past lives it lived, including this one, but it will not be "you", as your current personality, body and mind.* The values and perspective and appearance of a Spirit are very different than ones of your human personalities. You as a human personality only live once, ego and body die after each life, but the experience and wisdom gained stay with your Spirit. When in Spirit, you can take any shape you want, so you can show your spirit as the one you have just left behind, so that your loved ones can recognise you. You can show the same image, personality and mannerisms, but this is just an image, like a hologram. In reality, our spirit is a giant ball of light and energy. It will still be 'You', but not 'you' in the sense of the human character you currently identify yourself as. *Your current identity as a person is tied up with your current body.* So, in your *next* life, you will have a *new identity* that is tied up with your new *body, mind, abilities, experiences and memories.* But behind all these trappings of human identity lies the *ever-present real You.* You are a pure presence, formless and timeless, an integral part of the very fabric of reality, slowly evolving in consciousness. Your *human* sense of '*self*' always changes from one life to the next, just like an actor moving from one role to another. The *innermost Self that is <u>You</u> never changes.* This 'Self' is who and what you know yourself to be from each incarnation. *To put it in an easy context*: A '*personality*' is the result of social upbringing, culture, values, goals, morals, relationships with parents and siblings, presence *or* absence of trauma, etc. These circumstances will be different each incarnation. We get a new body in each physical life, but it is "*the soul*" or "*spirit energy*" with all its past life memories that inhabits the body.

Accidental Death?

I have already mentioned about our soul contract, but I want to mention death, and if there is such a thing as accidental death. So, we have made the plan before we incarnate, and our soul chooses when to leave the body. There are a number of *exits* in place and the soul may choose which one of these to take depending on the progress it is making. (I believe that we have five chosen exit points) No one dies by accident. We leave our body when our soul decides upon leaving, even though the human mind is not consciously aware. If say, a plane crashes killing 200 people on board, these deaths are not accidental as the souls of each and every one that died decided to use this as their exit. Once the soul has decided upon the exit, events will begin to unfold to make this happen. No matter how the death occurs *it is always the decision of the soul*. You as a human will not know about these plans. How then, (may you ask), do soul's get to choose when there are floods and fire and disasters that could kill them when they have not chosen to go? Well, this is where your guardian angel steps in to prevent you from being killed *(if this is not your soul's chosen time)* So, say you are booked on a flight and your guardian Angel knows that this flight will crash, your angel can do all sorts of things, like making a traffic jam so that you are late and miss the flight. You may even have a feeling that something is not right, and you make your own plans to change the flight. This will be a feeling sent by your angel guides. What happens if you die in a car crash! Again, this will be orchestrated by *'your soul'* as an exit point. If your soul has decided that it wants a quick exit, *it will choose the nearest option.* I have already explained that when it is your time to go, you will be met by your deceased loved ones and guides. You will have your life review and re-cap on the contract that you decided upon before incarnating. Your spirit can re-adjust, settle in, and get accustomed to the other side. During this time, your Spirit also reflects on its time on Earth. The life review is like a movie, where you will see all of your accomplishments, and all of your failings. People that you have helped and people that you have hurt. Your spirit gains perspective on these experiences so that you can grow as a soul and transition to your next lifetime (when that time comes) The period of reflection can take a few weeks or many years. During the life review, you are surrounded by Spirit guides, and you will review the lessons that you were meant to learn while on Earth. Starting from birth and extending to the great return, you will see *every event* in your life playback to you as though on a giant movie screen in front of you. You will be surrounded by love and support, with no judgement.

You will now understand that reincarnation has a purpose. It is for spiritual advancement as a human being. There isn't enough time in a single lifetime to address all the many facets of soul development. So, in the Afterlife you are again offered the opportunity to come back to the 'Earth Life School' and to choose what aspects of life and experience you want/need to explore in the next life. These will depend upon the decisions you made whilst watching your life review and deciding upon what you need to learn of address in order to become a more advanced soul. It is through a series of chosen lifetimes that you spiritually evolve into the *Best Spirit You Can Be*. The afterlife is our true home, with these many brief (relatively speaking) lives in between, here on Earth. Death is of the body; the soul is a permanent entity that is constantly evolving. We ask ourselves many times "how can this child be so wise at such a young age" "Where do they get such knowledge". The answer is, because they have been on the Earth plane before and have bought back with them knowledge from previous lifetimes. Some are able to remember past lives for a *short time* after birth. Reincarnation makes the experiences of this lifetime meaningful and purposeful. The body of matter (*our solid Earth body*) is dependent on the spirit body for its existence, and the body of spirit is dependent on the body of matter for its expression in the world of matter. The experiences of the body of matter, determine the growth of the spirit. If a person is ill, sometimes the causes are purely physical and that is why we need medical intervention. *Everything that affects your body of matter, affects your spirit*, and what affects your spirit body, then affects your physical body. There are many diseases that have no real physical causes but *start with the spirit*. If the spirit is not balanced, then the outer (body of matter) suffers. For instance, Anger effects the spleen. These things cause maladjustment, upsetting the perfect balance. When the body becomes so diseased (dis-eased) that the body is completely upset, then the spirit can no longer express itself through the body. It then severs itself and death takes place. This is what happens also in old age, there becomes a gradual loosening in the adjustment between the two bodies before the spirit will detach itself from the body of matter. People will ask, why do people come into this life with broken bodies and hereditary diseases. *We come into the world with the body that the soul needs from inhabiting a 'challenging' body. The* soul needs to learn from the experience from the point of view of the evolution of the soul. Remember, *we choose our body before we incarnate*. If we have chosen a 'differently-abled' body, it can be for us to experience the difficulties and challenges that it may present. *It can also be for the 'care givers' to learn compassion*. There are many reasons for this, all for the development of each individual that is part of your life. But all discussed as a whole before incarnation.

Q: *"Why can some people be healed by healing mediums and not others"*.

A: "As a spiritual healer myself, I *channel loving energy* through to the person that is seeking help with either mental health or physical illness."

Healing can help the patient to become mentally stronger, and can give some satisfactory pain relief, and an overall spiritual wellness. Not everyone can be healed if it *does not help their spiritual growth*. They may be having to deal with some suffering because of the *soul's choice*, chosen before incarnating. The soul will have chosen to live with the disability or an illness for what it needs to learn lessons from, or for what others can learn from. Therefore, it would not be beneficial for the soul to be healed by a healer. A healer can alleviate pain, but not necessarily cure. We all have to understand the spiritual laws. The reason that we take on certain bodies in each incarnation *must not confuse the evolution of the soul with the evolution of the Earth body.* You will usually find that a person who starts their lives with a material defect have very loving souls.

Medium ship and messages

A reading with a true medium can help you with life—and specifically if you are grieving from losing a loved one. As a medium, I am often able to bring evidential and specific information that no-one (only the sitter) would know. This is proof to the sitter that there is no trickery involved. I connect with my Guide '*Fast Cloud*'. He will relate information that can re-establish a connection and offer a certain level of evidence that the soul survives death. This suggests that not only can we continue to communicate with loved ones on the other side, but that we will be met, on the other side of death, with people who can help us transition. Belief in an afterlife comes much easier to some people than others, and it is a mediums job to bring comfort and proof to those who seek it. How lovely would it be to be able to say to your deceased mother, "mom, I really need to know you're with me right now." "Will you please appear before me so that I can see you?" — and then watch as she appears! Unfortunately, that's not how spirits operate. Any signs you receive from the other side are not usually given in the most obvious ways. The signs given to the medium through their guides can be quite cryptic and are usually given in symbols. They will try to send signs that you will relate to. They *want* you to recognize them. I get the most obscure things sometimes in symbols. I will explain to the 'sitter' the symbol that I see and when it has meaning for them, they light up and know that we are connecting to a loved one on the other side. I always work with love and light and only ask for 'good energy' to connect with me (through my guide) I seek only to bring love, enlightenment and truth to anyone that comes to me for a reading. Before I '*tune in*' to the vibrations of my guide, I ground myself by visualising my feet as the roots of a tree and feel them going down into the Earth. I surround myself with a white light and do some deep breathing (meditation) which will higher my energy vibration before I talk to my guide/guides. I thank them for their help before they give it. (*A vibration is a state of being, the atmosphere, or the energetic quality of a person, place, thought, or thing*). Everything in the universe is made up of molecules vibrating at different speeds. This includes trees, bodies, rocks, animals, thoughts, and emotions. Human vibrations are composed of everything from physical matter to the way you communicate the thoughts you think. In simple terms, some molecules vibrate faster, and some vibrate slower; there are higher vibrations and lower vibrations. When you are vibrating at a higher level, you feel lighter, happier, and more at ease, whereas lower vibrations feel heavy, dark, and confused. *Gratitude* is one of the quickest ways to amp up your vibration. Try it right now—stop reading and look around the room. Turn your attention to what you are thankful for in this moment (there is always something) You can't feel fear or anger while feeling gratitude at the same time. Therefore, when you feel yourself experiencing a low energy emotion, see if you can shift your attention to gratitude. Make gratitude a habit, and it will transform your outlook on life as you start to experience a spiritual awareness and appreciation for the little things. Call to mind someone who is easy to love and hold that person in your heart. Visualize him/her sitting in front of you and notice how you feel. A feeling of expansion, lightness, and happiness will take over your being, *and that right there is the shift you are looking for.* Love is the highest vibrating state of being and our soul purpose is to love and be loved. It's as simple as that. Finding any opportunity to give our love to others and to be open to receiving the love of others. That is what we are here to learn and embrace. *Love for all things and all people.* The path to that is kindness, tolerance and non-judgement. Always choose people's feelings, generosity, and kindness over material things. *Ultimately, gratitude, kindness, compassion, and love are the most powerful tools we can use to navigate our soul experience here.* A medium wants to bring that love from spirit to help heal the mourning or distress that the people they have left behind struggle to cope with. That is what a true medium will want to achieve. It is not '*fortune telling*'. Spirit won't give you the winning lottery numbers for instance. They can give you a glimpse into the future, just for you to have as proof that they know what is in store for you.

How to Channel and find your peace

Channelling puts you in a different state of mind. Some people will turn to a medium to advice when they eel they have lost their way, or indeed their power. When you begin channelling for yourself, you go within and find peace and a very loving energy. You may not get messages right away, but you are channelling the peacefulness within you. When you are in a calm state your body will automatically relax. The gentle wave of energy will flow through your body allowing you to relax further and go deeper within yourself. Remember that you are safe, and you are loved. Be mindful of the energy that flows through every part of your body, starting with your breath and visualising each part of your body relaxing, right down to your fingertips. Just stay

within this feeling. Your whole body, and mind
is still. You will find that by now you are so
relaxed you won't want to move. Your
breathing will have slowed right down.
Visualise roots growing from your feet and
going deep into the ground. Breathe deeply and
you will find yourself in an even deeper state of
peace. Visualise yourself lifting up through the
blue sky and through the clouds and just be.
Feel the comforting peace as it gets stronger
within. You may notice that beautiful scenes
flow through your mind as you move closer to
your higher self. Your subconscious will take
through a journey spiralling upwards. You may
find that you see images in your mind of people
and places which have connection with who you
are and who you have been. You will feel deep
love within and around. This is when you are in
a deep state of meditation. There is nothing to
fear. It is good to practice mindfulness for
relaxation whenever you may be in a state of
stress and just want to find peace for yourself.
You may find that you get enlightened
'messages' come to you while you are in this
state of relaxation. You may even see yourself
in a past life. By mindful meditation/channelling
we become more aware of ourselves and the
energy that we project. When you are ready to
come back down to Earth energy, just breath
and become aware of each part of your body.
Do this slowly, taking long slow breaths, until

you are ready to open your eyes. You are working with your energy, and you are slowing down the energy to return to that state of waking. This is a form of meditation which is a state of consciousness that is completely different from the normal waking state. During meditation your mind is not focused on the external world or events taking place around you – the mind becomes clear, relaxed and inwardly focused.

The aim of meditation and channelling is to experience peace and happiness. The mind is the biggest obstacle in achieving this goal. Meditation can be used as a means for calming yourself or letting go and teaches you to explore your inner dimensions. Practised frequently it helps you learn to feel more balanced and aware. The benefits include stress reduction, increased emotional and mental clarity, heightened feelings of peacefulness and calm, increased energetic awareness, and improved health. Also, it allows you to channel your guides and your higher self if you so wish. Eventually you may wish to become a medium to be that connection between guided messages and helping others. Becoming a medium takes time and thoughtful practice.

The benefits of becoming a medium/channeller

A reading with a true medium can help you in your life by easing your grief. While it may never take away the pain of losing a loved one, or the sadness of not having their physical presence around, a medium, by bringing through highly evidential and specific information that nobody else could possibly know, can re-establish a connection, and offer a certain level of evidence that the soul survives death. This suggests that not only can we continue to communicate with loved ones on the other side, but that we will be met, on the other side of death, with people who can help us transition. I know that I have covered mediumship in an earlier chapter, but I want to clarify a few points. Belief in the afterlife becomes easier for some than others. You may not want or feel the need to believe, and that is totally your choice. I am only adding what I feel can be beneficial if you do. There are many people that will mock your beliefs. You may feel that this will create a barrier for yourself. You may feel that you are different and not wish people to see that you are 'different'. As I mentioned before, one person actually said that I was talking to the devil! Some people are very cynical, and again that is their choice. A lot of people have strict religious beliefs. This is where I say again, being spiritual is a way of life it is not a religion. For me, my beliefs and experiences have given me a better understanding of who I am, and the reasons that

I am here this time around. One of the reasons for this incarnation is to do service and being a medium helps with that also. I feel that I can bring peace and clarity to people that feel the need to connect with themselves or indeed their loved ones that have passed on. At first, when a few people made derogatory remarks or 'mocked' my beliefs, I would feel very self-conscious and even a little self-righteous. Now that I have worked my way through that and come to the self-knowing that I am happy within myself and happy with my beliefs, these comments no longer upset me. Each and every one of us are different and on our own journey. What we wish to believe is totally ok. We have all chosen the journey that our soul needs for growth. Channelling has helped my person growth enormously and I feel that I am a 'better' more enlightened person because of this. We all go through challenges and conflicts within our journey of life. I feel that this is where we grow. Understanding why we have these obstacles enables you work through them and find balance. When you are able to channel, the highs and lows of life don't seem to impact your life so dramatically. Again, it helps you to regulate balance. I believe that what we have been going through during the pandemic (more on that later) we are all wanting to 'find ourselves' and our purpose, and many are experiencing a spiritual awakening. We have all been thrown into chaos and fear due to the pandemic, but going through it, our lives have taken on many changes. People are searching for a meaning and a purpose. If you are feeling the 'want' to channel, take slow steps and let whatever is meant, to come to you. don't try to force things to happen. They will happen when the time is right. Just talk to the voice of your soul. That part is the easy part, and that's a good start.

Q: *"So what do we look like when we go over to the spirit side of life?"*

A: "What we look like now in human form is solid and dense"

The Soul is higher intelligent energy and energy can take on any form it desires or requires. Your Soul group helps to create the human you. When we return to our soul origin, our energy becomes much lighter because we have ditched the heavy body. Depending on which dimensions/vibration you are experiencing, your spirit can look just like body you have just left, but lighter, transparent and glowing. As we reach the higher vibrational levels, we become more like cloud energy. However, we can still take on an image for our loved ones to know who we are. I have explained in an earlier chapter, that when my daughter Emma was aged 10, my Mother passed away. Emma saw her when I was saying goodnight to her (after she had passed) She said she there was nothing unusual about her appearance. She looked exactly as she did before she passed. This example shows how spirit energy can show themselves to you as you would remember them. Energy can take shape in many ways. Have you ever thought that you have seen a ball of light or shadow move across a room Or even caught a glimpse of something out of the corner of your eye somewhere? Or even witnessed a mist or cloud of smoke form before you. Sometimes you sense the energy presence. If you answer yes to any of these, then you have had an experience with someone from spirit.

Coincidences or synchronicities

Your guides and loved ones catch your attention by putting things in your path. Like I mentioned with feathers, for instance. They can also let you know that you are going to connect with something or someone before you do. So, when I began noticing some obscure words that came into my head, which then produced an actual occurrence later the same day I wondered what was actually happening. I will explain:

I had the name *'Odette'* come into my head one morning. At first, I did wonder if it was someone from spirit wanting to connect. Then that evening I was watching a series on Netflix.

The episode that I was watching had the normal main characters, but during this episode a new character was introduced. Her name was '*Odette*!' Coincidence? You may think so. The next day, I had the word '*canasta*' come into my head randomly. That very evening, I continued watching the same series. Halfway through it, one of the women said: "she is about as difficult as a game of *canasta*"! Then, the very next day, I had a song come into my head. "*I won't give up on us*". I wondered if it was a message for me or just a song playing in my head, as sometimes that happens to us with no specific meaning. *That evening*, whilst watching the same series, this very song was played! These are all random '*coincidences*' but I came to realise that it is one way that spirit let us know that they are living along side of us. They know what is going to happen before we ourselves know it. to be, before we, ourselves know it. So, when you have things happen to you that you think are a little weird or strange, it is probably a deceased loved one or your guides connecting with you.

I could write a whole page of similar incidents like this, but I don't feel that there is a need, and you would probably become bored! **Your departed loved ones and guides may communicate with you through a song title or lyric that reminds you of them at the exact time** you are thinking about them. They may also try and provide you with clarity and guidance through a series of songs with a resounding theme or message that answers a question you have about a particular situation. In our dreams, we're often left with lasting impressions and insights that help direct us forward in our waking life. Lights may flicker or we may get disturbances with television sets and any electrical appliances. Of cause you don't have to accept what I write; I just want to help people to understand that the simplest of '*odd*' happenings can be a loved one letting you know that they are around. As I mentioned, spirit know in advance what is going to be played out in our lives. Nothing is coincidental, everything has a meaning.

The word "synchronicity" has become popular for describing coincidences that seem to come out of nowhere. You think someone's name, and a few minutes later the person calls. You want to read a certain book, and without telling anyone, a friend suddenly brings you the book. *Synchronicity* is defined as a meaningful coincidence. We can sometimes overlook what could be a beneficial experience because we condition our minds to fall into the same patterns. 'I know what I know' is certainly a limited mindset. Fortunately, your higher 'self' and your spirit team have a way of sending you messages now and then that nudge you away from fixed views. Synchronicity is one kind of message. It says, "There's more in this world than you are allowing yourself to believe."

Q: *"Can we trust our feelings, and intuition?"* *"How do we know if they are guiding us on the right path?"*

A: "We are told to trust our gut feelings, which is also our intuition guiding us." "Acknowledge your feelings in the presence and understand that these feelings are what is the truth for you".

We can feel that there are two people inside of us. One that says its' ok to do whatever, and the other tell you no don't do that! Your intuition arises as a feeling within your body that only you experience. Have you ever experienced a nagging feeling of unease about a situation? Suddenly felt suspicious about someone you just met. You can't explain your feelings logically, but you know something isn't quite right. Or maybe a rush of affirmation or calm floods inside of you after a tough decision, convincing you that you're doing the right thing. Gut feelings can evoke a range of sensations, some not unlike the physical feelings associated with anxiety. Other, more positive sensations might seem to confirm your choice. Some people describe gut feelings as a small internal voice, but you'll often "hear" your gut talking to you in other ways. These feelings tend to come on suddenly. The feelings seem to come from no-where, and they are not random.

Example: What if you suddenly feel a strong urge to cross the street? There's no obvious reason behind your impulse, but you can't ignore it, or the tingling at the back of your neck. A few seconds after you cross, the sign on the building ahead comes crashing down, right where you would have been walking. You stare in disbelief, heart pounding. How did you know that would happen? It is called the gut feeling, because that is where we feel it. However, Gut feelings are pattern recognition systems designed to keep you safe and well, but sometimes they can hold you back from thriving based on old fears.

Example: Say you were cheated on in the past and you're convinced your newest partner is a cheater, too. You might be right—but it could also be projection from the previous *trauma that you haven't processed*, and you're just attaching it on the next person that comes along. Or, alternatively, you could be projecting your idealization onto someone you're just meeting because you really want to find love. What you think is your intuition telling you "They're the one" could just be another projection. With that in mind, pairing your gut with the logical mind or getting some outside perspective from a friend can help. Someone who is suffering with anxiety, may find it difficult distinguishing intuition with anxious fears, and that becomes challenging. Intuition comes from a *calm and mindful state* that is not the same as anxious emotional feelings. Therefore, your gut and intuition takes self-awareness and trust. It is everyone's journey to learn when the energy is accurate. As you connect more on a spiritual mindfulness journey your instincts will become clearer and more accurate.

Psychometry

One of the ways I connect to spirit is by Psychometry. This is a psychic ability where it is possible to "*read*" the history of an object by touching it. I receive impressions, thoughts and feelings from the object that I am holding. Some mediums use a crystal ball. It is all about connecting with energies. The connection between psychometry and our aura is based on the theory that the human mind radiates an aura in all directions, and around the entire body which impresses everything within its orbit. All objects, no matter how solid they appear, are porous containing small or even minute holes. These minute crevices in the object's surface collect minute fragments of the mental aura of the person possessing the object. It is my goal to provide guidance and support to help others to connect with their inner knowing so they may realize their purpose and embrace the best version of themselves. Also, to help people with a further understanding of spirituality and the soul's purpose, and how to help the '*self*' find peace. This then will also help with health, and healing of the spirit. Spiritual wellness involves finding your life's meaning and purpose, and understanding the values, beliefs, and morals that guide your actions. We come here to fulfil a mission. No matter how big or small this mission seems to be for us, it's important. It's our unique mission. We are here to complete our soul's duty. I am trying to help you connect with your soul on a deeper level and help you understand your soul's mission. As I have state a few times throughout this book, *spirituality is not a religion* it is a way of life, and it is discovering a sense of meaningfulness in your life and coming to know that you have a purpose to fulfil. Many factors play a part in defining spirituality, faith, beliefs, values, ethics, principles and morals. Some people gain spirituality by growing in their personal relationships with others, or through being at peace with nature. Spirituality allows us to find the *inner calm and peace* needed to get through whatever life brings, no matter what one's beliefs are or where they may be on your spiritual journey. The human spirit is the most neglected aspect of our selves. Just as we exercise to condition our bodies, a healthy spirit is nurtured by purposeful practice. The spirit is the aspect of ourselves that can carry us through anything. If we take care of our spirit, we will be able to experience a sense of peace and purpose even when life deals us a severe blow. Knowing that there is a '*bigger picture*' helps us to understand some of the difficulties we may be experiencing. By understanding this, we can deal with life's challenges in a more understanding way. A strong spirit helps us to survive and thrive, even in the face of difficulty. Meditation is a way of relaxing the body and quieting the mind. It encourages a deepening of consciousness or awareness. Alternatively, some people find Yoga beneficial to overall health. Throughout my life, I have connected with people that have helped me with deepening my knowledge of life, and how I have been able to help others. With my counselling I have learned to listen very carefully and only reflect back what has been said to help the person draw their own conclusions. Counselling is about building trust. It is being noncritical but **supports you in making progress in your life and goals, whether that's helping you overcome fears or improving your sense of self.** With the E.F.T. therapy, I have been able to help people to overcome their fears and phobia's. My spiritual healing as helped me to give peace, relaxation and often, pain relief. My spiritual knowledge has been a major factor in my life. I have been able to help others that have asked for further knowledge.

This is how I understand that I am here this time around to do service. I hope to help others to become centred, more peaceful, more attuned to the higher vibrations. I can sometimes give clarity to questions about what happens to our loved ones when they pass over. This in turn, uplifts. Also, it helps me to understand that there is a '*bigger picture*' to everything, and that things are often '*meant to be*'. It has helped me to understand that we are all on a different pathway, and that I must not be judgemental. I have had to do a lot of *self-healing and soul searching* before I felt that I was able to spiritually awaken fully. I had to learn that you cannot just '*jump in*' and try to help others with their problems. You have to wait to be asked, otherwise you are just adding to your negative Karmic slate. Everyone is on their own pathway and seek their own knowledge. Therefore, *only offer help where it is asked for*. You cannot heal the world. As I said earlier in the book, some people will only find healing when it is in their soul's interest to do so. Not when we as Earthly beings think they should! Also, we can all say, he/she should do this/that. I wouldn't do that, that is not my way! Well, NO, it may not be the way you or I think another should act or think, we are all individual and are learning at different levels. We need to *learn to accept others and accept that they may not think the same way they we do*. It does not mean that we are right, and they are wrong. They are just *different opinions,* and we are all at different stages of our involvement. Therefore, try not to judge others. When we judge, it blocks our spiritual growth. Be mindful and try to catch yourself before you speak or send that hurtful email and do any potential harm. You can't get your words back. *Pause,* see if you can understand where the person may be coming from. Try to rephrase your critical internal thought into a positive one, or at least a neutral one. After all, we really don't always know the reasons for someone else's behaviour. Never underestimate the pain of a person, because in all honesty, everyone is struggling in their own way. Some people are better at hiding it than others. It takes practice to look for the goodness in others as our minds naturally scan for the negative. *We all make mistakes.* That is why we incarnate, so that we can have experiences and learn from them. When someone does something you don't like, perhaps think of it as they are simply solving a problem in a different way than you would. Or maybe they have a different timetable than you do. This may help you be more open-minded and accepting of their behaviour.

The Dalai Lama says: *"People take different roads seeking fulfilment and happiness. Just because they're not on your road doesn't mean they've gotten lost."*

When we feel happy with ourselves, we do not feel the need to judge others so critically. So, the answer is to find happiness and peace within yourself. One night I remember lying in bed and thinking about my mother. I wondered if she would be proud of the person I have become. The following morning, I awoke with the music I always associate with her. This being Annie's song by John Denver. Later that morning, I realised that I was humming to myself. I stopped in my tracks when I realised the words in the song were: *I see your true colours shining through... I see your true colours that's why I love you.... And then, you are beautiful... like a rainbow.*

This is just one of the ways that our loved ones can connect with us. We just have to be open minded. So, as I have mentioned, we can receive messages through music, dreams, electrical interference, feathers. There is a saying: "When Robins appear, loved ones are near". A lot of people associate birds with messages from their loved ones. Our loved ones like to place significant objects on your path to remind you of their presence. They can be objects that were sentimental to them or you. You may see what appears to be an apparition, blurry outline or even as a figure of light. Some people see orbs of light. Out of the corner of your eye, you may see something move, but then when you actually look, there is nothing there. Some people do actually see spirit as if they were alive. I explained in an earlier chapter about how my daughter saw her nan (my mother) just after she had past. She saw her as if she were still in her earthly body. No matter what signs you are receiving from your loved one, take a moment to thank them and be open to interpreting the signs in a way that feels right for you. If you can quiet the mind, you start to connect with the higher vibration spirit world—you can focus on that vibration and connect with loved ones. And that is where you get this amazing connection and beautiful energy that can assist you in your life and help you in healing. A few nights ago, I was sitting with Mike and holding his hands. Because his strength has decreased, he is feeling vulnerable and emotional. This has obviously had an impact on me, and we were feeling a loss the way life was for us before this. Normally, I am the one that preaches about being positive, and we all know that having a positive outlook on life is good for our mental well-being. There are times though when we are faced with certain problems/challenges and our emotions need to be dealt with openly and honestly. This was one of those times when we gave in to our sadness, and just sat holding hands. Suddenly I felt a surge of energy connection with a presence and a shape to the side of me. It came as a shock as I want expecting it. I felt the powerful surge of energy run through the whole of my body and into Mike's hands. The energy was bringing love and compassion. I knew instantly that this was his mother coming to reassure and give peace. My body shakes involuntary and my muscles twitch as a spirit energy connects with mine. It depends on the spirit energy and intention that it brings that depends on the level that it impacts me. Grace's energy was definitely very powerful and stayed with us for about five maybe ten minutes before the energy lessened and finally retracted. It impacted us both greatly. After this experience, we both felt an overwhelming sense of peace and upliftment. We discussed changing our thoughts to more uplifting ones and looked for the positives that we still have. We enjoy our days at the nearby country gardens, where we can sit by the lake listening to the birds while enjoying a picnic or lunch in the cafe. It changed our thoughts to the fact that come the spring we would enjoy time back there. I awoke the *following morning* with the words to a song:' *We'll gather lilacs in the spring again, we'll walk together down a country lane'.* You see how immediate this message was and how very apt once again. You simply cannot put these down to coincidence! Everyone has their own unique experience with spiritual energy. There is no right or wrong way to feel. You have a different vibrational frequency and perceive reality from your own unique vantage point. You also have your own blocks, limiting beliefs and other issues. No one else has this exact combination of attributes – you're unique!

Q: "Can you explain how the soul is energy?"

A: All matter is merely energy condensed to a slow vibration.

Everything is energy, and *everything* is connected to *everything* else. The water in the ocean and the clouds in the sky. The trees and the animals. You, me, and the world around us. Everything comes from the same source and returns to it. Everything is one. Thoughts and feelings are energy as well, so *everything* we think and feel has an influence on *everything* and *everyone* on this planet. In this way, we create our own reality, because mind rules over matter.

Q: *"How does spiritual healing help?"*

A: "A spiritual energy healing is like having your car battery charged". "The energy is there for you to distribute and use in your continued recovery process." "This happens naturally and unconsciously". "The body has received a boost and the healing will continue." "You may notice you need more sleep, exercise, hydration or different nutrition after your healing as the body rebalances and adjusts to the changes that were made."

Q: *"How is energy healing different from conventional medicine?"*

A: "Conventional medicine is generally targeted to one area of the body, is studied in a logical fashion and attempts to treat all bodies in the same way." "However, energy medicine is holistically approached and treats each person as a unique individual." "As the spiritual energy passes through your system, it creates change within your energy field."

We are spirit, soul, and body. All three demand our attention, and if one of them becomes imbalanced, there can be an issue in all three areas. Our spiritual and mental health are uniquely connected. **For example:** Negative thoughts left unchecked can become negative beliefs, and these negative beliefs are the lens that we use to view our overall experience in this world. What you will find is when we allow the negative ideas and beliefs, we attach to different negative experiences to go unchecked, they can leave us feeling isolated, powerless, and vulnerable. These intrusive thoughts will trigger corresponding emotions of anxiety, depression, foreboding, fear, etc. If we hold onto negative thoughts and emotions, a negative belief system is formed, which begins to impair your personal and professional relationships. Just as when we get an infection in our physical body, our pain sensors send a signal to our brain saying, *"Hey, something's wrong here that needs attention!"* If attention isn't given, then the infection can lead to more severe circumstances. It's the same with our emotions. When deep sadness, depression, or anxiety manifests, our emotions are telling us that something with our mental health needs attention. Try to recognize if there are negative thought patterns that have crept into your mind. If so, then take action in shutting those patterns down. Many individuals have experienced incredible trauma in their lives. Sometimes the thoughts and beliefs that the individual attaches to the trauma can be worse. If someone is assaulted, the event itself is difficult to deal with, but the intrusive thoughts of *"I'm not safe," "No one will protect me," "People cannot be trusted,* "can continue long after the event and cause serious issues. If we become depressed or anxious about an event, the first question to ask is *"What am I thinking and believing about the event?"* When the body cries out, experiencing injury or illness which demand our attention; we are being offered an opportunity to heal ourselves on many levels. We often go straight to the medical doctor with our ailments, seeking immediate relief. Patients and practitioners alike are often quick to mask the issue with pharmaceuticals, inevitably prolonging the symptoms and healing process. When we begin to see the importance of addressing the deeper more psychological and spiritual aspects of our inner workings alongside our medical treatments, we begin to see that the body-mind is not made up of separate parts, creating pain or dysfunction for no particular reason. We are reminded that it is the integration of systems, the interconnectedness of the whole which is so specific to human health, happiness and well-being. Trauma, grief, anger and fear are all very natural human emotions we are sure to experience throughout our lifetimes. However, if we are left to sort through our own emotions feeling unsupported, these feelings can become stuck or stagnant within the bodies postures, systems, meridians or chakras. Often when we open ourselves to receiving holistic healing work, practitioners can detect places where the "energy" has stopped moving or may be moving sluggishly. Energy moves through the body in many ways, and we do see from modern research that different systems can be traced to certain emotions. *For example:* grief is often manifested in our lungs and respiratory system while anger shows up in our digestion or as irritable bowels. As we open to this interpretation, we begin to understand the importance of not ignoring our emotions. The main concept behind the mind-body-spirit connection is that we are all more than just our thoughts. We are also our bodies, our emotions, and our spirituality … all these things combine to give us identity, determine our health, and make us who we are.

Mind: Your mind is your thinking mind (both conscious and unconscious) that is responsible for your beliefs, thoughts, and actions.

Body: Your body is the physical aspect of yourself that carries you through life and allows you to experience the world through your five senses.

Soul: Your soul or spirit is that intangible part of you that you might refer to as your essence.

Apache Blessing

"May the sun bring you new energy by day, may the moon softly restore you by night, may the rain wash away your worries, may the breeze blow new strength into your being, may you walk gently through the world and know it's beauty all the days of your life."

I felt that I wanted to include this blessing to bring your attention to the beauty of nature and how it can lift the spirits when we attune to it.

Q: *"How can I stop being so negative"*?

A: "Just simply STOP.! *YOU*, are in control of your own thoughts. You can change a thought at any time you like…Just Change it. In order to break out of the obsessive thinking patterns which maintain feelings of anger, resentment, bitterness and rage you need a method for changing your thinking patterns. However, trying to repress you thought and feelings is not the answer, as they will just cause them to go underground and come out in another way. You need to redirect your thoughts, but you also need to deal with the *underlying feelings too*. This is where forgiveness comes in. It works on many levels at the same time. It helps you redirect your thoughts and to let go of the unhappy feelings associated with those thoughts. A good way to help with negativity is by practising mindfulness.

Q: *"What is mindfulness?"*

A "Mindfulness allows you to become more aware of the pattern of your thoughts".

Then learn how you can change those thought patterns to a more helpful mindset. You don't have to meditate, although this is a good practice, but it will help you if you can find clarity by looking more clearly at how you are feeling and what you may be constantly dwelling on. If you feel that you spend a lot of time caught up in your thoughts, worrying about the future, or dwelling on the past, this may keep you in a state of negativity or even fear. Mindfulness is thinking about how you can improve on these thoughts. Maybe you may feel that exercise could help. Changing thought patterns to look at a more positive way of dealing with your problems. It is how we relate to ourselves, and others. So many of us spend our days just running from moment to moment. We are busy, have demands coming from several different areas of life, and simply don't feel like there is time to stop and allow mindfulness. Find a time for yourself, and just sit quietly thus paying full attention to your thoughts, being mindful is the opposite of rushing around and multitasking. When you are mindful, your taking your time. You are in a relaxed state of mind.

Q: *"Why doesn't my life go the way I want it to go"*?

A: "Life is an ongoing process of creation." "*YOU* are creating your reality every minute."

The decisions you make today, may not be the decisions you make tomorrow. You make things difficult by changing your mind. Therefore, be of one mind and of a single purpose and don't take your mind off it until you have produced it in reality. Keep choosing the same thing. Try not add negative thoughts to the mix. Keep focussed and keep positive. What you have chosen to manifest *before you incarnate* will come to fruition if you just let it. Take the stress out of situations, by remembering '*IF*' it is meant to be, for your soul progress, *then it will be*. There are spiritual laws of request. If you want help, then *you must ask for it*. When you are ready to ask for help you are ready to receive it. You will get an answer. You just have to be open to receive. You may switch on the television, or pick up a book, or even hear some music that will give you an answer. Again, remember, that spirit is only allowed to help for your spiritual growth. They cannot and do not interfere with your *'free will'*. This brings me back to where I have explained that YOU cannot change another person. Only the 'other' person can choose to change themselves. No matter how unhappy you are in a situation wishing the other person would be more like YOU want them to be. If you are unhappy with the way someone is treating you, then YOU have to decide to change the situation, or even look at the way you are behaving to cause the situation to be negative. If you can't change a situation, change how you *think about it*. As you now know, earth is a place of learning, and lessons are presented to us by making our outside an exact reflection of our inner world. If you are angry within, then you will attract angry people in your life. If you are self-critical and constantly beat yourself up with your thoughts, you will attract people who will reflect this by putting you down or some even physically hitting you. The person who feels safe, secure, loved and happy inside, will draw people into their lives that love them. You may have chosen to have difficult people in your life this time around. Maybe they are unkind or controlling. This is where you have been given the opportunity to experiences these lessons in order for you to face and deal with and become the best person that you can be. There will be *a reason why you have chosen to have these people in your life.*

LOOK WITHIN, to alter beliefs and attitudes in order for *your* outer world to change.

WE CANNOT CHANGE OTHERS – WE MUST CHANGE OURSELVES.

Remember: We create our reality with the thoughts we think all the time, every day. Our thoughts dictate the decisions we make

Q: "Why can't I find happiness"?

A: "Maybe, subconsciously, you don't feel that you deserve to be happy"

You may have a boulder of negative memories and beliefs which are causing even more negativity and UN-happiness. One thing that you can practice is to *forgive.* When you can find forgiveness, you will begin to find happiness within. People sometimes convince themselves that vengeance is 'justified' and that vengeance is sweet but you will never meet a person who is truly happy, and at peace with themselves, if they are also vengeful. Yes, there can be a form of satisfaction in a vengeful act, but it is sickly form of satisfaction and there is *nothing healthy or life-enhancing* about it. Vengeful people live in fear and anxiety. They may adopt an air of confidence, but they do not tend to sleep well at night. They believe so much in vengeance that they cannot conceive of anyone else not feeling the same way. They are waiting and wondering when those they have harmed will come and do vengeance on them. *They are not in charge of their own life as their life is dominated by anger.* There is no satisfaction in playing the role of the 'angry victim'. Forgiving someone does not mean that we have to accept their behaviour or hurt, but toxic anger, rage, hatred and resentment causes more harm. *These feelings stress the body and mind and can even create health problems.* When we feel unloved, or hurt we usually believe that '*other*' people are the cause or the source of our feelings. We perceive that they are rejecting us or being unkind or insensitive to us. But feeling unloved is ultimately the result of an unresolved conflict we have within ourselves. To highlight again: *We choose challenges and also challenging people to be in our life movie for the lessons we both need to resolve.* Once you come to terms with the fact that there is a much bigger picture, then you can begin to understand how life on earth and your life story/movie works. These lessons are what you need to resolve (with Love in your heart) and you will not find peace within until you do. If you *do not* resolve the challenges in a forgiving way, then you *will keep getting* the same lesson given to you until you do. If it is not in this lifetime, then rest assured you will have to come back in another life to find resolve. You have to balance all Karma. Two people that are in conflict need to find forgiveness and understand that the lesson has been given to balance past life conflicts with that person. This WILL continue to until you find forgiveness and tick the box that you have passed your exam.

Q: *"Why do I keep getting the same kind of negative people come into my life"*

A: "We are like magnets, and we draw towards us everything and everyone that comes into our lives".

Remember we have chosen people to play parts in our story of life before incarnation. However, we draw these people to us on the Earth plane by our thoughts and emotional energy. As I have mentioned, if we think negatively all of the time, then we will attract negative people and situations into our lives. The inner attracts the outer. Ultimately, we have to learn whatever it is our soul has chosen through these experiences. It is how we choose to deal with these situations as to whether we pass the exam we set ourselves. To put it in simple terms: 'We have a Karma slate.' If we treat someone with negativity, then we chalk up a negative mark on our slate and have to then we will need to experience that negativity ourselves in another lifetime. Life isn't about being perfect it is about finding balance so that we can become the best version of ourselves. It is only when we have completed these tests with satisfaction within the soul, that we can know that the next time around, we *will not* have the same tests.

Q: *"Why are people so critical of me"*

A: "The same as the answer above basically". "If you are critical and judgemental of yourself, then others may treat you the same way."

It is the way you are expecting to be treated (*subconsciously*) Change your thought patterns. Write some positive affirmations about yourself and say them to yourself whilst looking in the mirror. Tell yourself that you ARE worthy of love and that you are *willing to accept love in your life.* When you do this, you will no doubt release pent up emotions that are causing a blockage to your happiness.

Q: *"If someone has made me feel second best and unloved which has caused me trauma, how do I deal with it without negativity?" "I'm not sure that I can forgive"*

A: "Firstly you need to be able to let go of the pain "It's possible that you may have conflicting feelings about wanting to be with this person, but also have the feelings that you cannot forgive."

You will remember that I said *we choose people that offer us lessons.* You may not feel strong enough to deal with this lesson at this current moment in time. Ask yourself, what is this lesson showing me about myself? What outcome do I desire? The important thing is that you have to LOVE yourself. If you are critical of yourself, then others will see that in you and will also criticise you. Find something that you like about yourself and focus on that. If you are always in a negative state of mind, people will avoid you and they will criticise. It is human nature to do so. Forgive yourself for not being perfect! Do things that make you feel good. Once you find forgiveness and happiness within, it is so much easier to forgive others. *The inner reflects the outer!*

Life on Earth is a team game

Life on Earth is a team game. It is vital to learn the rules so that you can participate and make your contribution. A game of football would be a free for all if everyone did their own thing, so players are taught the rules before they go onto the field. In the same way we are taught universal laws before we incarnate. Life on Earth has turned out to be a free for all as people have forgotten or chosen to disregard the rules. When people take themselves too seriously, they are critical and judgemental of themselves and others. Many feel tense and out of control. Often people have to feel superior, so life then becomes a power struggle and disharmony prevails. I feel that this year in particular (2021) that the mass consciousness on our planet is changing. People want harmony and a different way of living. Due to the Covid pandemic, people have come together to help each other in so many ways. So many acts of kindness, and a generosity of the spirit. It has however had a negative effect on some as they became isolated for so long. I will focus more on this in a later chapter. Some advice for someone that is struggling to find peace from the stress that this may have caused would be to maybe find a meditation or yoga class. Besides the need for humility, this pandemic has increasingly drawn attention to numerous social and economic inequalities, injustices and imbalances apparent both in our societies and throughout the world. Socially and economically disadvantaged people are more likely to suffer from the coronavirus and other diseases as they have no, or limited, access to quality health and social care systems. Some live in overcrowded houses and hence find it difficult self- isolating and may experience insecure employment, unemployment, or forms of financial insecurity. This impacts negatively on both mental and spiritual health. In addition to social and economic inequalities, attention has been directed towards the imbalance's humanity has caused within the natural environment. Reports suggest that there has been an improvement in the quality of the air and in the wider environment due to the lock-down as this has created less pollution. So now, an opportunity has been provided to reflect on the role of humans in causing environmental degradation. This includes global warming and consequential rising sea levels, changes in weather patterns, the rapid loss of many species, and the destruction of natural habitats. *Our human actions have contributed to these environmental problems.* So maybe now is time for us to change certain factors and be more aware of our responsibilities to the planet. *The pandemic as highlighted the need for change.* A change of mind-set on human well-being for all. We need to eradicate poverty and strive to live within the framework of the values and guidance given by the spiritual laws, in order to achieve peace in the universe. Whenever you feel *a strong emotion coming on* — a response to pain or pleasure, success or failure, extreme stress or thorough relief — say to yourself, "*This, too, will pass.*" We watch the news and worry about the economy and the state of the world. These things deserve our concern, but our *worrying about them endlessly* is not useful. Worry captures our consciousness, diffuses our attention, and makes us prone to making mistakes.

Disharmony and Intention

This brings us back to disharmony in the body, causing anxiety and stress. Anxiety is having too much fear and worry. Some people feel worried and stressed about many things. Often, they worry about even small things. Some may experience a panic attack which is a sudden feeling of extreme anxiety. When we are worrying and our thoughts are going round and round in circles imagining every possible outcome, we are in the dark. Imagine there is a light switch in your head. When you are considering doing something, while still examining the possibilities, the light is off. As soon as you are clear that you will do it, say to yourself *I intend* to do this, and the light switches on. Clear decisions move you from feeling stuck to the feeling of freedom. Intentions are more powerful than wants, wishes and hopes. Intention releases a force that makes things happen. Whatever you aim for in life, if you gather the energy and sight on your target, the might of the universe is unleashed behind your vision. Even if you do not actually accomplish your intention, you have set a powerful force in motion. Imagine an archer, he pulls his bow back and holds it *in-tension (**with intention**)* as he aims for his target before unleashing his arrow. Intention is taken into consideration however when assessing Karma. The karmic balance sheet of our thoughts and deeds have inevitable consequences.

For example: If a child runs out into the road into the path of a car and is injured. Does then the driver bear karmic responsibility. It depends on his intention. If he was driving sensibly – he does not. On the other hand, if he was drunk or angry and driving carelessly- he does bear responsibility at a spiritual level and will have to repay in some form.

If someone has evil intent and focussed on hurting, harming or creating havoc, then a black mark is earned in their soul record. The intention has gone out into the universe, and it noted. The creeper of beliefs and fears about rejection and hurt take a stranglehold on our heart. It causes us to cling to relationships *or* to withdraw. We stop loving when our mind takes over and we see imperfection in another. Then we connect *ego to ego*. Your ego is the fear of your lower personality, and this forms a boulder which blocks the flow of love. Success is a state of mind, not a particular achievement. When your all is focussed on a specific goal, there is a moment of elation at the moment of achievement. Then you have to set another one and start gain. The law of abundance is very simple. If you want more friendship in your life, be friendly to others. If you want more happiness in your life, *remember that thoughts, beliefs or memories that make you feel sad, are past.* They have no reality in this moment. If you want more caring and nurturing in your life, remove the barriers that stop you from receiving it. *Challenges/lessons* are sent to us to see how we respond and deal with them. Remember, *we are all responsible for our own destiny. We have chosen these lessons before we incarnate.* We are responsible only for ourselves, and others are responsible for themselves. As I have said earlier, we do not have the right to carry someone else's burdens or assume that others want our help. Help should only be given if asked. If we go ahead and interfere with another person's progress, this will result in negative Karma and another test will come forward to us differently disguised. Listen to your intuition and trust it to guide you. Chances are, at one point or another, you've had a 'gut feeling'. Maybe someone instantly gave you a bad vibe, or you had a sudden and unexplainable urge to skip an event. But what are gut feelings, or "gut instincts," really? And should we always trust them? Our gut feelings or instincts are similar to our intuition, though often a gut feeling will involve some sort of physical feeling as well— which isn't always the case with intuition. The difference between gut instinct and intuition is that gut instinct is not a reliable guide to building innovative processes in creative thinking. Affirm that you are what you want to be. Speak your words with energy and intent. Make sure that your affirmations contain *only positive words* and have faith. Faith activates the response from the universe. Every time we focus on something, we are calling it towards us. With every though and belief we invite people, situations and material things into our lives. When they arrive, if we don't want them, we try to push them away again. The unconscious mind and universal mind work exactly like computers. You cannot tell a computer not to bring up a certain file for it cannot accept negative instructions. It will assume that you do want the file and bring it up. Your conscious mind can discriminate between negative instructions and positive ones, but *your unconscious mind cannot tell the difference. Don't, can't* and *won't* are words which invoke the law of resistance. *Whatever you resist, persists. I am healthy, goes into your computer as a command. I deserve to be loved, draws love.* If we have been resisting for a long time, it may take a while for changes to occur. Write a list of what you do want in your life. If two people want to push a boulder in a certain direction, they will both stand on the same side of the boulder and push so that it moves. If, however, you stand opposite each other and push, it will only move to the extent that one is stronger. This is what your inner personalities do when they struggle. They resist each other, and we stay stuck. If one part of us is afraid of commitment and the other part of us wants a stable relationship, then we create a pull-push situation. The relationship will stay stuck. Resistance will result in delays. Again, look within and decide what you truly want and what your vision really is. Quite resisting and send out enthusiastic energies to draw the positive to you. Resistance is a result of our mind being attached to having things a certain way rather than the way they actually are. It is a mental habit of the ego. Stress happens when your mind resist what is. Changing your thinking will take some time. You need to practice healthy thinking every day. After a while, healthy thinking will come naturally to you. Attention is the focus of your thoughts, words and actions. So, watch where you put your thoughts. If you give too much attention to worry, or fear you energise it into creation. Churning worst case scenarios in your mind or continually talking about your fears are powerful ways of drawing them into your life. Try to focus on a positive situation. Decide on your vision, focus on it and give it your full attention. Water represents emotions. If emotions are blocked, they stagnate so that relationships become stuck. If your emotions are a torrent, then people may be frightened to come close to you in case they get swept away/ or drown. However, if the river is peaceful, then people will want to sit by it. Watch the flow of your emotions and notice the effect it has on your relationships. If a cupboard is crammed full, nothing new can be put into it. If you hoard either money, old resentments or old idea's, there is no space for new to come in. To allow new to come in, you have to let go of the old. If you hold onto old emotions of those old memories, you will prevent fresh and happier things from coming in. Throw away old rubbish and shift your consciousness to attract something better. Open the gates for new beliefs and memories to come in. Notice and stop your *negative thoughts* or 'self-talk'. 'Self-talk' is what you think and believe about yourself and your experiences. It's like a running commentary in your head. Your self-talk may be rational and helpful. Or it may be negative and not helpful. There is a later chapter, 'Food for thought', which includes ego v intuition.

More Questions and answers

Q: *"Why are some people mediums and others not? What does this depend on"*?

A: "This depends on the evolution of each spirit."

Being a medium is a condition which you choose and know before incarnating, and when used correctly, it helps this person to advance more quickly in their evolution through the help given to other people. I have realised that this is part of my pathway in this lifetime.... doing service to help others. A medium is someone who is able to communicate and channel energy between us as humans and the higher realms. When we pass over, we transition from the physical being to the spiritual being...and mediums are sensitive and intuitive enough to hear, feel, and see information coming from the other side and channel that energy.

Q: *"Why aren't all messages clear from our guides?"*

A: "Firstly, our spirit guides function on a different vibration, higher energy levels. We as humans' function on lower energy levels and so the energy has to connect. It takes a lot of hard work for them to connect with us. Messages can come in all shapes and colours. Most spiritual messages and experiences have an element of *synchronicity* to them.

As I have explained previously, spiritual messages and experiences can show up in many forms: A song, a recurring series of numbers, a dream A gut feeling or intuition, weird/ unexplainable things like lights going on and off or the scent of your grandmother's perfume when you are alone in the house. Sometimes, these messages may repeat for us to help us learn or integrate the message that is being presented. Our guides will try to share their guidance with us, but will do so typically in a quiet, non-obtrusive kind of way. The truth is, there are messages all around us, and they happen every day…but they usually are not glaring neon signs saying, "Do this!" For us to receive the message we have to be open to the message and be aware of our surroundings and what is going on around us. One of the biggest challenges to interpreting the messages we receive from our spirit guides is releasing our expectations and ego. So often we ask a question, and we have an answer that we want in our minds. When we come from that perspective, we run the risk of twisting and turning each message or input we get to give us the answer we desire. I have included some dream interpretation in another chapter, to show how I have received messages in dreams. You have to be open to what you are receiving and resonate with what you are given. You will usually get that 'aha' moment, when you might think, oh my goodness the dream or the words to a song gave me the answer to thoughts that I had been churning in my head. Our guides will give us clues, and we interpret the meanings that resonate to us. It may not always feel right, but you will 'feel' what is right for you.

Q: *"What about changing relationships?"*

A: "Change" is a pretty full-on concept. We don't want to be forced into it against our wills, but sometimes it really is exactly what we need. There's a big difference between being asked to be someone you're not and growing to embody everything that you can be. Sometimes, you really do need to change to be in a relationship — here's why: You should never stop growing. When you look back over the years, you'll probably notice that you have changed. Spiritually speaking we choose our partners. We all have soul partners and everyone in our lives has a purpose. As I mentioned in Karma: To learn the act of forgiveness, someone must take the responsibility to deeply hurt you. Thus, providing you the choice to either forgive them or stay resentful. To know how to be independent and strong, someone must ensure they abandon you at your worst hour. Thus, giving you the opportunity to either stand up for yourself, or fall down and succumb to your circumstances. So, everyone you meet has signed-up to help your soul's evolution. *YOU* have signed-up too, to deal with them. Even the annoying and challenging ones. You have decided who will be part of your life. Say then, that you have chosen your husband for the purpose of producing children. You will go through your life lessons with this person until maybe the children are grown and you may find that you have nothing to offer each other in soul growth. Your life is orchestrated for you to meet the next person that your soul will have chosen for the lessons and experiences that the new relationship brings. When a change is needed, you will know because you will find the dynamics change within you both. You will go through situations that will challenge you and you will notice will eventually notice that things are not good for you. When you have learned what it is you need to learn from each other, you may go on to meet someone else that offers you the next lessons that you need. We should not be afraid of changing relationships. We are supposed to have changing relationships throughout our lives. It may be friends that you outgrow, or they you. Each of you will have shared the experiences that you have needed from each other, and then you will go in different directions. Some of cause, will stay with you forever. We can often get fixated on the loss and feel hurt or rejected by them. It is healthy to have changes, because each new person will bring new lessons, challenges and experiences that you need for growth.

Q: *"How do the elements affect us as an individual?"*

A: "In astrology there are four elements given to the signs: water, air, earth and fire. These four elements are reflected in us, and they play a role in how we interact with each other. It is all a matter of finding the natural rhythm of the four elements and how they organize our daily experiences and overall life"

I am an Aquarius which is the water bearer, which astrologers believe represents the gifts of truth and pure intentions that they bring to the world. An Aquarian is said to be self-reliant and optimistic. We are born within the elements that defines our personal traits. As we all know, the zodiac is composed of 12 different signs — each with its own personality traits, strengths, weaknesses and characteristics. Your zodiac (sun) sign is tied to your exact day of birth. This ties to your core personality and psychological profile — hinting at what is important to you throughout your lifetime. A quick reference to the 12 signs is:

Aries: March 21 – April 19

Element: fire

Symbol – Ram

Taurus: April 20 – May 20

Element: Earth

Symbol: Bull

Gemini: May 21 – June 20

Element: Air

Symbol: The twins

Cancer: June 21 – July 22

Element: Water

Symbol: Crab

Leo: July 23 – August 22

Element: Fire

Symbol: Lion

Virgo: August 23 – September 22

Element: Earth Symbol: The virgin

Libra: September 23 – October 22
Element: Air
Symbol: The scales

Scorpio: October 23 – November 21
Element: Water
Symbol: Scorpion

Sagittarius: November 22 – December 21
Element: Fire
Symbol: The archer

Capricorn: December 22 – January 19
Element: Earth
Symbol: Goat

Aquarius: January 20 – February 18
Element: Air
Symbol: The water bearer

Pisces: February 19 – March 20
Element: Water
Symbol: Fish

Relationships are very complicated especially between a man and a woman. Why? Because both partners invest most of their need's physical, financial, emotional within their romantic relationship. It is rare that relationship among couples doesn't run into a few bumps, however, the real problem arises when instead of resolving the conflicts, you blame or tell hurtful things to each other, which can at times turn too ugly and maybe become impossible to resolve. Astrologer's, say that relationship problems stem mainly from—ego and insecurity. Complicated relationships are challenging, but there are ways to navigate through the ups and downs to find relationship success. (Unless it is your destiny to change relationships) The strengths of your Sun sign can help you find peace within and also with your partner. If, you seriously want your relationship to work, then knowing how to use the positive energy of your Sun sign will give you the possibility of quickly moving through conflict to a renewed state of closeness with your partner. So, astrology helps you understand how to rise above patterned behaviour and connect with each other.

In a nutshell:

Aries: Aries have a great magnetic personality. Aries have a bundle of energy that attract others towards them. *Aries feel*

that it is sometimes better to lose the argument rather than lose the trust and love of their partner.

Taurus: Taurus is the most dependable and reliable of all zodiac signs. when The Bull gets angry, it can destroy or wreck everything in his path, but Taurus will work hard to provide his loved one's financial stability and comforts in life.

Gemini: Gemini is the sign of the twins and has two distinct sides to their personalities. They are superb with words, can charm anyone with their demeanour and also have brilliant humour. They lack patience and, in their restlessness, they sometimes throw away most precious loved ones for some distant dream in their heads and may live to regret their hastiness. Gemini can suffer more from emotional problems than the rest of the zodiac signs.

Cancer: Sun sign is ruled by Moon, the planet of mind. As is the waxing and waning of the Moon, so are the mood swings of Cancer. You may come across a Cancer person, laughing its contagious laugh and later in the day withdrawn deep into its shell. To keep up with the mood swings of a Cancerian can prove to be quite challenging for some. However, it is hard to resist when they surround you with love and care. However, watch your words for they never ever will forget what you said or did to them even many years later.

Leo: Leo is a fiery sign and full of energy. You may get attracted to the energy of a Leo and get wounded by their pride. They may make you feel like the most wonderful and special person in their lives. Leo, the Lion, will always care for you, even if they don't show. If you open your heart to them, they will open up to you and reflect that love back. They will always want to have the last say, (even when they know they are not right.)

Virgo: is an earthy sign and the most practical and methodical sign of the zodiac. They are gentle and quiet, but they quietly observe and notice the smallest details before they go in for war with you. They won't go into any conflict without fully weighing the pros and cons and gathering all information. Most people don't like to be examined and analysed to correct flaws or mistakes, but Virgos can seldom stop them from correcting the mistakes of others. This may often bring conflicts in relationships.

Libra: the sign of scales, is ruled by planet Venus. They hate conflicts, so they often prefer to find a compromise rather than stand their ground and deal with the discomfort. They can be good-natured but can also be sulky at the same time. They can be happy one moment and sad the next moment. They are not moody; it's just that they are unsure and indecisive. The golden scales of the balance go up and down.

Scorpio: Secretive and possessive, Scorpios prefer to handle conflicts on their own and will not let others know the intensity and inner turmoil. They tend to be totally calm on the surface but are actually in desperate need of help and support. The intensity of their feelings can be scary at times because they are trying to control the situations and their inner powerful sensitivity.

Sagittarius: is a fiery sign and is ruled by planet Jupiter. They can say or do things with interior motives but may land them with a foot in their mouth because being diplomatic is not their virtue. They are unafraid to be direct and blunt. Sagittarius is the least aggressive of the rest of the fire signs and would much rather push a problem to the back of their mind than deal with it. They like to keep their life fun and carefree and put them in serious situations, they start getting fidgety and uncomfortable. Once they are angry it is hard to control, and this may bring serious problems.

Capricorn: is a hard-working earthy sign of the zodiac. Capricorn is ruled by planet Saturn, and they often face delays in getting what they want in life. Stability, tradition and family are important for them. When faced with a conflict in a relationship, the first thing any Capricorn will do is turn to family. For them, money, duties and stability in life are important. They may seldom appear emotionless when discussing matters of great personal significance, which is far from truth in reality. They like to be in control in any relationship and this may bring problems with it.

Aquarius: Free-spirited and do not like conflict in relations and will run away from conflicting situations. It is probably the most unpredictable sign of the zodiac. They are most confused about their own actions and probably don't even know how to react to any kind of situation. They are visionary; their ideas are much ahead of their time and people think of them as eccentric.

Pisces: They are dreamy but very intelligent and live in their own world. Pisceans are very sensitive and emotional people. They often hide their hurts and tears behind the mask of laughter. They aren't the people who are quick to jump into an argument or conflict. It is difficult to hold a Piscean in a conflicting relationship. Very little excites them but if you toss a stone in calm waters, face the torrent of sarcasm at your own risk! They are extremely intuitive.

This may help you to understand yours and other people's natures, and why you feel more aligned and compatible with some people and not others. Every person is distinctly unique and therefore have different goals and purposes. By understanding your Zodiac, it can help you to identify and understand your life purpose.

Q: *"So you say that we exist as spirits before being born and we have lived other lives"*?

A: "Yes". "In actual physical life, the circumstances and tests that spirits encounter are related to the decisions they made in other past physical lives and also during the period of life in between incarnations, when not connected to a physical body".

Q: *"What proof do we have that past lives actually exist, I mean, that life exists before birth"?*

A: "There are testimonies of people who have memories of past lives, which can be spontaneous (*especially in children*) or induced through regressive hypnosis."

There is a considerable amount of studied cases of the reincarnation of people who *'remember'* a *'past life.'* I experienced this for myself when I regressed to the girl collecting herbs in the year 1465 and so I know this to be true.

Q: "*Couldn't it be a result of peoples imagination*"?

A: "It is possible that *some* cases could be the result of a vivid imagination or for some other reason, but there are *many* cases in which people remember very specific details of a past life which have been historically confirmed."

They remember places, events, names in great detail, many of which occurred in countries where the person has never been in this current life. The most striking cases are those of small children who suddenly start speaking a foreign language which they have never heard in their current life, this being a memory of the language that they spoke in their past life. They are usually children between 2 and 5 years old, who start talking to their parents or siblings about a life they have had in a different place and in a different time. The children are usually strongly attracted to the events of that life and frequently insist that their parents let them go back to the family where they affirm that they used to live. This also applies to a lot of adults. Again, I resonate with my life as a child living with my Dakota Indian family. When I was young, (in this life) my siblings would watch westerns where there were wars between the British and the Native American Indians. I noted the plaited hair, boned bodices on the Sioux

Indian men, and the many beads that they wore. I was fascinated by the Sioux tribe, and I never wanted them to get hurt and so I feel that my subconscious was connecting with my past life even back then. To this day, I feel an affinity with the Sioux Indians, and I enjoy watching tribal dances. I feel emotion when I listen to their music. This former life must have been a 'good life' and I have carried back the love from that time. Also, my guide, 'Fast Cloud' is a Sioux Indian, who was my father in that life. I remember another message from 'Fast Cloud'. He asked "Where are your beads? "I carved many beads for you when you were a child". This was just his way of reminding me that we shared the life as father and child.

We are the sum total of our past. How we emotionally deal with our past directly influences our present life. When we reflect inward and uncover those emotions, we continue to carry inside us, we can begin to understand what drives our life patterns.

Q: *"How does our past influence the present?"*

A: "After your last life and before being born into this one, you reflect on what you have learned in previous lifetimes, and reincarnate to experience, learn and balance your previous lifetimes' experiences".

We keep getting born again and again (reincarnated) in order to settle our give and take account. According to how we have lived in our past lives, and how we have used our wilful action in each of them, our personality has been shaped. The personality traits stored as impressions in our sub-conscious mind continuously get moulded/reinforced by our actions and thoughts in any given lifetime

Q: "*What is astral travel?*"

A: "It is a temporary separation from the body."

we can leave our body and come back without death occurring. The spirit is separated from the physical body which, as I said before, is only a garment that is used in order to be able to act in the physical world. However, this separation is only temporary and there is always a bond between the two which is never broken, and which allows you to go back to your physical body. It´s called the silver cord that joins us."

Q: "*What is the silver cord?*"

A: "It´s the bond of union between the astral and the physical body, like an umbilical cord which provides the physical body with the vital energy it needs to continue living in the absence of the astral body".

Clairvoyants usually describe this 'cord' as a very elastic kind of silvery thread that can be extended, to the point where, however much the astral body is separated from the physical body, the cord always stretches as much as it needs. In other words, it lengthens to great distances when the spirit separates and travels far from the physical body.

Q: *"Where do you go when you separate from your body?"*

A: "Wherever your thoughts take you".

Those nocturnal visits give us human beings energy and experiences which will help us later on in physical life, because there, we are assisted by more advanced spiritual entities who advise and help us. This usually happens in our 'dream' state or if someone has been in a near fatal accident.

Q: *"What do you mean when you say that we have a spiritual family?"*

A: "Each and every one of us is loved by a multitude of spiritual beings." "Starting with the highest *vibration/energy* and continuing with your spiritual guide, *who never leaves you*, and a great number of other spirits."

Many of them are already deceased friends and relatives from this and other lives. Besides that, each and every one of us has a soul mate, your other half, (*higher self*) a spirit energy who is perfectly in tune with you, the perfect partner for whom you will begin to feel real love. Some souls may become incarnate at the same time as you and may or may not be part of your blood relatives, or they may simply be friends.

Q: "Why does my father show more love to my sibling than me?"

A: "We've all experienced existence over numerous lifetimes, and as a result, have been part of different family dynamics time and time again." "Remember that we have all chosen each other to incarnate with for the soul lessons that we need to progress."

You will have shared other lifetimes together and you will have come together this time round to balance the scales. So possibly you may have done harm in some way to whoever your father was to you in a previous incarnation, and so this time around you are feeling the hurt, to balance the Karmic slate. After all, we can rarely understand another's perspective until we've lived in their shoes for a little while. We tend to keep repeating the same mistakes in this life until we manage to sort ourselves out and break the cycle. We may need a few lifetimes to break free from repeating more intense behaviour cycles. It depends entirely on what you have to teach each other."

Q: "*Why do people believe in a God that rules over everything?*"

A: "In the Universe there are many beings at different stages of evolution, with greater and lesser capacity to create than ours, according to their level of advancement." "Because of the law of cause and effect, they must have been created by some previous process, by something that has always existed and will always exist, and who has established the laws and principles of everything that exists, and that is who some call *God.*" (*Whatever or whoever <u>you</u> believe God to be*)

Q: "*What or who then is God?*"

A: "Love, wisdom, justice, truth, humility, generosity, sincerity, sensitivity, understanding, compassion." "The highest consciousness"

Q: "*What is cosmic consciousness?*"

A: "Cosmic Consciousness has the following characteristics: It is a Presence".

It is a very soft Presence, gentle, delicate, smooth and flowing. Like a delicate and soft cloud. It feels like light itself, but more like the substance of light, not as rays of light, but as a flow of light, as an ocean of light. It is "light upon light". It is Love. This conscious substance of light is soft, gentle, tender and sweet. It is loving. It is as if one becomes an ocean of Love that is conscious. So, one can call it conscious love, or the Loving Light. In traditional literature this is sometimes referred to as Universal Love. It is both Consciousness and Love in the same There is no sense of individual or personal boundaries in this aspect of Being.

Q: *"If God is Love, why does he/it allow wars and hatred?"*

A: "We are all born with free will so that we learn from our mistakes".

The evil in the world does not come from a *God*, but rather from human beings in the process of evolution that, through not knowing the spiritual laws, act against each other. People fight and kill for personal reasons. It is often from greed, or different belief systems. Wars can also begin out of fear. I have highlighted the word 'God' in italic because we all have our own ideas of who/what *God* is. I, personally do not see *God* as a separate superior being, existing in some other realm, overlooking human affairs and loving or judging us according to our deeds. *God* is in each and every one of us, the most intimate and undeniable aspect of ourselves. <u>*God* is the light of consciousness</u> that shines in every mind. *It is the highest consciousness.*

Q: *"Why does a God allow Earthquakes and disasters that kill thousands of people" "Why do they have to suffer"*?

A: "Earthquakes are part of a cleansing progress in the evolution of the material world." "Death is not a disaster, it is *freedom from the material world, freedom for the soul.*"

Each person that 'dies' in these 'happenings' are there because of *past lives.* The soul will have chosen this experience because of *soul evolution.* The pathway to soul growth is not an easy one. The soul that goes through agony, pain, illness and sorrow comes out the greater soul. This soul will then understand the suffering of others and will be able to offer empathy. Everyone must go through every experience, either on Earth or in spirit." "*There is a lesson to be learned in everything.*"

Q: *"Why do I need to believe in a spiritual journey? "What is it?*

A: "A spiritual journey is a journey we take to find out who we are, what problems we need to overcome in this life, and how to come to peace with the ourselves and others."

However, like everything in life, embarking on your spiritual path is a choice. In life you are presented with several choices leading to new stages of development. So, at certain points, you have choices that may bring challenges. Life is full of ups and downs, challenges and changes. It is how we choose to respond to these that we choose to progress and find our true *self.* As I stated earlier in this book… we are not human beings having a spiritual experience, we are spiritual beings having a human experience.

Q: *"Why are children born with defects, such as being blind or dis-abled?"*

A: "The soul returns to experience these 'defects' to learn from the experience". "It is also for the people that they are connected to, to experience caring for them." "It is all about cause and effect". *It is all evolution of the soul."*

Q: *"So is the same to be said about children that are born into poverty and filth" "It seems so unfair"!*

A: "The answer is yes, *Evolution of the soul."* "Each soul returns after sitting with its spirit counsel for maybe years, discussing what it needs in order to progress." "Each soul chooses the different experiences it needs to balance Karma, and I say again for *the soul to progress and to find the true self."*

Q: *"Can you explain why there are still births, or why babies die soon after birth, so only live a short while?"*

A: "The mother and the potential incoming soul both made this decision together, *by prior agreement."*

Of course, once we incarnate our memory of this is wiped clean and so the mother won't remember this agreement. The incoming soul will also have agreed not to enter the foetus to allow the mother to experience sorrow. Maybe it is to help her finally work through a loss that she experienced in a prior incarnation that she hadn't dealt with. Again, _all experiences_ are for the soul growth, '_evolution of the soul_'!

We are born into situations chosen before we incarnate, for whatever our soul has decided upon for the experience that it needs. I think by now you will be understanding that our lives are pre-destined and that there is a point and a need for everything that occurs in our lives.

Q: "_so when we do 'die' do we stay with the family we are on the Earth this time around?_"

A: "If there is LOVE between you, then yes." "Loving families stay together on the other side." "One of them may return to another incarnation before the other, but they will stay connected and return to each other _again and again_." "The bond will always be."

Q: "_If there is a spirit world, why do we forget it?_"

A: "We are given amnesia at the moment of birth and forget the past lives we had and our life in the Spirit World between physical lives." "If we remembered the Spirit World, we would not be able to achieve what we incarnated here for." "Say for instance that you and your partner became enemies in this life, you would have the opportunity to meet again in a different life to reconcile your differences." "By forgetting previous events, you will both have the chance to act spontaneously and without judgement."

Each reincarnation is to give you the chance to recommence, to fix some past mistakes, get over disagreements, past hurts and to learn how to forgive. Your memories would be in the way of all that.

Our choices influence the course of our lives and ultimately our mental health. When we truly forgive, we can live our authentic lives and be content. If you feel that your actions caused hurt to someone, then make amendments where it's possible and rectify any wrong doings through either apologising or exploring alternative healthier ways you could have managed the situation better so that you don't make the same mistakes. Focus on growth – learning from your mistakes and growing from your experiences is crucial to your soul development.

Q: "What is my soul?"

A: "Your Soul Is the *'real you'* a special substance that is non-physical and immortal".

Your soul temporally inhabits your physical body. Your soul is the part of you that consists of your mind, character, thoughts and feelings. It is our soul that provides us with a kind of inner voice, a moral compass and direction. It is our soul that we hear as this 'little voice inside' reminding us that there is more we can become, and it is our soul that suffers when we don't nourish it by integrating a spiritual component into our lives and striving to give our lives meaning and purpose.

Q: *"If Our spirit guides know that we need assistance, why do we have to ask them to help?"*

A: "First of all, let me be clear, that your spirit guides and helpers can help you on your pathway and give you nudges to put you in the right direction".

However, we are born with free will, and the universe is not allowed to interfere with that. They can give us certain nudges to help us get on the right track.

Receiving answers from above

I have explained about how spirit connect with us, and I want to add my latest connections. As I said, I get most of my answers in dreams and songs. While I have been writing this book I am understanding more about '*why*' I am '*here*' this time around and '*who*' I am. Two nights ago, I dreamed that I was climbing a cliff. I got to the top and was able to look down, feeling pleased with where I was and how I managed to achieve this. I consulted the spiritual dream interpretation, and this is what the meaning of the dream represents:

Dreaming of climbing a cliff:

You are making an important transformation in your life, *mostly inner*. You are *getting to understand yourself truly*. It shows that you are in the process of *self-discovery*.

This dream was very meaningful in itself, but then the following morning, I awoke with part of a song that I was humming to myself. The words didn't come to me instantly, but as I continued to hum it over and over, the words came into my head. The song, I realised later was one of the Beatles hits called '*baby you're a rich man*'. However, the part of this song that I was constantly humming was: "How would you like to be one of the beautiful people, *now that you know who you are.*"

So once again you see, how spirit connect with us through dreams and music. You may get your messages in different, sometimes subtle ways. My dream together with the song was reiterating the message that I am beginning to understand who I am. To add to that I do feel that *I am rich* in Love from my family and my friends.

Types of Dreams and how to recognise them

Not all dreams are spiritual in nature or worthy of interpretation. In my experience, dreams fall broadly into two categories – *spiritual dreams and non-spiritual ones*, and you need to work out which type your dream is before you bother interpreting it. As humans, we need to dream partly so we can hash out and process the emotional experiences of our day in order to deal with negative emotions. Therefore, sometimes dreams are simply '*Emotional Processing*' dreams. These are the dreams often make *no sense* — they usually appear to lack meaning or *feel a bit chaotic*. Sometimes emotional processing dreams are rich in symbolism, but the symbolism can feel too cryptic for any interpretation. Sometimes this is simply a '*stress dream*' where something distressing, or challenging is happening in your dream. The subconscious, when we're asleep, often attempts to find solutions to our problems, or it may just hash out and consider difficulties & dilemmas that we're going through (but in a more meaningful way than the emotional processing dream). These difficulties or dilemmas are often outside of our conscious awareness. The subconscious contains many messages for us about our lives, our unmet needs, our unfulfilled or forgotten desires, our unacknowledged feelings, and the hidden dynamics of our relationships. A dream from the *subconscious* differs from the emotional processing dream in that it contains clear and often very clever symbolism which appears to make much more sense than in a processing dream.

How to recognise a spiritual dream

Spiritual dreams can fall into a few different sub-categories. Let's look at the first one:

Visitation Dreams: This is a common type of spiritual dream, and it is when you are visited by a deceased loved one, a guide or an angel while you are asleep and in the astral. How can you recognise a *visitation dream*? You will usually know it when a deceased loved one comes to visit you in a dream you will *feel deeply impacted by the experience* – often a deceased loved one will send you some loving energy in the dream and this sense of love stays with you, often for hours or days after you wake up. Angels can also pass on positive energies to us in dreams. Sometimes *visitation dreams* can also be healing dreams, where you meet a celestial being and wake up feeling healed or reinvigorated in some significant way.

Spiritual Insight Dreams: In this type of dream, you receive a message from Spirit, and it is clarifying something for you or advising you in some way – sometimes the dream can contain a *word, a symbol or a song lyric* that is highly relevant to a problem you are working out in your life. Spiritual insight dreams can sometimes look like messages from the subconscious, in that both types of dream are often rich in symbolism, but the difference with a '*spiritual insight*' dream is that these almost require no interpretation. These come complete with an interpretation to the dream, within the dream. The key difference between the two is that the *symbolism* in *spiritual insight* dreams will be crystal clear, whereas subconscious dreams can sometimes require more pondering. You will know when there is a message for you in the dream because it will *resonate with you*. As I explained in *my dream*, sometimes you will get song lyrics to accompany the dream. So just be mindful of what kind of dream you have had. If a dream resonates with you, has impact and stays with you for days, then you can be sure that it is a *spiritual* dream and that you need to pay attention to what the message holds for you. I remember a vivid dream that I had years ago:

The dream:

I was standing on a beach and a continuous tidal of huge white waves came rolling towards me, bringing with them all of my deceased loved ones and many more. It brought me happiness joy, and the feeling of well-being. We're guided on a daily basis by our spirit team, which includes ancestors, guides, angels and elemental spirits or other guiding forces. Dreams just happen to be one of their favourite ways to send messages. Spirit guide dreams carry important messages for our healing, growth, and alignment.

These dreams can guide us to:

Discover our purpose in this life - Recognise what we need to heal in ourselves - Feel inspired and see things in a greater perspective in challenges that we are facing.

Yet another dream I will share with you show the *cryptic* messages behind the meaning, and how our spirit team give us messages that can help us on our pathway. Lately, I have been feeling emotional stress over Michael's ill health. This has escalated into some worries about the future as to whether Mike would be well enough to travel. Our passion is Africa and we have holidayed their many times. We had originally planned our next trip for February 2022, but due to the pandemic and Michael's health, I had been throwing problems around in my head, and allowed myself to feel negative! One night, after voicing each other's concerns, I had another insight dream.

The dream:

I dreamed that I was in an airport, and I was singing… '*We are going on an aeroplane*'. Then suddenly I was in Africa! The strange thing was that there were *Tigers*! I would normally think this weird as we all know that Tigers do not live in Africa! However, in my dream, an extremely large tiger put all four paws around me, and I was held captive by him. Although I was a little afraid to begin with, I soon began to realise that he was being very gentle, but supportive! I was talking to him inside my head, and eventually I said to him "let's go and find your cubs". He released me and an African guide led me away. You will probably be asking yourself; *how can this dream be a message*?

Firstly: *To dream about an airport*

It means that you will go on a trip to a faraway country. You have been planning to see a destination that you want to go to. This trip would be like '*medication for your stress and worries'. So, you see how this fits in with the dream so far.* The fact that I was stressing about it all.

Secondly: *To dream about a Tiger*

A tiger in a dream carries a spiritual message. Why are tigers who are threatened routinely not traumatized?

To dream of a tiger is about how you can grow spiritually to become immune to '*traumatic events in daily life'*. Think about your life for a moment. Imagine a life free of fears. The tiger has appeared to help you move forward into a journey that is free from the '*stress and pressures'* of the world. The tiger appears in dreams when you know secretly you have *'negative energy'* within, but you hold the internal wisdom to heal yourself. It goes on to say...If you have been going through a storm or *trauma* recently then the tiger appearing can be an *assurance that you can fight to the end and truly get what you want.* I have added this dream to show that some dreams are quite *cryptic,* and it is best to search for the meaning behind them. I always use *the spiritual dream meanings.*

Characters that guide you through the dream: Have you ever met a character in a dream that shared a clear message or pointed you to a specific place? These guiding characters in your dreams can be spirit guides. Guides can take the form of a *close friend, stranger, or other familiar face* to get us to pay attention. For example, if you're most comfortable with a best friend sharing a message about your next steps for work, a spirit guide *might become your friend in the dream.* When a dream has an impact on your waking thoughts, it will be because it has something to teach you. There is a specific message from your higher being. There will be something from these experiences that you are having within your inner psychology that you need to hear with your waking consciousness.

"One must recognise the potential that your dream holds for your spiritual journey" "There is nothing more real than a dream" "Dreams are our souls' way of broadcasting wisdom to us every night" Dreams tell you what you really *know* about something, what you really *feel*. They point you toward what you need for growth, expression, and the health of your relationships to person, place and thing. They can help you fine-tune your direction and show you your unfinished business. Author Tom Robbins once said that dreams don't come true; they *are* true. When we talk about our dreams coming true, we're talking about our ambitions. So why are our dreams so cryptic? Dreams convey messages in the language from which your soul originates; *images, impressions, knowing and feeling. Your subconscious mind may translate symbolic messages into words for you,* but at the heart of every dream image is a meaning beyond words. It helps to understand that in true dream messages (rather than random dream scenarios), your inner self is always guiding you towards being the best version of yourself that you can be in this lifetime. That is the only motive your inner self has with any truly instructional dream, and it's up to you whether you pay attention or not. Dreams can be very chaotic as you try to understand the language that your unconscious self is trying to relay to you.

Psychic protection.

Our own anger, fears, depression and desires can invite unwanted 'negative' energies to invade our psyche. Even feelings of guilt. Therefore, *any negative emotions* can draw *negative energies* unto us. Teenagers especially are often vulnerable because of hormone changes, changes in vibrations and often anger or frustration. If you are unhappy about the feelings, you are experiencing you can safely guard against these negative influences. Negativity is toxic to your entire system. Firstly, reduce time spent around negative people, and don't let yourself be pushed into doing things that you don't want to do. One of the quickest ways to calm yourself down and get back to a state of relaxation is to practice meditation. Find a quiet place and close your eyes. Observe your thoughts as they pace through your head and do not label them as good or bad. Take deep relaxing breaths and feel the weight being lifted from your shoulders. If you are not one for meditation, you can also start walking or jogging to lift your spirits and drive the negative energy away. This is especially important when you don't feel like doing anything at all and feel like you are getting sucked into a black hole of negativity. Make a mental note of the *number of times you complain* in a day. When you do so, you will realise a lot of times, the whining and moaning were completely unnecessary. *The more you whine about what is irritating you, the more you pay attention to what is upsetting you and then you complain some more. Focus on the solution* instead of moaning and complaining as it doesn't solve anything. There are different types of energy sources. Some are physical, some are emotional, and some are spiritual.

Physical – energy is generated by the response of the environment—what you take in by nourishment, and what you expose yourself to as far as chemicals, compounds, and electrical currents. These energies are either giving to your body or depleting your body.

Mental – energy is based on electrical currents, which are stimulated by knowledge and data that affect your neurological system, your neurons, and your nervous system. If the mental stimulation you are receiving is not of the same quality as the high-frequency current that releases certain chemicals in your body, it will create an adverse effect on your emotional quality as a human being. And then there are the:

spiritual – energies. The ones that are in lower form are based on *fear, guilt, judgement, doubt, shame, hate, and anger.*

The ones in the *higher energy forms are based on love, compassion, bliss, elation, playfulness, joy, ecstasy, pleasure,* and every higher vibration that connects you to unconditional love and acceptance. From how you are with your children, to how you are in your relationship, to conversations you're a part of, to what you're taking in visually, to what you're eating, to how you connect with yourself and the inner conversations you have with yourself, *you are creating energy, either positive or negative.* You need to identify the energy sources that are affecting your life and make a change to your belief system. *Negative spirit energies attach themselves to your negative thoughts and can make you feel worse.* They miss the comforts of the physical world and often want to express them by attaching themselves to the energy fields of the living. It is important to keep a *healthy/positive attitude* as much as possible. If you're feeling stuck, negative, sluggish, it may be due to some bad energy in your field. Stuck energy can gather like unwanted guests at a house party. The most effective way to combat an energy traffic jam is by smudging. Smudging can clear your emotional, energetic, mental, spiritual, and physical body—as well as your environment (home, office, or other physical space). It helps tackle any bad feelings you sense looming, clears the energy in your field, and allows you to start anew. I refer to the 'negative' energies as *lower-realm energy*. All energy teaches us something, but we do not want to hang onto the lower energy because it is not healthy. A *lower, denser vibration* may make you feel *exhausted, overwhelmed, angry, helpless, and even produce jealousy*. However, we do need to let our emotions surface, but then take a step back to ask yourself what you are actually feeling, and why. When *anger* is continuously suppressed and not healthily expressed it can morph into deep resentments, unconscious sabotaging behaviours, etc., like when someone is trying to manipulate you. Fear based; *lower realm energy* is the root of this. Learning to strengthen your own force field and maintain your energy within, no matter the external circumstances is a skill we all need. There are many ways to release negative energy and keep energy flowing through us in a healthy way. One of the words that I know I keep using, is balance. We have to find ways to balance our emotions which affect our energy. As you are all probably aware, meditation is a good way, or a healing session with a trusted practitioner. Take a bath, as this is a wonderful way to purify the aura of any negative energy and re-nourish your spirit. Adding in some essential oils such as *eucalyptus, cedarwood, lavender* along with some *Epsom or sea salt* works to calm the body, mind and spirit. Remember that we incarnated here as humans to be able to experience the *entire range of human emotions* on the scale. If you have negativity energy pulling you down, try switching your thoughts to *love and compassion.* **Love** is the gateway *lifting you up and strengthen you.* It takes a lot of practice to become the spiritual person that we wish to be. We need to reflect on *truth, reality, and understand our true purpose in life.* Finding true *self-knowledge,* frees up our minds and hearts, allowing us to choose a clear pathway. Because we are human, we are ego-centric human beings. In order to become more connected to our higher self, we need to reconnect to our highest self. This is one of the greatest journeys we can embark on, especially during uncertain and uncomfortable times like these. **The simplest way to activate your connection to your highest self is by sitting still.** The ego is an unconscious aspect of the mind. Our brain, made of physical matter, contains the mind, and the mind is the source of human consciousness. The importance of connecting spiritually is *focussing on the positive.* Let go of materialistic thoughts. When you look beyond the material you realise *what-makes-us-us*. It isn't about what we have it is about '*who we are.*'

To explain more about the negative energies on the Astral plane:

Lower astral entities intrude our energy fields when our auras are deplete. When we indulge in *negative thoughts and out-of- control behaviour*, especially the misuse of alcohol and drug abuse, we weaken our auric energy shield and risk invasion. As I said earlier, un-evolved enterties miss the physical world and want to express themselves, and so they impinge their 'wants and needs' through us. They retain the mind-set that they had whilst on the Earth plane, and so if a person was an angry person whilst on Earth, it is more likely that he/she will retain this until his/her spirit learns differently. Therefore, the negative energies will feed off our *negative behaviour and emotions* and, in some cases, can *actually influence us to more negate behaviour.*

Simple: The more negative you are, the more negativity you will create.

More about the Aura and how it protects us

Its purpose is to protect your physical body and keep away negative vibrations, which could potentially cause you harm. So, your aura or auric field also contains information about your life, such as your emotional and mental thoughts, beliefs and memories. The Chakras which are the seven wheels of spinning energy, are also found within your auric field. These little spinning wheels, can create changes in its colour and shape. No two auras are exactly the same, as we are constantly shifting our vibrations due to changes in our thought patterns. When we are low in energy and feeling down, our aura naturally shrinks to reflect this. When we are happy, our aura naturally expands radiating outwards. This strange phenomenon, explains why we are more attracted to happier people and less attracted to more negative people. Unless of course we are also negative, then we are naturally attracted to other negative people. So the saying goes, 'if you want to manifest a happier life, spend more time with happy people.'

"There are two ways of spreading light: to be the candle or the mirror that reflects it."– **Edith Wharton**

The human Energy field

1. The Etheric Layer

This is the layer closest to the physical body, and the layer some therapists can see during treatment. Sits approximately two to four inches away from the physical body and can be seen as a faint *grey/violet* mist. This layer is connected to the *base chakra.*

2. The Emotional Layer

This layer sits directly outside the etheric body, extending one to three inches. This layer is connected to the *sacral chakra*, and holds all our emotions, feelings and sensitivity such as joy, sorrow, love and hate. This is seen as Orange.

3. The Mental Layer

This layer sits directly outside the emotional body, extending three to eight inches from the physical body. This layer is connected to the *solar plexus chakra* and contains all our mental thought processes such as rules, regulations, judgement and discipline. Usually, this layer is represented by the colour *yellow.*

4. The Astral Layer

This layer can extend out to about one foot. It is the bridge between the lower vibrations of the physical plane, and the higher vibrations of the spiritual. Connected to the *heart chakra*, this layer is represented with green or sometimes a beautiful *rainbow colour.*

5. The Etheric Template

This layer extends out about two feet. Connected to the *throat chakra*, this layer represents the blueprint of the physical body and looks much like the negative of a photograph. It is seen as blue

6. The Celestial/Causal Layer

This layer can extend for up to two and a half feet. Connected to the *third eye chakra*, this is where your spiritual connection begins and the process of enlightenment. The colour is Indigo.

7. The Spiritual Layer

This layer can extend for up to three feet. Connected to the *crown chakra* and protecting all the other layers it vibrates at the highest frequency and is often seen as a *brilliant white or golden light.*

Reiki practitioners and holistic therapists/ spiritual healers are well known for the powerful work they do with this natural healing energy. Once any blocks and tears have been repaired within your chakras/auric field, there is no doubt you will feel more energised, balanced and calm. The aura is spiritual energy, or life-force, which is present around each of us from birth (and before birth, as the foetus develops) until around the time of our death. Usually just before death only a narrow band of spiritual energy remains, linking all the chakras in the centre of the body, and shortly after physical death, no aura can be detected, because the life-force no longer exists.

A few more questions and answers

Q: "*What happens to murders when they pass over?*"

A: "They will be troubled souls having to face the horrors of not being able to restore physical life to their victim." "They face a miserable time until they feel strong enough to reincarnate with the sole purpose of atoning in the physical world for what he/she did." Hence – Karma.

Q: "*What about people who commit suicide?*"

A: "To commit suicide is to end your soul contract and those lessons that you came to the physical body to learn in the first place".

People that commit suicide may think that they have solved their problems, but actually, they have only postponed them. They are what is known as the suffering souls, because they see through their life review how their *thoughts, feelings, intentions and actions effected other people.* They will be helped to make the decision on what lessons he/she needs to learn and then return to Earth in a new incarnation to work out his/her Karma and find balance.

Q: *"What about when a person's soul has decided to die because the person is very sick"*

A: "The Angels and guides will stay with them through the whole transition." "The soul may slumber for some while until it feels strong enough to make the adjustments to move to a different plane where we will be with our loved ones." "This will also be one of the chosen exits decided before incarnation." "As I say, I believe there are five exits to choose from."

Q: *"Can you explain briefly the passing over from Earth to the spirit world"*

A: "After death, the soul finds itself suddenly relieved of the weight of the body, of the necessity to breathe, and of any physical pain." "A sense of soaring through a tunnel and a very peaceful, hazy, dim light is experienced by the soul." "Then the soul drifts into a state of oblivious sleep, a million times deeper and more enjoyable than the deepest sleep experienced in the physical body."

In the first state, people are essentially the same as they were in life. They have all of their memories, they have the same beliefs and attitudes toward things, and they may even manifest the same surroundings that they had on earth. Some find it hard to come to terms with and need help with the transition. When a soul first enters the spiritual world, it usually meets friends or relatives who crossed over before them. Spouses will be reunited, although not necessarily forever, this depends on the bond that their souls have. The spiritual world is a place where a person's inner nature becomes the whole of their being. If two people were truly of one mind on earth, they will live together as spouses in *heaven* too. However, if their personalities are fundamentally different, they will eventually part ways. Those who did not find love on earth, will eventually find their perfect match in *the spirit realms*—no one is ever alone unless they wish to be. All forms of vibration function in harmony with one another. All forces live in peace and conscious helpfulness. Souls recognise one another in the astral world, and it is here that they realize the indestructibility of love. Friends and relatives become the new arrival's guide to the spiritual world, (*heaven*) and, with the help of good spirits, the person's true inner nature will gradually be revealed. This first state might last anywhere from a few hours to a few years depending on how long it takes for a person's outer nature (*what they outwardly say and do*) to harmonize with their inner nature (*what they truly feel and believe*) In the second state after death, the person becomes aware of the deeper parts of his or her inner nature. They start saying what they *really think* and act according to what they feel without worrying about appearances or making other people happy. They act according to their *inner values*—the way someone on earth might act when nobody else is watching or when they're sure they won't get caught. People who are truly good inside will be kind and generous to others, while people who are inherently evil will be openly selfish and cruel. While we can all be generous or selfish sometimes, inherently good spirits will reject the selfish thoughts and work to rid themselves of those impulses. Inherently evil spirits will justify their bad behaviour and thereby embrace it as part of themselves. At this point, *like is drawn to like*, so the sorting out begins. As I have already said, no judge passes sentences of guilt or innocence—we seek out kindred spirits because that is where we feel at home. We have our life review, and it is *we that judge ourselves.* We see the wrong doings that we may have carried out along with the good that we have done for others. For people who *are ready* for the higher realms, there is a third state, a time of instruction. It is a time for learning about *heaven* and how to lead a life that allows one to experience it. At this point, the person is already in touch with the community in *heaven* where he or she will ultimately live, but still has a lot to learn about that community—what it does, how the individual can contribute to it, how the community can fill the individual's need. People who have joined a community of *negative spirits*, however, will continue to *descend farther and farther into misery* until they reach those people who are most similar to them. This *is not a punishment*; it is simply the place where they feel the most comfortable. If they have freely chosen a path that is the opposite of love and wisdom, there is nothing more the angels can do for them. The most merciful thing to do is to let them live the life they have chosen. This is what some people term as *hell*. There is no devil with hot fires raging! The devil (if you like) is the *negative energy* within the soul and the negativity is what you may call the fire! It's important to note that all human beings arrive in the spiritual world as equals. Regardless of their religious background or their personal beliefs, regardless of their nationality, gender, or race, all people have an equal chance to go to either *heaven* or (*their hell*) That decision is made by the individuals themselves, in the form of every choice they've made to act in either a loving way or a selfish way. Remember the story of Jack (in the spiritual story) who acted out of selfish needs lived in a negative place until he realised the need for change.

Q: "*What is heaven then?*"

A: "Heaven is a *spiritual state of existence* where the utmost happiness and harmony is found."

There are seven planes and each of the planes has its own particular energy, which is best described as a vibration. The frequency of vibration is what makes the planes different from one another and the spiritual and physical inhabitants of the planes different as well. The higher the frequency of vibration, the faster the atoms move. For instance, the molecules in the solid objects of the first plane move *very slowly*. The molecules in the plants of the second plane move *more quickly*, and so on throughout the planes. These vibrations are the essence of life in all its forms. The vibrational forces of the planes have both vast and tiny proportions that, once understood, can be influenced by the power of pure thought. The planes are divided by thin veils that take the form of beliefs that are programmed into the subconscious mind of every man, woman, and child on this planet. When we arrive at the *Seventh Plane of Existence*, we learn how to drop these veils of belief so that we can realize we are not separate from the planes but connected to all of them. Each plane of existence is subject to its own *conditions, rules, Laws, and commitments.* The first six planes have illusions within them, but the Seventh Plane is the essence of truth and divinity. The planes are so vast that the human mind can't comprehend them. The seventh is the plane of the *Creator of All That Is*, the energy that flows through all things to create life. Here we have the realization that we are part of *All That Is.*

Q: "So the Astral plane is the next level beyond the physical?"

A: "Yes, the astral plane is the level beyond the physical, the realm of dreams, spirits, and psychic phenomena, the substance and vehicle for contact between the material and the mystical".

Within the astral plane, there are numerous densities and vibrations, commonly divided into lower, middle, and higher planes, each associated with a distinctive sound and colour. As you pass through the planes, you rejoin with the rest of your entity, then with other entities, becoming more and more merged with the total consciousness of the Universe. You slowly release the separateness that you took on in order to experience the Physical Plane as you learn to accept and tolerate others as being part of yourself. In the 'higher vibrational planes, you are in contact with the harmony-first, then emotionally. It all sounds very complex, but basically, we pass through the planes as we grow and progress. The planes represent the different states and conditions through which the individual soul passes along the way. As mentioned earlier; every plane of heaven is supervised by hierarchy, a group of advanced souls dedicated to helping our soul's progress. We arrive at the grand central where it is decided if we need to sleep for a while. We open our eyes to a world of colour, insects and birds, trees and waterfalls, beautiful gardens and perfect nature. The feeling of love is overwhelming. As you reach the higher planes of awareness you live in a less dense atmosphere, and a deeper peace. To understand the universe, think of how waves behave. Think of waves, as energy that is constantly in motion. Thoughts, emotions, beliefs, and attitudes effect the flow of energy within the body. *Everything vibrates. Life energy is movement.* Energy frequency, holds memory and information about us. Heaven is the universe, so think in terms of *energy, frequency* and *vibration.*

Q: *"Are there such things as nature spirits?" "If so, what are they?"*

A: "Nature spirits are just that, spirits of nature".

We have become disconnected from nature, and we see symptoms of this disconnect everywhere. We are changing nature on a global scale. We've become disconnected from nature and lost sight of the fact that earth is our home. Most of us spend more time on social media than we spend outdoors in nature. We are stressed, depressed and overwhelmed. We feel disconnected and difficulties arise with higher rates of physical and emotional issues. So. you ask, "what are nature spirits?" Everything is alive and has consciousness. There is Spirit in all things. Flower spirits, tree spirits, water spirits, land spirits, devas who hold the blueprint for different places and different plants, and the elemental beings of earth, air, fire and water. The more you deepen your connection with the earth, the more in tune you'll feel with nature spirits. People that want to connect and feel grounded, imagine roots coming out of the soles of their feet. Become aware of the earth beneath you, the sky above you, your heart in your centre and breathe – long, slow deep breaths. Notice your surroundings. Pay attention to where you are, the season, the time of day, the plant life, insects, birds, evidence of animals, feathers, etc. Be here now. Be open to the idea that there is a world beyond your everyday senses that you can tap into if you genuinely want to. Spend time outdoors, Slow down to nature's pace. This will put you in touch with the spirits of nature.

Q: "*How can I be a more caring/spiritual person*"

A: "Show empathy and compassion"

Compassion is a very natural impulse that we have, and it's a natural sense of concern that arises in us in the face of a pain or a need or suffering and accompanied with the wish to see the relief of that situation or wanting to do something about it. It's easier to feel this for someone who you care about, because in order to generate compassion you need to be able to identify with the other person and be able to make the connection. In the case of total strangers, when someone has been, say for example, hit by a car in front of us and they're bleeding and screaming, at that moment most of us are capable of experiencing compassion instantaneously. Compassion helps us connect with others, mend relationships, and move forward while fostering emotional intelligence and well-being. Compassion takes empathy one step further because it harbours a desire for all people to be free from suffering, and it's imbued with a desire to help. This shows love and love connects us spiritually. Right now, during the pandemic, we are seeing magnificent acts of kindness, generosity and heroism from key workers and medical staff worldwide. We are showing gratitude, communication and empathy on a global scale like never before. Even though there is so much pain, anxiety and despair, there is also so much positivity, peace and progression being shown. It is in these extraordinary times that we are susceptible to each other's energies, as well as our own. It is often only when limitations are put upon us, that we are forced to recognise and realise what we can each really achieve, and properly see what good we have around us. To become a more caring, spiritual person, show acts of kindness. Be grateful for your life and the lessons that it gives you. Recognise that there is a purpose to your life and live it in the best way that you can.

Q: *"How can I learn to Love myself"*

A: "Self-compassion involves treating yourself the way you would treat a friend who is having a hard time—even if your friend is feeling inadequate or is just facing a tough life challenge" *"Practice self-kindness."*

Individuals who are more self-compassionate tend to have greater happiness, life satisfaction and motivation, better relationships and physical health, and less anxiety and depression. When we are mindful of our struggles, and respond to ourselves with compassion, kindness, and support in times of difficulty, things start to change. We can learn to embrace ourselves and our lives, *despite inner and outer imperfections*, and provide ourselves with the strength needed to thrive. Our self-criticism tends to undermine self-confidence and leads to fear of failure. If we're self-compassionate, we will still be motivated to reach our goals—not because we're inadequate as we are, but because we *care* about ourselves and want to reach our full potential. While conducting my counselling sessions, I advise people to write a letter to themselves, whenever they feel inadequate or when they want to motivate themselves to make a change. Think of an imaginary friend who is wise, loving, and compassionate and write a letter to *yourself* from the perspective of your friend. Write a letter as if you were talking to a dear friend who was struggling with the same concerns as you. Write that letter from the compassionate part of yourself to the part of yourself that is struggling. After writing the letter, you can put it down for a while and then read it later, letting the words soothe and comfort you when you need it most. Another good time to write a letter is when you want to say something to a person that may be upsetting you or have hurt your feelings and you want to forgive them. You don't send the letter to them, but when you write it down, it takes away the constant negative talk to yourself. Any moment you notice a surge of a difficult emotion—boredom, contempt, remorse, shame—pause, put your hand on your heart (this activates the release of oxytocin, the hormone of safety and trust) Empathize with your experience—recognize the suffering—and say to yourself, this is upsetting or this is hard, or this is scary, or this is painful or ouch! this hurts, or something similar, to acknowledge and care about yourself when you experience something distressing. Repeat the phrases below to yourself (or some variation of words that work for you)

I will be kind to myself: This breaks the automaticity of our survival responses and negative thought loops.

I accept myself: I give myself the compassion that I need: I am worthy of love:

I use the above in my E.F.T therapy sessions also to unblock deep rooted fears that have caused negative beliefs within the body.

Continue repeating the phrases until you can feel the internal shift: The compassion and kindness and care for yourself becoming stronger than the original negative emotion. Let the thoughts, emotions, feelings, or sensations you have recognized *simply be there.* Typically, when we have an unpleasant experience, we react by piling on the judgement or by numbing ourselves to our feelings. We each have the conditioning to live for long stretches of time imprisoned by a sense of deficiency, cut off from realizing our intelligence, aliveness, and love. The greatest blessing that we can give ourselves is *self-compassion.* Many times, in your life, you might fall back and think that your circumstances are controlling you, but, on the contrary, *you are the master of your circumstances, and your thoughts.* The magic begins when you realize how worthy you are. The way you treat yourself determines the way how others will treat you. Self-limiting beliefs prevent us from achieving success in our careers and lives. ... Simply, they are negative self-perceptions that live in our conscious and subconscious rooted in past experiences, comments by others, values and beliefs of our family and friends, and even messages from the media. The first part of overcoming self-limiting beliefs is to identify them, understand their impact, identify their source, and assess their validity.

Q: *"Why do certain people feel the need to be a victim"*?

A: "The desire for empathy is crucial for them in that the mere experience of a harmful event is not enough for the emergence of the sense of being a victim". In order to have this sense, there is a need to perceive the harm as undeserved and unjust. Let me be clear, there is a difference between actually being a victim of trauma or a tragic event in life and having a victim mind-set. People who *think the world is against them* are *victims of their own making.* They embody helplessness and resignation. They avoid responsibility for their lives. I don't think people consciously want to be a victim. It may be their way of being 'safe' within their comfort zone. If life isn't treating them the way they want, they sometimes can't deal with it and unknowingly give their power away. The attention, sympathy and time that a person can get from *victimhood* is validation that they really are a good person and if circumstances were *just different*, they would obviously be thriving. It's a way to *'save face'* in the midst of any kind of failure. For some, this way of being was role-modelled by parents or other caregivers and has been the only method to deal with things that don't go the way they are supposed to go. A victim mindset can also be created by very legitimate concerns that are not getting addressed, and as such, a learned helplessness is established. This person has learned in the same way that we learn anything — repetition of a particular pattern over time — speak up, get ignored, speak up, get ignored, speak up, told to shut up. The complaint was legitimate, but it ceased to have a *commitment to change* overtime as the person has learned nothing will change. For people that recognise this in themselves, there are life coaches and self- help organisations. Meditation is a good start. In today's society as we are exposed to increasing numbers of images and stories of other people's success. The constant barrage can make us feel helpless and unsatisfied, which is a shame because this way of thinking leads to people feeling angry, unhappy and resentful.

Q: *"Why is life so unfair, why do some people have more than others?"*

A: "If you regularly think that life isn't fair and that you deserve better than you have, or you feel like people treat you unfairly and take you for granted then you may suffer with victim mentality". "You probably spend a lot of time dwelling on how bad your life is but feel completely powerless to change it".

It is important to remember that you have chosen what your soul needs for its growth. As I have explained, it is due to Karmic debt. We come into the situation we are born into to learn something from the experience.

Q: *"So I have chosen to be poor in this life?"*

A: "Much as the answer above, you have chosen what your soul needs this time around".

Poor is not determined by the amount of money someone has; it's determined by his mind. There are very poor people in this world who are able to share the little they have and there are very rich people who are unable to share the abundance they have. Poor or rich 'money wise' is just what it is, the attitude towards sharing might be something that's brought into this life from the past. So back to Karma then, it is how our actions from the past and the actions of those around us in the past shaped us. We are all responsible for our own actions. So, in this life you are given the opportunity to resolve past actions.

Q: *"Why do I attract selfish people into my life and how do I deal with them"?*

A: "There are many reasons why you may be attracting selfish people into your life" "I think that this question calls for a basic understanding of how we attract people and things into our lives"

According to the laws of the universe in which we live, one is through Karma. You may have a *karmic debt* to pay to this person. It could also be because you allow people to step on you, so people see no harm in using you for their own benefit. Selfish people may focus on you because they feel threatened by your strengths, or they believe you can be easily manipulated and used. Selfish people are mentally and emotionally deprived people. It could also be that the selfish person was born to parents who denied them basic love, care or attention. Such depravation was made up for it with selfishness as they grew older. They developed the belief that they have to *steal* love, care and attention to fulfil themselves. Such belief translated into selfishness. The human brain always tries to compensate for what it's starving for. It's its way of trying to make up for what's lacking. *It's a survival mode.* Selfishness (especially when it's severe) often comes from the upbringing of the person, and unless they want to face the facts and reconcile with their past, and themselves, it will remain in them. Selfish people probably don't realise that they are being selfish. They maybe just assume that they are nice people who care about their own happiness more than anything else. But on their journey towards finding happiness, they carelessly walk over other people. A relationship with a selfish person means that they extract your love and affections, without giving back in return. They feel that their needs are greater. Often selfish people can be manipulative and seek to control people and circumstances to achieve what they want. We can all be selfish to a certain extent. While normal levels of self-love, self-value and self-confidence are important for people to function well, there is a line between these characteristics and being a little too self-absorbed, arrogant or just plain narcissistic.

For example: Some people are always trying to make others believe that their own world is the better one, while others will always cut you short and try to air their grievances when you wish to air yours. Others can talk for hours about themselves, making you feel like you are of lesser importance. If you have someone that is being selfish, here are some ways you can deal with them. Firstly: acknowledge that this person is selfish for whatever reasons they have found themselves to be. Every relationship requires some give and take. I would suggest being compassionate towards any person, no matter what their traits. People are functioning in the context of their life experiences. People who are 'selfish' tend to have been raised in environments in which their feelings, thoughts, and needs were probably not valued. As I have stated in a previous chapter, you can only control your own actions, not anyone else's. This means trying less to control another person's negative behaviour, but more about setting boundaries and thinking about how you react.

Q: *"How do I set boundaries without upsetting others?"*

A: "So firstly, we need to understand that boundaries are important" "Boundaries are not necessarily standing against another, even though there are people that are not good for us"

On a deeper level, maybe you were not able to stand up for yourself as a child. Maybe now you are not being true to yourself. Maybe you feel the need to please others by saying yes, all the time. Believe me, I have been this person. I tended to think that because I am (what I feel) a loving person, I expect others to be loving towards me. It doesn't always work like that. There are many that are attracted to the loving energy, but naturally there others that may 'put on you' because you are nice! You can often be 'taken for granted'. So, at some point we have to wake up to this and ask ourselves, why we allow people to walk over us. It is ok to say no, and I am only just beginning to practice this myself. We have to have some form of defence and be able to realise when is a good time to have this. We often find that people that are manipulative or need to be in control, try to control those of us that don't say no. It is important then, to look after yourself and instead of saying ok I will do whatever it is that you need me to do (even though deep down you really don't want to) but to just say, I am sorry, but no.... I don't feel that this is right for me. Or … no thank you. So instead of being defenceless, you are setting boundaries.

Q: *"Why do some people feel the need to lie constantly"*

A: "Lies take on all shapes and forms, from omission of details to flat-out false-hoods" "It's almost reasonable to say that lying is instinctive because even young children lie without realizing it" "Being lied to can be frustrating and it often breaks the bond of trust between two people, causing problems in the relationship" "Knowing the reasons why people lie, however, can shed some light on the problem and help us understand the people who feel the need to lie".

Self-defence

Many people lie because they want to protect themselves from an unpleasant situation or conflict. Think of young children who lie. They lie to make sure that they don't get into trouble. Children lie to avoid unpleasant consequences. Adults do the same. Many people lie because they know they've done something that will anger the other person. A woman might lie about the cost of the shoes she purchased, and a man might lie about which buddy he was going to hang out with. These lies are strictly to avoid a fight. The person may not have done anything wrong, but would prefer not to have to justify, explain or face an irate spouse.

To Spare Feelings

Some people who lie often do so with good intentions. We call these 'white lies' or lies that occur when the person wants to avoid causing someone else pain. A husband may lie to spare his wife's feelings, or a father may lie to avoid his child's tears. To some, a white lie is nothing more than a reason or excuse rather than an untruth. Each individual must decide if telling a white lie is justified. If keeping someone from being hurt unduly means omitting the truth and no damage comes from the fib, then most people not only feel it is justified, but necessary.

To Protect Feelings

While some people who lie want to protect the feelings of others and spare someone else pain or hurt, many people lie to protect their own feelings, self-esteem, self-confidence, or other personal emotion. Someone who says, I didn't want that job anyway, when he/she really did, is lying to protect himself/herself. A child who yells out, 'I hate you!' may be trying to protect himself from feeling hurt or to reject others before he is rejected.

To Present a Good Image

Many people want to present a good image Sometimes for work-related reasons. Think of a job interview where a person might dress well and attempt to impress the interviewer in order to land the job. People who lie for image reasons often do so because they want to cover over a blemish in their work history or avoid providing the real reason for termination of employment from a previous job.

To Be Liked

Everyone wants to be liked and being part of the group is important, as well as part of human nature. Many people lie simply to be accepted by others. A person may feign interest in something or agree with a statement he or she does not believe.

To Manipulate Others

We learn very quickly that we can manipulate other people. Whether we choose to do so might be a subject of debate. The fact remains that many people lie to get other people do what they want them to do. This is the human ego. People who lie to manipulate a situation or other people are often only interested in personal gain and fail to consider other people's feelings. By lying or omitting details, the person can achieve a personal goal. However, it is important to note that a lie manipulates a situation and a person's thoughts. Even a lie that is told with innocent intentions. What we *say and do* has an effect on others and even well-intended lies are a form of manipulation.

A Matter of Trust

Lying creates an uncomfortable situation because we expect others to treat us honourably and tell the truth. We expect not to be lied to and when the situation occurs, we lose faith and trust in the other person. There are some people (typically those with certain personality disorders) who lie frequently and do not care about the effects of their lies. This type of person also typically does not care about the treatment he receives from other people. Most people, however, care how others treat them and knowing they were lied to can be a breach of trust, depending on the gravity of the lie.

Compulsive and Pathological Lying

A more serious problem with lies occurs when lying becomes compulsive or pathological. The differences in the two may be subtle, but it's important to understand each. A compulsive liar uses lies as a way of life. Lying for any situation or no reason takes the place of honesty. A compulsive liar lies because it serves the person in some odd way, and he/she takes comfort in lies. Telling the truth just doesn't feel right to a compulsive liar who will bend the truth to fit his/her own needs and desires. Compulsive lying can be accompanied by other personality disorders like narcissism. While the person delving into compulsive lies feels secure, the lies often hurt and damage relationships, family and friends. Compulsive lying is an addiction and becomes difficult to stop once it has become a way of life. *Some people need to feel special and loved and so they create stories and lies to make them feel better about themselves.* None of us are without faults and I think that if we can accept people for who they are and look at the deeper reasons '*why*' people are experiencing life in their own way, it stops us from being judgemental which is in itself a negative emotion. *We are creating positive and negative thoughts all of the time.* Our thoughts and emotions can affect our health. Emotions that are freely experienced and expressed without judgement or attachment tend to flow fluidly without impacting our health. On the other hand, repressed emotions (especially fearful or negative ones) can zap mental energy, negatively affect the body, and lead to health problems. So then, it is important to recognise our thought and emotions and to be aware of the impact that they have on ourselves and others. A person's faith or spirituality provides a means for coping with illness and reaching a deeper kind of inner healing. Coping means different things to different people, it can involve finding answers to the questions that illness raises, it can mean seeking comfort for the fears and pain that illness brings, and it can mean learning how to find a sense of direction at a time of illness. In the face of a serious illness, we are often challenged by a range of emotional reactions that can be unfamiliar and more intense than anything we have ever encountered. We feel ourselves vulnerable and in need of a stable and solid support. We need to realise that everyone is on their own personal journey, seeking their own truth. In order to truly grow as a soul, we have to understand that no matter what people are like, they are who they are, just as you are who you have chosen to be!

Q: *"How can I be positive all the time, when they are so many challenging things going on in the world?"*

A: "I realise that I have focussed quite a lot on staying positive and focussed". "However, it is true that it is difficult to remain positive throughout".

None of us can go around with permanent smiles on our faces, we would look like we were on some sort of 'drug' or maybe even a bit 'crazy'. We have to go through different emotions depending on what we are experiencing at the time. The past two years in particular have been difficult for most people. Emotional health, financial struggles to name a couple only. Lock-down itself was difficult to deal with. With so much going on in the world, and so many negative news stories, it's sometimes easy to forget that there are plenty of day-to-day difficulties that we faced even before the pandemic. So therefore, it is ok to feel down and out of sorts. It's ok to show our emotions. We can all have emotional meltdowns. That's ok, it's a natural process, but the reason to bring positivity back when all around you is failing, is so that you can pull yourself out of the dark and back into the light. If we don't do this, we will stay stuck in a black hole of negativity. It is the act of looking for the positive, that bring us balance.

Q: *"How can I stop worrying about my loved ones dying?"*

A: "First of all know that your fears are rational". "We have probably all experienced these thoughts from time to time"

"It is when your thoughts become dark and irrational that they can turn to anxiety and even depression"

Many people struggle with the fact that they believe life ends in death. When a family member dies or when they think about their own death, the mystery of death touches people personally. Some feel anxious about the way death cuts us off from people we love and care about. They may be frustrated or disappointed by how little solid evidence they feel there is about what people experience after death. Some even wonder what the point of life is if it ends in death. Thoughts about what happens to us after death may bring up questions about the universe, we live in. Is our universe friendly or not? Does human life have purpose and meaning? If we are religious, we may wonder what God's purpose for our lives is. It's one thing to understand that death is inevitable and that things may be out of your control, but it's another to be at peace with that knowledge. Allow yourself to feel emotions. Often people can spend a lot of time worrying about the 'what ifs' and this can interfere with their ability to function properly and can rob us of our joy for living. Understand that there is a scientific reason for why your brain comes up with constant worries. You're getting an illusion of control, which keeps you searching for more.

Stay grounded by reminding yourself not to indulge in the act of worrying, as worrying won't change the inevitable happening. Try to focus on the good times that you have had and can still have with this person and take the focus away from them dying. How can you enjoy the times that you still have if you are in a constant state of worry about the future? By focussing on the end, you are missing out on the story that is now. I have included a chapter on the 'circle of life' which will help to highlight how we don't ever really part from each other. If you feel that you are suffering from anxiety or depression because of irrational thoughts, there a chapters that highlight how to find help either from within or via a trained therapist.

I hope this helps.

Angels and feathers

Michael's health has been a concern for us and so I channelled with my spiritual 'team' and asked for their support in helping us to get through whatever fears and challenges we might both encounter. As I have mention earlier in the book, when I ask for guidance or help from them, I get my answers either in *song, dreams* or very often a *feather* will appear. An angel is a messenger, and they will work with birds to deliver feathers as a way of letting you know that they hear you and want to help and support you. Because Mike has not been well, he has lost a considerable amount of weight, partly due to not being able to swallow or digest food properly. During the first few days of worrying, I experienced so many feather 'messages. The first was on a trip to the grocery store. I was feeling a little emotional, and my trolley was heavy, and the wheels were crooked, thus making it difficult to push up the incline to my car. Out of the blue, a lovely man came up to me and asked if he could push the trolley for me. I felt overwhelmed by his kindness as he delivered my trolley to my car and then proceeded to tell me to have a lovely day. I reached for my car keys to unlock the door and noticed a large *black* feather lying beside the door. I have always thought about white feathers being the ones to notice and have never given much thought to black or other coloured ones. Upon returning home I decided to research black feather messages. The meaning of a *black feather* is *protection and safety.* They are a good omen (not at all what you might think) It went on to say: "*The healing process that one is going through will soon be complete and you will be able to let go of things that don't serve you anymore".* "They are also a sign of *encouragement* to remind you to keep going *even though you may be facing some challenging circumstances".* "*The feather is motivating you to have faith and trust".* "Trust

*that all will be resolved to your best interest"
"These feathers can also show you path to self-growth and freedom to achieve whatever goal you set your mind to!"*

So then, to see black feathers is a *positive sign* and you should be thankful and blessed to have them in your path. The message goes on to say, *"you will start to live as your authentic self."* That was the night that I had the dream of climbing the cliff. Basically, explaining about me being on the *path to self-discovery, and knowing who I am.* This was just reiterating what I have already discovered. There were numerous feathers that came to me over a period of a few days. One feather appeared right beside my foot. I had closed my eyes enjoying the sunshine, and thinking about my life, and also about Mike. I opened my eyes to find the large black feather. Yet another, black feather floated down actually *on to my shoe* sometime later. The messages from these feathers are very meaningful right now. The following day, I counted *11 black feathers* all within a very small radius of my front door. Even though I know that feathers are around naturally, when they are in a specific place or given when you have asked for a sign, then you need to accept that they are messages from the universe. The number 11 in angel numbers represents a transmutation of your personal power to a higher more spiritual level. It illuminates our 'inner teacher' and reveals that we have *great powers of intuition* which makes us highly *empathetic* (which I already acknowledge that I am in this lifetime) I remembered having had the song: Baby you're a rich man: How does it feel to be one of the beautiful people, *now that you know who you are!!* As you can see each one of these messages is connecting with the pathway that I am currently on in this stage of my life. On a daily basis, I was finding *white* feathers on our doorstep and others that would be in obscure places. One day, I collected Mike's watch from the repair shop, and as I opened the door a white feather floated right in front of me. When I got home, I made my dinner (as Mike was working) I was thinking about him and the fact that he was still working even though he didn't have his usual strength. I had noted that this was between *5pm and 5.30pm* when I sat to eat my dinner. Later that evening when Mike came home, he told me that he was looking out of the window at work somewhere around that time as they had a lull in the orders. He looked out of the window and a white feather blew across from the carpark and attached itself to the fence right in front of him. It stayed there for 5 days! I know that Angels send us these signs to show that they are listening and helping us with our prayers. The *white feathers* are a sign of *faith and re-*

assurance. So, our messages were that we were being sent protection (black feathers) and re-assurance (white feathers) Angels do not have feathered wings, despite the images that you may find. Their wings are more like solar flares as they are not made out of matter. This is why they work alongside of the birds for the feathers on their wings. They blow these feathers into the right place, often where you wouldn't expect to find one. The other way to get messages is through song. I have mentioned this before, but literally, while I was typing this, I received a message from my daughter. Her youngest daughter, Florence (aged 5) asked where '*Bob*' was. (Bob was my eldest sister's husband) who passed to spirit eleven years ago. She said that she thought that *Bob* was holding her hand. She also said she wished that he didn't have to go! I was thinking about this and instantly got the song in my head '*singing in the rain*'. I googled the lyrics to the 'Gene Kelly' version, and there were two lines that were actually *high-lighted* on the page: They are: '*What a glorious feeling – I'm happy again" "I'm dancing and singing in the rain"* The perfect words sent through song to say that Bob is most definitely happy on the other side. I have so much evidence of life on '*the other side*' and I hope that other people that are searching for proof for themselves, find inspiration in my accounts. On speaking with my sister that evening, she said that she had a memory of Bob when they were on holiday in Spain. It was raining, and he stared singing the song. So, you see that was another message to say that Bob is around and connects with us. My sister feels his energy, especially when she needs re-assurance and upliftment. Her daughter, and granddaughter also feel Bob's presence. Emma (*my daughter*) had a strong bond with Bob from an early age. The strongest memories of her fun times with Bob were at Christmas time. She would help wash the dishes after dinner, and he would make her laugh. Very often, when she is washing the dishes at home, she will feel Bob's energy around her. This is one of the reasons that she can differentiate between Bob and her Nan (*my Mum*). When she feels my Mum's presence it is usually when she is sad, and she will reach out to her Nan for comfort. She will feel the impression of my Mums hand on her brow. All her thoughts disappear, and she falls asleep. One particular night Emma was going through an upsetting incident, and she sent her thoughts to my Mum to give her reassurance and comfort. Emma felt her hand on her brow, and her hair was actually brushed back from her head. So, when you are feeling upset and in need of comfort, send out your thoughts to you loved ones and angel guides and then *have faith*, that you will get their help. They truly do connect with us. Children function at a higher level of consciousness than adults, at an *expanded level* of consciousness. They are closer to the spiritual realm. Children are good mediums because of their purity of energy, and benevolent energies from the other side (angels), particularly those who may have been close to you on earth, might try to communicate to you through them. Children haven't yet learned to be manipulative or twist truths, and so they will speak the truth.

Back to Angels and feathers: Our angels like to send us signs to let us know that they are listening and working on our prayers and requests. As I stated earlier, symbols like feathers are most important when they are meaningful to the person that receives them. If I find a feather floating into a certain spot where one should not be, like inside my home, it has a deeper meaning. When your attention is drawn to a feather, it is there for a reason.

FEATHERS AND THEIR MEANINGS:

White Feathers: white is the most common and often considered the symbol for purity, which is very much aligned with the meaning of angels. White feathers can also be a sign from the angels that your loved ones in Heaven are well and have successfully crossed over into the spirit realms. Especially if the feather floats out of nowhere and gently lands in front you. It is often the person you are thinking of at that time.

White is also a symbol of *faith and protection*, and when you find white feathers in peculiar locations the message is especially significant. This is often just to reassure you that your angels are around you, working with you, and answering your prayers. They are confirmation that you are on the right path and definitely heaven sent.

Grey feathers: are a call to return to peace. Grey is also neutral and can be a sign that the answer to your question is not yes/no or black/white. It is time to go within and find your centre and tap into the void to help you to refocus and find the answers that you seek. It is the colour that helps you go in-between and see more than meets the eye. When the information you need is about the mental or emotional world, a grey feather is telling you there is an alternative point of view you may not have seen yet. It says the situation is not as hopeless as it seems on the outside and that the challenges of present are not the final outcome. If it has a silvery tone to the grey, then it is a sign to be persistent. Keep moving forward with intention and resolve. Keep yourself a bit grounded and know that you are protected by your angels.

Brown feathers: Signify grounding, home life, and stability. Brown shows you there is an energy of respect, grounding and balance between the physical world and the world of the spiritual. It signifies the importance of connecting with the earth and the now or the present moment. It also serves as a reminder of setting healthy boundaries. Keeping a balanced perspective and reviving your energy and creativity are reminders a brown feather brings.

Black feathers: Are a reminder of the *protection* of your angels, and a signal that spiritual wisdom is accessible by you so go within. You need a break from the world. Black Feathers send a message of reassurance you are not alone. It reminds you to discover the rich gifts that have been buried deep inside you. It's also a symbol of spiritual knowledge. Black feathers have long been associated with wisdom, which is why it's essential in the headdress of Shamans and spiritual leaders of ancient peoples. Seeing a black feather can mean that your angel is gifting you with spiritual knowledge and wisdom beyond this world, and that you must remain open to new information and insights that will come your way. What a feather means to one person will vary to another. Even when each particular feather symbolizes something unique, its interpretation will depend on where you are in life, spiritually and emotionally. Because the language of the spirit realms is incomprehensible to mortals like ourselves, angelic beings manifest their message through signs and symbols, like the ones in the feathers they leave behind. Angels make it easy, sometimes: a person who has a close link to their psychic powers can '*feel*' the angelic message simply by touching the feather. For those who need a little more help, it's best to ask yourself some questions when you encounter an angel feather:

What were you asking for when the feather appeared?

How is your life going right at this very moment?

What was the first thing you felt when you saw or touched the feather?

Once you answer these questions, the meaning of the feather will be revealed to you personally. But above the specific and personal message it brings you, the most important takeaway from a feather sign is this: the ever-loving and ever-benevolent Divine is with you, and with it, you can accomplish all things, great or small. Trust in the love and the light, and you will never be alone!

Angel numbers are another way in which they get our attention: If you see consecutive numbers repeatedly such as 11:11 (my favourite) then there is a message for you. 11:11 signifies that an energetic gateway has opened up for you, and this will rapidly manifest your thoughts into reality. These are the Angel guides who oversee synchronicity. While these numbers have many different meanings depending on your situation, they are usually associated with creativity, motivation and innovation. I mentioned earlier in the book that I kept having these numbers crop up over and over, until I decided to look for the specific message that was meant for me. Upon reading the meaning, I felt inspired to write this book. There have been <u>so many more</u> incidents where I have either picked up my phone to send a particular message, and times when I have felt the need for reassurance. One morning I woke with a tune playing in my head. I recognised it as a Native American tune from a CD that my friend Marion had given to me. The night before, I had been talking to my spirit team asking for healing for Mike. Marion sends 'distant healing' for him also. I always feel a strong connection with my guide 'Fast cloud' when I hear Native American music. I picked up my phone to message Marion to share this with her, and the time was 11:11 I felt sure that my spirit team are confirming that Mike is receiving the healing and support. There are all the other times that 11:11 have popped up in different ways which I have mentioned a few. So many times, I have had these numbers come to me. Another one I had a few times was 17:17 These suggest that we use our creative power to take control of our lives in a way that enables us to *pursue life's purpose.* It means that your life will revolve around *enlightenment, peace and clarity.* These certainly resonate with where my journey has taken me. When I went through a troubled period, feeling the need for peace, and also strength, I had the numbers 21:21 crop up on a couple of occasions. These numbers are telling you to enjoy the *peaceful period* that is coming your way. They will bring lots of *positive energy* to help you to feel yourself again. When we crave peaceful periods in our life, these numbers appear to give us strength to overcome difficulties. These details are very true and so very apt. Each time, I get an important message that helps me with my journey in this life. When you see these numbers *repeatedly*, your angels believe you aren't realizing your true potential, and they are reminding you to recognize your own worth. They want to reassure you that you are a strong human being who is on the brink of taking a leap forward on your spiritual journey. People can become sceptical when you talk about angels. Some think of and angel image as a large white being with extremely large, feathered wings. However, angels are pure spirit and do not have an inherent physical form. They are being of light and can take on any form. They are powerful beings and they do not need wings to fly. They don't have gender either. Angels have intellect and will and so exercise knowledge and love, but they do not have bodies or live an embodied form of life. Each angel is essentially a centre of consciousness without a body. Angels exist in an altogether higher order of reality, which is not a physical environment and is not conditioned by space, time, or material limitations.

Discovering that life is a 'school of learning'

When we are faced with challenges, some people react with negative emotions. '*You hurt me, and I will hurt you back*', sort of attitude. Recently I was faced with a negative situation. My instinct was to be angry as I was hurt by the comments made to me. I felt that I wanted to turn my back on the person that had said the harmful comments. I contemplated what I should do, and I realised that this person can sometimes present challenges, but that is why we have certain people in our lives. *We are sent challenges to see how we deal with them.* Think of yourself in a classroom sitting an exam. It is whether or not we 'pass' the exam as to where we go next in life. As I mentioned earlier in this book, *we choose lessons and people we want to offer those lessons before we incarnate.* Because our memory of this is wiped clean before we arrive on Earth, the lessons are set before us to see *if we can deal with them in a positive way or not.* If we do not learn to deal with them in a positive way, thus passing the exam, we will *be sent further tests in the form of challenges.* I had decided upon *accepting the 'upset' as a challenge.* A few days went by, and I kept noticing the numbers 22. I looked up this in my Angel number book and it said:

"You are at a crucial point on your journey which will help you understand the <u>relationships</u> and <u>spiritual assignments</u> that will support your growth!"

Once again you see that this could not be more apt, and just goes to prove that the angels/guides are actually with us and let us know that they are supporting us in whatever way they can.

I realise that by taking notice of the messages that are being sent to me, that I am actually making progress on my spiritual journey through this life. We are learning every day of our lives. The day we stop learning, is the day we die! Angel signs are the signals and omens that signify the presence of angel guides in your life. As I have previously mentioned, Angels are very real. They are spiritual beings who exist within a *different frequency band.* They can send us warning signs if it is for our highest good, but some people aren't open to these beliefs and therefore often don't get the message. Guidance from the angels can be subtle, and in many cases when we "*miss*" receiving the messages angels are attempting to convey, they will use signs and leave clues and hints which serve to nudge us in the right direction and remind us of their support and presence. When you are open to receive a sign, you will find that there's almost always something deeper behind it and signs often come hand in hand with receiving a flash of inspiration, a message, or getting an 'aha' of understanding and recognition about what will now serve and support you and manifest positive changes and blessings in your life. Finding feathers in obscure places is *one way* of knowing that your Angel guides are near. Or you might feel a warm loving energy which often feels like gentle tingles on the surface of your skin. This is a positive feeling, although it may feel a bit strange. It happens when your vibration begins to raise due to being in the presence of a higher being/frequency. Angelic energy is powerful, and so when you're in the presence of these energies the actual lighting around you may show signs of an increase of energy. This angel sign could take the form of the lights around you (like a lamp in your room) flickering. It may also take the form of a light turning itself on with no clear reason for why. When an angel/higher energy, directs their awareness towards you, that awareness carries an almost *electrical energy*, which is why electrical devices like lighting acting a little weird is a clear sign! Your lights may flicker. You may feel a gentle breeze, or a lovely scent. Your loved ones can let you know that they are around you by sending you a smell of their perfume or tobacco that was personal to them. Some members of my family know when my father is around because they can smell his distinct tobacco scent. I know when my father is close by as I have a piece of classical music that 'was his favourite', come into my head. Then as I mentioned in the healing section, I feel his hands over mine. They will send messages through the songs that you either have in your head, or maybe when you just turn on the radio. If you wake up in a morning with a particular song in your head, and it won't go away, you can be sure that there is a message in it somewhere. It won't be the whole song, but you will find that the same part of the song keep repeating itself, or certain words will stand out, and again you will get that 'aha' moment, when you realise that the words resonate with you. Angels are beings of *love and light*. You may experiences little flashes of colour or light from seemingly no-where. A dear friend of mine, feels a tingling or moving sensation on her crown chakra when her Angels and guides are near. You may experience a gentle touch or think you have seen someone walk past you when there is 'no-one' there. Or you may feel chills. They will draw your attention to things in whatever way they can. You may '*hear*' a message *in your mind* or hear a whispered voice which seems to appear out of thin air. Don't assume you're making it up! If you can't really hear what is being said, ask your angel to speak a bit louder so you can understand. Hearing the guidance of your angels is a beautiful sign of their presence and is common when you are in need of comfort, reassurance, or angelic guidance. While they are supporting you, there is a limit to what they are able to do without interfering with *your 'free will'*. As mentioned earlier, there are many spirit guides and helpers, so when you feel frustrated about a situation, or confused about what step to take next, send your problem to your angels and guides. They are there to help you in whatever way they are allowed to do (*for your soul's growth*). We choose *the main experiences* in our lives before we incarnate, and so in order to fulfil our '*contract*' there are some *challenges* that we have to face, and our guides *are not allowed to interfere*. They can, however, help to guide you through it. So always send up your thoughts to them and remember *to thank them always*. I went through a stage of concern for Mike, even though I know that none of us will depart the Earth until our soul has decided upon an exit point. I admit to feeling a little negative about life in general. Our loved ones, and spirit guides are always aware of our feelings and as I have already said, one way they relay messages is through dreams.

The Dream:

I dreamed that I was walking along a road besides a cliff. I looked down to see clear crystal blue water, shrouded by a soft mist. Above, two extremely large birds (like the ones in Avatar) soaring above, weaving and gliding gracefully over and around each other. They were a magnificent bright turquoise blue. I felt total and complete peace just watching this beautiful scene. I awoke feeling very positive about everything.

The colour turquoise dispels negative energy and aligns all chakras bringing inner calm.

Here, you see I received a healing dream/message. A couple of times after that I noticed the numbers 13:13, I researched the meaning of 13.13 and it states: *Guardian angels are communicating with you. This is a sign of spiritual enlightenment. You are chosen for great things.* So again, you can see how spirit connect with us and bring us re-assurance. We just need to accept and have faith in their signs. Angels speak to us in synchronised ways, which basically means that we will see something over and over again, so much so that it goes beyond mere *coincidence*. Mike had to go for a small procedure, and I sent out thoughts to his deceased parents and asked them to be with him. Mike rarely dreams (*or doesn't remember them*) but that night after his procedure he dreamed that he was waving his parents off as they left him. I hadn't told Mike that I had sent thoughts to them and so this could not have had any bearing on his dream. This proves to me that his parents had indeed been with him throughout and then when they were happy that he was OK, they waved goodbye.

I am adding these dreams/messages just to show readers that *we do receive help and guidance* if we *trust and accept* what we are given. Even the smallest sign can be enlightening. I am always eternally grateful for the spiritual knowledge that I have been given and the constant upliftment and guidance, together with validation that I do receive answers from spirit. You may have had a dream that holds specific significance, or you may see a number *repeatedly*, or perhaps several friends have mentioned the exact same *particular* book, event, or workshop in the space of a very short time period. *These are not coincidences, but meaningful timing.* Each one of us is connected to spirit, and they are trying to communicate with us every day. Maybe just to let us know that we are not alone and that they are there to assist us in whatever way they can. Because we have free will and choice in our lives, our guides will not tell us what to do and will wait for us to ask for help. While sometimes it might feel like life would be much easier and simpler if someone (a higher source) just told us what to do, it wouldn't be an educational and learning experience as we need to figure it out ourselves. So, our guides and loved ones will try to share their guidance with us, but will do so typically in a quiet, non-obtrusive kind of way. The truth is, there are messages all around us, and they happen every day…but they usually are not glaring neon signs saying, '*Do this*!' For us to receive the message we have to be open to the message and be aware of our surroundings and what is going on around us. For it to be a message, all you have to do is go about your regular day-to-day activities, and the message will present itself to you. *You don't have to force it or do anything different* — except being open and aware of what is around you. You'll know when you are getting a message because you'll have that feeling of it being synchronicity and special to you. Watch for the feeling that arises within you! Connect to your intuition. Are you seeing/hearing a variety of messages that align with the issue you are currently having that point to a solution for you? If you are getting messages through your dreams, you might want to try a dream interpretation dictionary to give you some guidance. I always use the spiritual dream dictionaries. You will feel that the dream symbolizes something for you. If you have a song stuck in your head, write down the part of the song that is replaying in your head. You might not have the lyrics completely correct, but don't worry about that. Sometimes it is more about the concept than the actual words. Don't think about the entire song, just the part that is coming to you. How does that part relate to your question or situation. Always thank your spirit team for help and guidance. This then brings me back to gratitude:

Keep a gratitude journal and add to it every day.

Be grateful for your life - Be grateful for life's lessons and the people that bring you the lessons.

Tell someone you love them and how much you appreciate them -Notice the beauty in nature each day.

Nurture the friendships that you have, good friends don't come along every day - Smile often.

Include an act of kindness in your life each day.

Avoid negative speech and destructive behaviour.

Help other people that ask for your help

Remember to compliment your friends and family on matters that will cheer them

When you think a negative thought, try to see the positive side in the situation. Try to begin the day with a *positive attitude* rather than a negative. Gradually you will become a happier person, and a more grateful one. Negativity drains your energies. People that are always complaining and critical, are very toxic people and are a constant drain. You will notice that there are people who always blame others for their problems. They play the victim. These people have problems to deal with their own issues, and do not take responsibility for their own actions. It is, therefore, easier to put the blame on some-one else. Some people actually thrive on getting your pity, and even though you want to help, they probably don't want it. This is where I say again, *only offer help if it is asked for.* There are people who like to constantly speak badly about other people. Some will try to control your opinions about topics, and others will point out all the flaws in your behaviour. Some might seek your company in judging others. What they all have in common is that after every interaction with them you feel *emotional fatigue and stress.* Truly effective stress management involves a mix of habits and thought patterns that minimize the stress you encounter in life and increase your ability to cope with the stress you must face. There are several habits that can help to relieve your stress. These include, meditation, exercise, and *focusing on the positive.*

Surround yourself with positive and supportive people. You need to let go of grudges, toxic relationships and negative thought patterns. We need to recognise our feelings and deal with them. *Let go of anger.* It serves no purpose, only to make you feel *even more stressed and negative.* It is a downward spiral. There are people that we cannot help, *unless* they ask us for help. By interfering in someone else's pathway, *you are creating more negative karma for yourself,* and you are not letting the other person learn their own lesson. Remember, we have '*all*' chosen the pathway that is right for our soul's growth, whatever challenges that may bring. So, by interfering without being asked to do so, could ultimately change the destiny of the person dealing with the problem. Also remember this…. *You cannot change another person*; you can only change things *within yourself.* If someone or something is making you very unhappy, then *YOU* have to be the one to change the course of events. Don't expect the other person to change. You can inspire another, or support them, but you cannot make them change. If you cannot change a situation, change how you think about it! How often do you say,

"*I wish this person would be different, or do this or that differently*" By trying to force someone do something, even if (*you think*) it's for their own good, requires either coercion or manipulation. It requires intervening in their life in a way that is a *boundary violation*, and it will therefore damage their 'growth' and as I said earlier, add a negative to your Karma list! I realise that I have expressed a point of view more than once throughout this book, but sometimes we need reminders about how we are experiencing and learning all of the time. Even though I have been fortunate to gain a great deal of knowledge on 'life' and how we can help ourselves and others on our spiritual pathway, I am still learning, and I hope that I don't sound self-righteous! I can maybe also sound a little boring on this subject to some, as largely it has become my way of life and the way I deal with situations. One thing my daughter said to me recently was, that she was very grateful for all the teachings that I have been able to share with her. However, she did ask my opinion on a situation, and she asked me to answer it '*like a mother*' and not in the spiritual sense. If she had asked my opinion and advice on this matter when I was younger, I would have probably given her completely different advice, as I would have been acting from the ego. However, I now see things from a different perspective and can only answer with the truth as I know it now! You get to decide what is right for you, you don't get to decide what makes another person good or bad (in your eyes). People will choose their own values and if they don't deal with their own experiences, then there won't be healing for them.

Breaking the cycle:
A lot of people, whether religious or not, tend to think in defeatist terms. When we see signs of social decay, we shake our heads, blame the politicians or media and lament the passing era. Breaking the cycle of futility means that we have no obligation to engage in the problem. How can we help ourselves? Forgive yourself, first and foremost. Whatever the "issue" is (cruelty, theft, adultery, murder). Forgive yourself!

Forgiveness isn't something you feel; it is something you do. To forgive is to release. There will always be challenging time within the family circle. Conflict, stress and spending time in each other's company can cause argument. It can be difficult to keep children shielded from adult arguments when things are uncertain. Speaking in spiritual terms, we are born into the families that can offer us what we need for our soul growth. The person that you resent so much, may have been someone that you have loved in a past incarnation, or had a hate relationship with and this time around you are balancing this behavioural pattern. In order to break free of the obsessive thinking patterns which keeps us feeling anger, resentment, bitterness and rage we need to find a method to change our thinking patterns. Trying to repress your feelings is not the answer, as they will just cause them to go underground and then they will manifest in another way. I know that I stress on the importance of forgiveness, but I feel that by understanding someone else's actions (whether you agree with them or not) can help you deal with them in a more constructive way. We are all on this pathway of learning from each other and also paying back Karmic debts. So then, discovering that Earth is a school of learning, and that life is a series of experiences maybe we can see the lessons behind the actions.

"We are the sum total of our experiences. Those experiences – be they positive or negative – make us the person we are, at any given point in our lives. And, like a flowing river, those same experiences, and those yet to come, continue to influence and reshape the person we are, and the person we become. None of us are the same as we were yesterday, nor will be tomorrow."

BJ Neblett

when events and changes happen in our life, we have a part to play in this from conscious, and unconscious intention and direction we set for ourselves.

"For the meaning of life differs from man to man, from day to day, and from hour to hour. What matters, therefore, is not the meaning of life in general but rather the specific meaning of a person's life at a given moment."

Viktor Frankl

Your inner critic

Our inner critic take affect the actions that we take. Ur inner critic needs to heal, like any wound. We can be afraid to get things wrong, afraid to be shamed or judged, or exposed. We need to recognise where our inner critic came from. Maybe your teacher told you that you would never amount to anything, or you Dad told you that you were worthless (These are just examples) The things that people say to make us feel un-worthy, un-loved or afraid, stay within and we may choose to believe that what they say are true. Also, you may be reading an article about someone else which maybe derogatory by putting them down, you may then make that decision that you don't want to be like them because you don't want to be judged in the way that this article is shaming the person that you are reading about. This is where our own inner critic develops. You may decide that you want to join a group, let's say a choir but your inner critic remembers someone saying that you were not very good at singing, then you are feeling fear. Fear of being judged and criticized.

That fear can hold us back because we allow that fear to stop us going forward and doing what we want to do. So, then it is time for you to look within and recognise where these self-limiting beliefs began. Who was it that said you couldn't sing? Why did they say it? Why are you going to accept that this is a fact? What are you giving up in order to hold on to these beliefs? Often, we begin to move towards something that we feel we might be good at, but we listen to that inner critic telling us that someone said you weren't any good! Some of this fear can be something that we have brought back with us when we incarnated, or it could be a memory from this lifetime. If you can't push past this trauma, maybe you could seek out someone that may be able to help. If it is just discomfort, then this may be part of your growth. If you can stamp out the fear and go with whatever it is you are wanting to achieve, then this will bring a new energy. You will feel liberated with what you have achieved. We may still get moments of fear of judgment, but the more we work on letting go of that fear, we begin to move towards our authentic self and move towards the things that will make us happy. Our inner critic is just emotions, energy and thoughts. We need to heal our fears, and we won't do this by hiding away from it. I managed to confront one of my fears with the EFT, but it may not be that simple in some cases.

Sometimes we need to go beyond the fear of self-doubt. You can listen to your fears, but don't let it be the biggest voice! Ask yourself what is the worst that can happen. The fear that holds you back is just a thought. You can change a thought and you can create a new you. IF you can't do this alone, ask your guides to step in and help you to find the way forward.

Spiritual Enlightenment

Throughout my life, I feel that I have gained a fair amount of spiritual enlightenment, and a deep understanding of the meaning of life and therefore if people ask for my opinion, then I answer them with the understanding that I have gained. Life is shifting in consciousness and so are we. We are changing and evolving, and I feel more and more people are connecting to the higher energies. We go through many stages in life. We experience many 'growing pains' as we learn lessons throughout life. So, as I understand it, if a situation or someone is making your life constantly miserable, then find a way to move away from it. Not an easy task, you might say, but the 'choice is yours and yours alone'. Always ask for help and guidance from your spirit team and they will help you to make the decisions that are right for you. I share my experiences, strengths and hopes so others see it is possible. I do not give advice unless someone comes to me as a counsellor, or unless specifically asked. All too often, I have stepped in to help with a situation without being invited to do so and it has resulted in me being stressed out! I have had to learn my lessons through this, and it has helped me to grow spiritually and look at where I need to step back from a situation. We cannot just point the finger at someone else. As I have said before, we each have our own lessons to learn throughout life, and unless we are asked for our help, we should not jump in and try.

I think the main reason that people will seek advice from a 'spiritual person' is to look at another perspective on life. Being spiritual, simply means that the person has attained more positive thoughts with a conscious awareness on a soul level. It is only thoughts that are different. I just like to point out that we all have a choice on what to think, but by changing negative thoughts into positive ones you can open up your mind and find a healthier pathway. You won't always be 'on top' of your thoughts. You can ask yourself, 'why' do I let things bother me in the way that they do? 'What do I want from life?' and 'How can I achieve it?' 'How can I best deal with my challenges?' You will always encounter problems along the way. It is what we choose to be our belief system. We can choose to stay positive. We can accept the challenges that are given to us as important lessons in our growth. We can choose to take our power back and look at the bigger picture. By realising that everything has a lesson for us, and we are creating our experiences day by day, even minute by minute. There is a MUCH bigger picture. We have to become the best person that we can possibly become in this life by trusting and embracing ourselves exactly as we are. This is spiritual awakening.

Q: "*What <u>exactly</u> is a spiritual awakening, and is there a way you can tell if you are having one?* "

A: "*awakening* happens when you are no longer filtering everything through your ego and focussing on the future and the past. Instead, you have an awareness of your individual 'self'. One of the first signs of awakening is *noticing*. You may be going through life on autopilot without giving much thought to who you are, what you want, and why you are here. Finding inner peace is paramount. It doesn't mean that you won't experience challenges in your life, it just means that when things do you aren't on an emotional roller coaster of anger, frustration, or despair. Dealing with challenges isn't always easy, but necessary to balance your energies. We are sometimes dealing with suppressed emotions that maybe circumstances haven't allowed us to feel. Emotional healing is paramount to our health and wellbeing.

When you find enlightenment and become your 'self' then you will be able to deal with emotions more readily and with a different mindset. We begin to rearrange who we are becoming and expand our energy. We handle this in our own time. We are governed by society to a certain degree, but we have to let go of rigid beliefs in order to move forward. Once you start to realise that you are on the road to enlightenment, you will not want to accept lies and deceit from others. They will become more apparent to you, and you will be in a place where you are not going to accept them. This will enable you to find your peace within. This will be finding out what works for you. You may need to take a step back from people in your life that are not serving you in a positive way. This does not mean that you have to cast them out forever. However, it is letting go of the stress and chaos that some people bring and choosing your own pathway and also accepting that other people may be different to ourselves. We are continuing to learn through every phase of our life journey. Others influence us, but we have to decide to be happy with ourselves and our life choices. Stop comparing your life to others and re focus your energy on the best part of you. So next time you find yourself comparing yourself to someone else, stop yourself and think whether it is fair to compare your life with theirs when you are only seeing a portion of their life, they want you to see. You don't have the full story. If comparing is how you evaluate your worth, you will always be losing, there is no doubt about it. In this game of life if your only objective is to reach a point where you are better than others in every way, well you are going to fail miserably because it will never happen. Part of what makes life interesting is learning from others. We all have a role to play in each other's 'movie of life'. There will always be differences, because these are the lessons of our journey. Often, we focus so much on the goal or destination that we forget the journey, disconnect from each important step, and stress is created, the sense that we are 'Not There Yet'. Yet happiness can only be found in the here and now, and has nothing to do with goals, destinations, or getting what you want. Take the focus off the future and live in the now. We don't always know where we are headed, and that's perfectly okay. Accept any uncertainty, doubt, trepidation that you feel; learn to love this special place of no answers! Life is full of potential.

"Spiritual awakening is not a goal or destination. Rather, it is an invitation to trust and embrace yourself exactly as you are, in all your glorious imperfection".

Increasing intuition: Have you ever thought of an old friend from school only to run into them in an airport the next day? Have you ever heard your phone ring and known it was your mother before looking? Have you ever felt an immediate and irrational dislike for someone or experienced the feeling when first meeting someone that you already know them? These are all signs of intuition. If thoughts, objects, and individuals all have energy, spiritually awoken human beings seem more apt to connect with this energy on a regular basis.

Having synchronicity: Along the same lines as intuition, there is synchronicity. but others believe that these subtle signs are guiding you. Synchronicity can manifest in the same numbers cropping up, meaningful names, words, or symbols. Synchronicity is a form of guidance from your higher self, or soul. It is a way of showing you that you are on the right track. It can be a form of powerful confirmation, a ray of guidance, or a sign of hope for those on the spiritual journey. where to go and what to do next in your life as you proceed through your spiritual awakening.

Increasing compassion: Empathy is your ability to feel what others are feeling. Compassion is an action that is inspired by your empathy. It literally means "to suffer with." People who are in the process of a spiritual awakening begin to notice both a more all-encompassing empathy and a more action-oriented compassion that feels normal, natural, and fulfilling. One area of compassion that is often forgotten is self-compassion. Be kind to yourself and practice mindfulness. With an awakening comes confidence and a deep sense of self-worth. Gone is the need to conform to cultural norms or remain politically correct. Instead, a complete sense of satisfaction with *'who you are'* and the choices you make is more fulfilling. You will realise that there is a mind-body connection. As Eckhart Tolle says: "You find peace not by rearranging the circumstances of your life, but by realizing who you are at the deepest level." "Spend time focused on becoming yourself fully."

Self-worth and self-esteem

There are many ways for a person to value themselves and assess their worth as a human being, and some of these are more psychologically beneficial than others. So many people lack a feeling of worthiness. I think that the first step in building self-worth is to stop comparing yourself to others and evaluating your every move; in other words, you need to challenge your inner critic. The critical inner voice is like a nasty coach in our heads that constantly nags us with destructive thoughts towards ourselves or others. This internalized dialogue of critical thoughts or "inner voices" undermines our sense of self-worth and even leads to self-destructive behaviour, which make us feel even worse about ourselves.

I have covered a part of this in a previous chapter, but I feel that I ned to add this to enlightenment because until we find happiness within, we cannot project it outwards.

More about messages and connections from our spirit guides

Our guides and loved ones can give us little snippets of information just to let us know that they are hearing our thoughts. As I have mentioned, often they are very cryptic clues.

For example: Michael had booked reservations for our next family holiday in Africa for 2022. Because of the Covid situation and Mike not feeling particularly strong, it is looking very unlikely that we will be able to keep the booking. I had been constantly turning this over in my mind, wondering if we would be able to return to Africa when it was safe for us all to travel. So then, not necessarily for the time of the booking, but anytime in the future. My friend, Marion who is clairvoyant and a Reiki healer, often sends thoughts of love and healing to both Mike and myself. She messaged me one day to say that she was on the bus going to work. She had closed her eyes, and suddenly saw (*in her third eye*) the word 'AFRICA' in bold letters. She said she knew it was for me. The following morning, I awoke with the words to a song: *I'm going to be an optimist about this!!!* and so you see how the two messages came together and gave me the answer that gave me hope. I know that we have to wait until it is safe enough to travel, and also for Mike to regain his strength. The following day I was travelling to do my weekly shop and had to stop at a junction to let a camper van out. I looked at the wording that was written across the top of the door. It said: '*One life-live it*'. Not only that, but the registration was: MI...me (the dots being the numbers) At a glance the registration read *my time*! As you already know, I am a great believer that these are not coincidences but synchronicity. Two events that come together for a purpose. They may be to give us a message or they may be that a situation happens that moves your life in a new direction. Even though I know how messages are sent to us I still felt in awe as I read the wording on the van. There are so many inspiring ways that we get messages. We just need to open to them and *believe*. It happens to everyone sooner or later: A certain number pops up wherever you go; an old friend you haven't seen in 20 years since school appears the same day, you're looking at her photograph. You're singing a song and turn on the radio-and the same song is playing. Such *coincidences*, are examples of synchronicity. The concept is linked to the psychology of Carl Jung who believed that such "meaningful coincidences" play an important role in our lives. Mike had to go to hospital to get some treatment for his illness. As we switched on the engine in the car, the time was 11:11. Then the following day I awoke with a tune in my head. The CD is instrumental music that I often play when I am giving healing, called, 'Eagles chant.' I wanted to share this with Marion as she was the one that gave me the CD and as mentioned, has also been sending 'distant healing' to Mike. As I began to type, I noticed that the time was 11:11. I feel that the angels are still sending support, and I feel strongly that Mike is receiving Marion's healing. These numbers are a reminder that we are all connected and asks us to align our thoughts and actions for our highest good and best self. It also reminds us that we are manifesting our thoughts and to keep them positive.

Taken from my Angel number book:

I realise that I have written a chapter on angel numbers, but I just want to add a little extra at this point.

Number 11:11 is made up of the powerful influences of the number 1, amplified and magnified by four. Number 1 resonates with the vibrations and attributes of new beginnings and starting afresh, independence and individuality, initiative and assertiveness, ambition and motivation, success and leadership, courage and strength, creation and creativity, self-reliance and tenacity, attainment, happiness and fulfilment, innovation, self-development and oneness with life. Number 1 reminds us that we create our own realities with our thoughts, beliefs, intentions and actions. Many people associate the repeating 11:11 with a 'wake-up call', a 'Code of Activation' and/or an 'Awakening Code', or 'Code of Consciousness'. It can also be seen as a key to unlock the subconscious mind and reminds us that we are spiritual beings having a physical experience, rather than physical beings embarking upon spiritual experiences. Upon noticing a frequency of 11:11's appearing repeatedly, you may begin to see an increase in synchronicities and unlikely and what you may term as 'coincidences' appearing in your life. At times, when you are about to go through a major spiritual awakening, the number 11:11 may appear in your physical reality and experience to signal the upcoming change or shift.

When Angel Number 11:11 appears repeatedly it signifies that an energetic gateway has opened up for you, and this will rapidly manifest your thoughts into reality. The message is to choose your thoughts wisely, ensuring that they match your true desires. Do not put your energy into focusing on fears as you may manifest them into your life. Pay special attention to your thoughts and ideas as these are revealing the answers to your prayers. Your positive affirmations and optimistic attitude will help to manifest your desires and help you to achieve your goals and aspirations. They will also assist you with serving your spiritual life purpose and soul mission. Angel Number 11:11 encourages you to look to new beginnings, opportunities and projects with a positive and optimistic attitude as these are appearing in your life for very good reason. Be an inspirational guiding light to bring illumination and enlightenment to others and to help raise spiritual awareness. Trust that the angels support you in your 'light- work'. Every time I receive or notice a sign or synchronicity, I just feel an overwhelming sense that everything is in order and that the Universe is looking out for me. Whatever they mean to you, I'm sure synchronicities can and will bring you the same amount of joy when you learn how to recognize them!

I have shared quite a few synchronicities that have given meaning to me. The one that probably stands out the most was the till receipt for £11.11

Give your worries to your spirit team

A little while ago, I had cause for some concern and so I gave my worries up to my spirit team. I found myself 'chatting' with my dad. It had been a challenging day and after mulling things over, I eventually fell asleep. You have probably guessed that I had a message! Well, yes, I did. When I awoke the following morning, I had a song in my head. The song was: *'I'll be there."* The words that resonated with me were: *'I'll reach out my hand to you…. Just call my name and I'll be there'.* So, you see, my dad was aware of my anguish, and he was telling me that he would hold my hand and support me. The next day, I was ironing, and I was thinking again about Africa and if we would actually return. I felt a strong connection with my father's energy, and so I just talked to him. I said, "Dad I know that you are only allowed to tell me so much, *BUT* I want to know if we will go back to Africa at some point" I also said that I *didn't need to be told when,* but just '*if*' it would happen.

I added, "*please do not give me a cryptic message in a song*". "I need *to see* a yes or a no in **BOLD** letters". "I need it to resonate strongly with me for me to know that it is a message from you". **That very evening**, I was just checking out my face book messages before retiring to bed. I was literally about to turn off my I-pad, when I saw a post. It was a link to a YouTube channel and the writing was in bold. It said: **YES (official)** Now some would say that it was coincidence, but I had that 'aha' moment and it certainly made me stop in my tracks. It was exactly what I had asked for that very morning…. A **BOLD- YES or NO**. I am sharing this with you, so that you can see how it works. Often the messages that you receive are cryptic. There are no rules on what a sign should look like: your favourite flower, an inside joke, the rarest bird, a cartoon. Just craft a message clear enough that *you know it when you see it*. The dreams, songs and other synchronicities, help me on my spiritual journey. Another way in which I Communicate with spirit is through Claircognizance which is "*clear-knowing*". This is done by focussing on the breath. Breath-work can be extraordinary to shift your energy. Breathe in through your nose really deeply and fully and slowly out through your mouth. Do this as slowly as you can, with your eyes closed. Do this three times. That alone will shift your energy into a meditative state, ready to receive messages.

Intuition: Intuition, as mentioned previously, is that sneaking suspicion that you feel when something is not right, but you can't put your finger on why. Learning to listen to your gut feeling has a lot to do with trust, which can be hard when fear is involved. To follow your intuition means that you *do not* have to put *conscious thought into making a decision.* When your intuition tries to communicate with you, it may try to get your attention by forcing you to notice little patterns throughout your life. Maybe you have been wanting to find a new job but afraid to take the plunge? Your intuition may subtly let you notice certain career articles or job postings to help get your attention. Have you ever had those "ah-ha!" moments when you're in the shower or driving your car? That's an example of your intuition trying to talk to you. When you allow your mind to rest, with maybe meditation, your mind opens up and allows your thoughts and emotions to flow through. Your intuition talks to you when you are less busy, when you sleep, when are you not trying to push for it, when you take your mind off what you are seeking. Your intuition is usually there to guide you in the right direction, but sometimes you miss the signs or choose to ignore them. However, if you continue to notice that your brain wanders back to a particular thought, then you might want to slow down and investigate why you're feeling this way. Another number that has been getting my attention of late is 17.17. I researched the meaning behind these numbers, and this is what it says: 17:17 suggests that we use our creative power to take control of our lives in a way that enables us to pursue life's purpose. We should trust our gut and intuition when deciding how to act, as we all have knowledge that we need this to move forward. Guardian angels are supporting you on your life journey. This number means that your life will revolve around enlightenment peace and clarity (*something I often seek*) The next sequence of numbers that cropped up after that was 21:21 This number is telling you to enjoy the *peaceful periods* and that it is bringing *positive energy to balance and help you feel yourself again. It brings strength to overcome difficulties!* Again. this shows you how once you accept on message, you get another. Sometimes for clarification and others to spur you on further.

"Follow your intuition, it will always guide you to the right destination" "Spend time cultivating gratefulness if you want to be happy"

The circle of life

Life is a circle; *the end of the journey is the beginning of the next.* Everything comes full circle. It is important to be aware of envy, jealousy and hatred because what we project, we also receive. (*Either in this life or the next*) Our pathways represent the challenges and obstacles that will be offered as great opportunities on our destined paths. These are the roads to follow through choice and free will in order to obtain deeper knowledge. These paths, reaching away from the core, may also render times of confusion, as this state of mind may develop because of you getting off the straightforward/destined path. When this occurs, the mind and soul are no longer in harmony. It is vital to listen to your '*intuition*' so that the lessons will be learned with greater ease, and the soul will rule rather than the mind/ego taking control. Once issues are resolved and the soul understands the worthiness to life, a straightforward destined path will be found again. Thereupon, more lessons will be learned, and if the choice is made to remain on the path of merit, the soul will return to the centre of the circle where love exists in the highest, most pure form imaginable. The soul is a permanent entity. When it is time for the soul to leave the body, it will take with it the same thought patterns that it acquired from the physical existence. If the physical life had been one of love, truth, honesty, humility, and gratitude, your soul will return to the home of happiness, the home you left in the ethereal world before entering the dense earth plane. In this light, you will have completed the physical circle that will continue in the ethereal world. The expansion of thought and all senses will continue to further your growth to wisdom that is inconceivable to the earth plane, as it is limitless. The ultimate achievement is to realise *the purity of the soul, the greatness of love that lies within*. The centre of the circle is where all will eventually want to be. If the circle of life is not completed, then you will go to school to re-learn the desired lessons, either in the spirit world or with reincarnation. (Back to Earth school) Once the lessons are learned, *then and only then*, will you be permitted to move on to the higher levels of wisdom. This is why it is so important to complete the lessons you need while on the physical plane, so it merely continues in the ethereal world. The soul is constantly evolving. You know it from your suffering. Every moment of suffering means you could have dealt with a particular lesson in a more constructive way. You may have a lesson that has not been resolved in a former lifetime and because you still haven't learned from it, it will keep turning up and you will therefore keep the suffering going. So, each time you return you have the opportunity to notice where you could have done better. As I have mentioned once or twice, *you choose to come to the earth plane*, therefore, make the best of *all situations* that will be nurturing to your spiritual growth. The circle of life never ends, it is just made more exhilarating for you as you continue your journey on your destined path.

"A heart full of love and compassion is the main source of inner strength, willpower, happiness and mental tranquillity"

So, live your life that the fear of death can never enter your heart. Trouble no one about their religion; respect others in their view, and demand that they respect yours. Love your life, perfect your life, beautify all things in your life. Seek to make your life long and its purpose in the service of your people. Prepare a noble death song for the day when you go over the great divide. Always give a word or a sign of salute when meeting or passing a friend, even a stranger, when in a lonely place. Show respect to all people and grovel to none.
When you arise in the morning give thanks for the food and for the joy of living. If you see no reason for giving thanks, the fault lies only in yourself. Abuse no one and no thing, for abuse

turns the wise ones to fools and robs the spirit of its vision. When it comes your time to die, be not like those whose hearts are filled with the fear of death, so that when their time comes, they weep and pray for a little more time to live their lives over again in a different way. Sing your death song and die like a hero going home."

Words of Wisdom: by Chief Tecumseh

Doing Service:

The greatest good is when you do service for others. I believe that I am on 'track' with my spiritual journey now. As you now know, I realised a while ago that I am here this time around to do service. By being a medium, I am able to raise my vibrations high enough to channel and connect to the other side. While it may never remove the pain of losing a loved one or take away the sadness of not having their physical presence around, a medium, by bringing through highly evidential and specific information that nobody else could possibly know, can re-establish a connection, and offer a certain level of evidence that the soul survives death. This suggests that not only can we continue to communicate with loved ones on the other side, but that we will be met, on the other side of death, with people who can help us transition. Psychic reading can be hard work because you're translating images constantly. It's almost like Pictionary or charades. We have to be careful not to put our own feelings into the mix, but also to interpret the messages clearly and lovingly. My intentions are to try to bring peace of mind to the sitter along with the love from their deceased friends/relatives. Therefore, this is one way that I am doing service for others. Another is with the counselling: I learned with my counselling how important it is to *just listen*. This is a therapy that can help to build trust with the client. Counselling is also about showing empathy and having patience. A counsellor will not judge in any way but will show compassion. I understand that I am Empathic. Being an empath, I am able to understand how people *feel*, and can show empathy. I feel that I can accurately recognise emotions by sometimes just looking at another person's face. These emotions can be quite intense. However, it helps me to understand where people are coming from. How and why, they are hurting, and I can fully sympathise.

To describe an empath: Empaths are highly sensitive individuals, who have a keen ability to sense what people around them are thinking and feeling. Psychologists may use the term empath to describe a person that experiences a great deal of empathy, often to the point of taking on the pain of others at their own expense.

However, the term *empath* can also be used as a spiritual term, describing an individual with special, psychic abilities to sense the emotions and energies of others. I will go into more detail in 'M*yself V my spiritual self*' as I am mindful that this might read that I am 'blowing my own trumpet' so to speak! This is not my intention. I am just listing some of the reasons why I feel that my biggest life lesson is 'doing service.' I have also been given the gift of being able to channel healing this time around, so that I can also give service in this way. My personal way of healing is to connect with my Guide and my deceased father and tap into the universal supply of energy and transfer it to people who ask for help. Healing is not of the body; it is of the mind! Healing can boost your system with the highest energies, which is 'love and light'. Healing can often clear many years of unwanted fear and negativity from your system. *This is the state of true empathy.*

I had the fear of frogs which led me to the practice of EFT which can also help to unblock negative energy from fears and phobias.

What is EFT and how does it work:

EFT works by tapping on the paths through which, 'life energy' flows. The energies or meridians help balance energy flow. By tapping on different parts of the body, it helps *balance energy* and reduce physical and emotional pain that is fear based. People can see an EFT practitioner for treatment or treat themselves using this technique. So, you see, all of these therapies that I feel connected to, concentrate on relaxation and help to reduce stress and anxiety. This in turn will help to increase a general sense of well-being. I mentioned in the beginning that my mother left us an invaluable legacy of spiritual knowledge, and she helped me begin my spiritual journey. I am sharing my spiritual beliefs and experiences throughout this book to help others on their journey of enlightenment. I have been shown enlightenment by finding a deeper mental awareness to '*self-realization.*' When you make the shift to a higher level of consciousness, you become more aware of reality as it exists beyond the confines of the '*self*'. When I was thinking about this, the idea for the name of my book came to me. '*Spiritual enlightenment.* Each and every one of you that finds interest in this book, will take from it whatever resonates with you. We are all at different levels of navigating through life, finding out who we are. To me, spirituality means knowing that our lives have significance and purpose in a context beyond a mundane everyday existence.

It involves exploring certain universal themes – love, compassion, life after death, wisdom and truth. An opening of the heart is an essential aspect of true spirituality. Because you have chosen to read this book, I guess you are on that pathway to wanting to '*find yourself*' or just to understand why we live with the challenges of this Earthly life. I know that I will still have lessons to learn and that I sometimes struggle with the challenges that come to me, but I can usually 'take a step back' and look deeper into the reasons 'why' I have challenges to face, and a more effective way of dealing with them. I have come to realise that my next lesson is to find patience. I live life in the fast lane, and sometimes struggle if someone slows me down. With Mike becoming less active, I noticed that I could sometimes get a little agitated when I had to slow down my pace. Was I losing my empathy? Maybe I had an empathy overload, a sort of burn out and was focussing on what I thought was a negative time, instead of looking for the positive. One particularly difficult day, which turned into a stressful night ended with me feeling very sorry for myself and having a good cry. I decided to take a leaf from '*my own book*'. I lay in bed and talked to my loved ones and my spirit team, asking them to *be with me* and to give me the *strength* and *peace*, that I needed at that time. Just as I was falling asleep, I had a hymn that I remembered from childhood days, 'play in my head'. I hummed the whole of it, not being able to recall the words. When I researched the hymn the following day… these are the words to the tune:

Sleep, my love, and peace attend thee,
All through the night,
Guardian angels God will send thee,
All through the night.
Soft the drowsy hours are creeping,
Hill and vale in slumber sleeping,
I my loving vigil keeping,
All through the night.

So *yet again*, you can see how my spirit team channelled their energy to connected with me, and I knew that they had heard my 'cry' for help. Your spiritual guidance team are *always* ready to support you when you need them. Knowing that there is always a supporting presence, can give you the faith and courage that you need to face your trials. As I have reiterated throughout this book, always remember to thank your team for the support they give to you. I would like to share part of a poem that my mother wrote before she passed. It is called '*the unseen guests*.'

Poem by my mother Flora Dorcas Rose

I sit within the twilight, surrounded by a love

no earthly man can understand this feeling that I have,

for every care is laid aside, and I remain at peace

Knowing that forever, Love will never cease.

Unfortunately, I don't have the original and this verse is the only part that I can remember, but she was describing the love from the spirit side of life. She describes it beautifully. The love and peace that we each feel when spirit are around us.

She signed it: *Florabunda Rose*.

"Love is patient, love is kind. It does not envy, it does not boast, it is not proud. It does not dishonour others, it is not self-seeking, it is not easily angered, it keeps no record of wrongs"

Self -Esteem and the blaming game!

So then: We should all practice Love: Loving *'yourself'* is critical to building a solid foundation of spirituality. You can begin to embrace and give love in your life. I think that the pandemic has been a particularly difficult time for a lot of people, and many are struggling with health issues. Depression and anxiety stealing their happiness. Depression is a mood disorder. It may be described as feelings of sadness, loss, or anger that interfere with a person's everyday activities. In a major depressive disorder, the feelings of sadness are constant. Anxiety disorders can make people feel self-conscious, anxious, nervous, worried, fearful or restless. People with anxiety may not be aware of how it negatively impacts their daily lives. Anxiety is your body's natural response to stress. While lowered self-esteem may put you at risk of social anxiety, having an anxiety disorder can also make you feel worse about yourself. In this way, these two afflictions interact to continue a negative cycle. Self-esteem refers to a person's overall sense of self-value. It is essentially your opinion about *yourself*.

It can encompass a range of factors such as your sense of identity, your self-confidence, feelings of competence, and feelings of belonging. It plays an important role in a variety of areas in life, which is why having low self-esteem can be such a serious problem. Self-esteem is about more than just generally liking yourself—it also means believing you deserve love and valuing your own thoughts, feelings, opinions, interests, and goals. Having self-esteem not only impacts how you feel about and treat yourself—it can also play a role in how you allow others to treat you. People who have low self-esteem often feel that they have little control over their lives or what happens to them. This might be due to the fact that they feel that they have little ability to create changes either in themselves or in the world. They may feel that they are powerless to do anything to fix their problems. This could result in becoming controlling over someone else… the need to find control. If you know someone who is struggling with anxiety or depression, support them to get help. Lots of people can find it hard to open up and speak about how they're feeling. If you recognise these signs, maybe let them know that it is OK to talk about their emotions and what they are experiencing. I have mentioned lots of alternative therapies which can help in previous chapters. If someone has hurt you, do your best to let go of that pain. We can all hang on to negative energy, which then creates blocks within our system. We have to go through the motions and emotions in order to deal with the negativity that has maybe got a strangle hold on your heart. Embrace the reality *that we all make mistakes.* Be the best you by practising '*self-love'*. Start to notice how you speak to yourself and see if you can negotiate a few kinder words. When you can love yourself, you can then love others despite their 'faults'. Love is the ultimate law of life. Everything starts with Love. Loving yourself doesn't mean being narcissistic. It is more about accepting yourself. Narcissism is a personality disorder where the individuals have an *inflated sense of self-importance* and a *total lack of empathy*. They believe that they are superior to most people and can only be understood by those who are also equally as special. Those with narcissistic disorders need constant reassurance from their peers, because their self-esteem is actually incredibly fragile. Those that practice' self-love' don't need recognition or congratulations for their accomplishments. They are well aware of their efforts and their success, and that knowledge is more than enough to feel adequate.

Life is like a camera Focus on what's important, Capture the good times, develop from the negatives and if things don't work out take another shot.

A lot of studies have shown that 'self-love' is the key to mental well-being, and it keeps depression and anxiety at bay. *Self-love is not about being selfish*; it is not being too tough on yourself. So next time you hear that little voice in your head telling you that you are not good enough or that you cannot afford to make mistakes; just ignore it. When we make a mistake, we are often too hard on ourselves. The first step of *'self-love'* is realising that we are only human, and it is okay to make mistakes. All we need to do is love ourselves and let the negative things pass through; eventually things will change, and bad times will pass. When we can love ourselves, we instantly change our perspective of the world. *'Self'*-love can give us a more *positive attitude* towards life. So, by loving the *'self'* we can accept the challenges that we have set ourselves (pre- incarnation) and deal with them more effectively and with less stress. It also means becoming comfortable with who you are. It means recognizing that someone else who didn't learn unconditional love has a hard time giving it. It means recognizing that most human beings hurt, and they pass this hurt along to other people. Understanding this can help you turn your attention from waiting and wanting someone else to make you whole, to realizing that *you have that ability inside of you*. Frequently people complain that if only others would change then they would be happy. "I wouldn't have any problems if only my husband would stop drinking" or "I would be happy if my wife would quit nagging me" or "If only my boss could recognize the importance of what I do" or "This world would be so much better if people weren't so rude" or "My day was ruined because of the horrendous traffic getting to work." All too often, people blame others for their personal unhappiness. Yet, most of us have the power to be happy if we only look inwards instead of outwards. I realise that it sounds like I am doing a lot of preaching, and maybe sounding like a bit of a know it all. I am only sharing knowledge that I believe can help others to understand what it has taken me many years to come to understand and come to terms with. Even though I was brought up knowing a fair amount of the fundamentals of our spiritual journey, I have had my own life experiences and challenges, and have not always dealt with them in a positive manner. I have had the same challenges come to me time after time, and I have ignored the '*golden rules*', or spiritual laws until I finally saw the patterns that kept repeating themselves. All of us have strengths and weaknesses. We all have advantages and disadvantages. Most of us have tragedies and traumas. We have successes and failures. We all have a balance sheet of the good and bad in our lives. The difference between those who are happy and those who are not, is that those who are happy focus on their approach to the world, not on their *expectations of the world.* They focus on what they can do, not on what others can do for them. They focus on changing themselves, *not blaming others.* Spiritual awakening is not a goal or destination...it is a constant invitation to *embrace yourself exactly as you are,* in all your strengths and imperfections. Throughout every moment of your life, trust and embrace yourself exactly as you are. Spiritual awareness is about being fully present and awake to each precious moment, coming out of the epic movie of past and future (*The Story of Me*) and showing up for life, knowing that even your feelings of non-acceptance *are* accepted here. It is about radically opening up to this extraordinary gift of existence, embracing both the pain and the joy of it, the bliss and the sorrow, the ecstasy and the overwhelm, the certainty and the doubt.

Knowing that you are never separate from the Whole, never truly lost. Often, we focus so much on the goal or destination that we forget the journey and disconnect from each step of our destined pathway. We create stress wanting to be somewhere else. Joy can be found in the *here and now*, and has nothing to do with goals, destinations, or getting what you want. Breathe, and feel the life in your body. Often, we don't know where we are headed, and that's perfectly okay.

"Follow your intuition, it will always guide you to the right destination" "Spend time cultivating gratefulness if you want to be happy"

"Until you change your thinking, you will always recycle your experiences"

"You are born as what you need to deal with" "Be patient. You'll know when it's time for you to wake up and move ahead."

"We come into relationships identified with our needs. I need this, I need security, I need refuge, I need friendship. And all of relationships are symbiotic in that sense. We come together because we fulfil each other's needs at some level or other."

I have added a few inspirational quotes that I think are helpful. Inspiration awakens us to new possibilities by allowing us to transcend our ordinary experiences and limitations. Inspiration propels a person from apathy to possibility and transforms the way we perceive our own capabilities. So, find your inspiration!

Just to re-iterate on types of ways to connect with your spirit team and how to trust them:

Clairvoyance: is clear-seeing or psychic vision. For example, when you do that quiet breathing and you close your eyes, you might see that there's a screen before your eyes. Some people call it their third eye or their inner vision, where they see something appear or they see an image flash image.

Clairaudience: which is clear-hearing or hearing a thought that's not yours. When we connect with loved ones or spirit guides from the other side, a lot of times it is like a quiet voice inside.

Claircognizance: an absolute knowing in your bones, and you can't explain how you know it. The claircognizant signs just might be your guides or your loved ones, sending you energy that you need to do something. It may be to point you in the right direction to connect you with certain people or maybe it's going to put you on a really important path. Where are you getting it from? You can't explain it, it's just *a knowing* that you have. When we honour those claircognizant messages, it leads us down the right path.

Clairsentience: which is clear-feeling, and that's when we intuitively feel out someone else's energy. The clairsentient signs feel like a *gut or intuitive pull*. It might be information for you on your life path or a reaction you have when you meet somebody new. You might feel really drawn to that person's energy, or you might have what I call an allergic reaction to that person's energy. Those are clairsentient signs that are guiding you, and they're being sent by spirit guides, or from loved ones on the other side. There are more tangible signs, outside psychic senses. Like electrical disturbances. Spirit love messing with our cell phones and flickering lights. They can send birds, butterflies, feathers, and even send coins onto our path. But the most powerful experience you can have is to ask for a *very specific sign* from the other side. These are the ones that I love. We're always looking for some kind of proof that loved ones are around and listening or that your spirit guides really exist and are with you. I tell people to ask for *their own version* of proof through signs and messages. My one daughter-in-law, (*Danielle*) shared a dream with me. She had been sending thoughts to Mike as she was aware of his ill-health. She asked that Mike would find the strength to fight and regain his strength. Just to point out that Danielle is an actress and so it was no surprise to her to find that she was dreaming about teaching Mike to act! Most of the dream was about her actually helping Mike to perform in an action movie. I consulted my dream manual about being someone in an action movie, and it said:

"Some situations or events have pulled the rug from under your feet, so nothing seems to be in your hands anymore. You will need some time to regain control over your life". "It goes on to say, that you will have enough energy to face every new challenge and obstacle that comes your way".

This dream was pointing out that Mike would find the strength to fight the challenges that would be presented to him with his illness. It is another wonderful interpretation of a spiritual dream. Our dreams come to us from our inner mind, our subconscious. Every night we experience this state of mind. We also tap into it any time we meditate, deeply concentrate, or listen to our intuition. The subconscious uses images from our waking life to communicate to us in analogies, in symbols. It is said that the presence of people of different sexes in your dream gives you a clue about your involvement with the different parts of yourself. People of the same sex represent your conscious, waking mind. People of the opposite sex represent your wise, inner, subconscious mind. A spiritual dream can give you insight on how to solve a problem that you are experiencing and maybe stressing over. As for remembering your dreams, a straightforward method is to create a dream journal. However, the ones that have a specific meaning will stay in your head for a very long time. When you are ready to tune into your guides and spirit team, they will know it. We live within the realms of spirit, and they are besides us every day. When you ask for them to connect, you will be aware of a different voice in your head. It will be different to your own thinking patterns. We are all familiar with the voice of doubt, the voice of judgement, the voice of self-blame etc; but the voice of your guides will be of encouragement and love. Your guides are a team, which connect with the source energy. They will relay messages to you, mostly through your main guide, but they also connect to other groups. Some who have incarnated on Earth and some that have not. They work with us on a soul level, soul energy and they see our broader journey.

When I first became a medium/channeller I would often question what I was given and wondered if it was my own thinking that was creeping into the messages that I was receiving. My mother told me always trust what you are given.

The power of mind over matter

I believe in the power of a positive attitude, and I read an article from a scientist who did a study of 50 people, some with life threatening illnesses. Those judged by their doctors to have high "spiritual faith" responded better to treatment and survived longer. Over 40 per cent were still alive after three years, compared with less than 10 per cent of those judged to have little faith. To understand mindfulness, we need to understand the effects of stress. It all begins in the brain. When you worry about something and you are determined that it is something of concern, the brain responds with stress chemicals through the body. Heart rate increases as well as breathing and the body prepares for fight or flight. When you continue to worry, the mind stays in this state of stress, exhausting the body's system. Mindfulness (*positive thinking*) slows all of that down. We can relieve our body's constant flood of stress chemicals and tension. This is done by accessing your subconscious mind, where this limitless power resides.

Your mind is the most powerful tool that exists.

To clarify: People who show a high degree of faith, self-confidence, who have the habit of meditating, and keeping a positive attitude respond better to treatments, and get less sick.

However, the opposite occurs in people under chronic stress, with low self-confidence, pessimism, and, ultimately, do not use their minds to help their bodies. These people are more likely to get sick, respond less to treatments, and have poorer health. Try to immediately erase any negative thoughts that produce doubt, fear, guilt, and remorse. Fill your mind with positive thoughts that generate a feeling of well-being. To calm and centre your mind, start a practice of mindfulness. At several points throughout the day, **stop** what you are doing and simply *focus on your body*. Turn your attention to what you are feeling, physically and mentally. *Be aware of the thoughts going through your mind.* Let them flow out and just watch them leave. *Don't judge anything* - just be in awareness. As you do this more and more, it will become more natural. This allows your mind to become calmer and more focused. Start journaling, so you can write down and reflect upon thought patters. If the brain expects that a treatment will work, it sends healing chemicals into the bloodstream, which facilitates that. And the opposite is equally true and equally powerful: When the brain expects that a therapy will not work, it doesn't. It's called the 'nocebo' effect. Our mind has the power to keep us healthy and the power to make us sick. It has the ability to block our potential or to allow us to reach extraordinary possibilities.

"Everything is energy and that's all there is to it. Match the frequency of the reality you want, and you cannot help but get that reality. It can be no other way. This is not philosophy. This is physics." - **Albert Einstein**

We have two minds! How often have you said, *"I'm in two minds about this"*? *The conscious, logical thinking mind and the subconscious creative, protective mind.* We have been taught that our conscious mind is in control, but it couldn't be farther from the truth. Our *subconscious mind* is running the show and it has decided seconds before the conscious mind is even aware there is a decision to be made. *Your point of view creates your reality, reality does not create your point of view'* A patient's survival rate can be affected simply by the means by which the doctor delivers the prognosis, it is fact we are affected by thoughts. If a person can be told that a pill will cure them, the placebo effect definitely demonstrates the power of thought. So why do we, as humans, continue to struggle? Why have we not chosen to change our life experiences and thought patterns. The answer is simply, *we have never been told we could.* Schools teach us to conform. Society frowns upon those who are different. We spend our lives trying to fit into a box that is designed for only one. Change is not possible unless *we believe that it can happen.* Why do we wish away the present moment hoping for something better? Our inattentiveness creates anguish and disappointment, because we're certain when we get what we want, we'll be happy. Yet, when it arrives there's, another desire waiting to take its place. Human nature always wants more to seek what is lacking in our lives. The problem is, we become fixated on *wanting and desiring, instead of appreciating* what is before us. Hence the cycle of suffering ensues. If we consider the present moment as perfect, *'what is meant to be'* will find its way into your life effortlessly.

To accept this moment means to appreciate that your present circumstances result from past thoughts and actions. You can do this by simply breaking old patterns of disbelief, and courageously believing — *knowing* — *that you are meant to be here, and that your life has a meaning*. If we cannot change outside circumstances to please us, *we must change our response to the events*. Begin by paying attention to the *thoughts* you have every day. Write them down. Is there a pattern to your thinking? Once you have identified the pattern, step back and take an honest look at your life. Are there *repetitive experiences in your life* and if so, do they align with your thinking? Every time you have a negative thought, try to substitute it with a positive thought. As I have said before, if there is something that you are not happy about and you cannot change it, change how you think about it!

"The spiritual journey is individual, highly personal. We don't all follow the same path. Listen to your own truth."

Everyone's journey is quite unique. We are not human beings having a spiritual experience, we are spiritual beings having a human experience. Earth is a school of learning, and the spiritual journey is a personal quest that we undertake to re-connect with our soul and find our authentic life purpose. We all ask the questions: *"Who am I"* *"Why am I here"* and *"where am I going"*. *"Who am I?"* Your identity is the foundation for your actions. If you don't understand who you are, you won't understand where you are going, or why you are here. Often people are dissatisfied with their lives and say, "There must be something else to this life." Life is not a bed of roses and we do struggle a lot just to survive here. The purpose of life is to *"live your life at the best"*. You have to be the creator of your life. If you want things to change, **YOU** have to change.

Q: *"How do I find out who I am and who I was in a former life?" "And does it matter?"*

A: "This may take some explaining, but I will start with the basics"

Time and space cease to exist when you begin exploring psychic dimensions. Instead, we perceive multiple dimensions of reality where all versions of ourselves are happening simultaneously. We do not disperse our identity on a timeline that starts at birth and ends at death. Our souls have cyclical lives, but there is a place in everybody's energy field called the Akashic records, holding their entire soul's history—past, present, future, parallel. And through these records, we are able to access any moment in a soul's journey. Our lives show us what we need to learn and when. When we become stuck and feel uncomfortable with where we are, then it is time for a shift. We decide what lessons we learn in this lifetime before we incarnate. We have a plan for the lessons we want to learn for our soul's evolution. Your life will show you when these lifetimes are relevant, and they come up to help you evolve past a block or a pattern of stuck energy. Every moment of your soul's existence is contained within the Akashic records of your soul's energy field. It can be located with clear intention to access these alternate lifetimes.

Fears/phobias: It's beneficial to humans to have fears of things that are dangerous to us, but many people suffer from phobias that are completely irrational. Fear of water, birds, certain numbers, plants, specific colours...The list goes on and on. For those who believe in past lives, *these fears may be carried over from a previous lifetime.* A fear of water may indicate past-life trauma, for example. Perhaps, in another manifestation, you met your end by drowning. I feel that my fear of frogs may have come from my life as a North American traveller who dealt with frog venom. Maybe I was poisoned? Then when the one jumped out at me from the greenhouse, it uncovered the fear!!

Strong passions: Strong passions can be evidence of a past life. To clarify: This is not a simple hobby-level interest in gardening or photography, for example. Nearly everyone has these sorts of passions. One of my passions is for Native American music and dance and I know without a doubt that this is due to my life in Dakota. Somewhere buried in your subconsciousness lies the memories of pivotal moments which have shaped your personality and have guided you towards the lessons that you are encountering in this life.

How to find out who you were: I was taken on a regression journey back to the past when I discovered that I had lived a life in England as a woman herbalist. There are trained therapists that can take you on this journey. However, it is possible to connect yourself and I will relay an article that talks you through an easy journey that you can make yourself.

Self -regression: First of all, find a place that is peaceful. I like to sit with my back straight and feet firmly placed on the floor. Some people may find it easier to sit crossed legged on the floor. Pay attention to your breath as it goes in and out. Breath in slowly and hold for a count of eight, and then release your breath very slowly. This practice slows down our breathing and higher' s our vibrations. Your attention may wander to other places, but simply bring your focus back to your breathing. Imagine roots from the bottom of your feet going deep into the ground. I then ask my guides to surround me with love and light. Then to begin regression, imagine that you are taking a journey backwards, along the river of time. Just close your eyes, let yourself get comfortable and take a few deep breaths to relax. For this exploration, allow your imagination and your emotional connection guide what you see and experience.

With each breath you take, let your conscious mind drift away, and give your subconscious mind permission to take over. No need to think or analyse. Simply oversee and remember.

To begin your journey, imagine that you are standing upon a dock next to the river of time.

Perched at the dock lay a boat set and ready to take you on a journey back in time, up the river.

When you are ready, simply step into the boat, sit down, and will it begin to move away from the dock. Your journey has begun. In your boat, follow the river back through the events of your past. See various events from your childhood that you do remember.

As the boat continues to flow upstream, you will move past the moment of your birth – a time you may not remember.

Now, just up ahead, see a tunnel approaching.

As you enter through the tunnel, the boat begins moving faster. This tunnel is your conduit between lifetimes.

Now is the time to hold on to the emotional connection to what you seek. Feel that emotion and restate the question which has sparked this journey. Why are you here, now?

When you emerge from the tunnel, and into the light, you will see a scene playing out that is from a time previous to your birth in this lifetime.

As the boat comes to a stop, take a few moments to allow yourself to watch the event as it unfolds.

Notice the people in the scene, how they are dressed, what they look like, the colours – you will even notice different sounds and maybe even smells.

When you are ready, you can set the boat back into motion downstream and back toward the tunnel. When you re-emerge, you will see scenes from your childhood of this life progressing forward. As if in fast motion, you move forward in time, past the events you remember, until you reach the present moment.

When you have returned to the dock from which you departed, exit the boat and return your awareness to the room you are in.

Finally, when you are ready, open your eyes and quickly write down what you have observed in your experiences on this day.

When I went on my regression journey, I began by looking up at a window. (Eyes closed) I imagined the window opening, and as my energy moved up, I could feel myself standing on the window ledge. The next step was to look up at the sky and merge with the blue sky. My energy vibrations rose higher and higher as my thoughts and visions took me up and above the clouds, eventually merging with the blue, and I was vibrating at a higher frequency. I was still aware of who I am today, but my I could 'see' myself as the child collecting herbs for my grandmother. I could see the vivid purple heather beneath my feet, and I could see that my dress was made of a 'hemp' cloth, and my shoes were brown leather. I knew that I lived with my grandmother in a type of cottage that was very basic. I knew also that I was collecting the herbs for my grandmother to make medicine. I was eventually brought back to my awareness and was amazed by what I had experienced. As I mentioned in an earlier chapter, today I believe in herbal medicine and prefer to use it to manufacture medicines (where possible) If you find that nothing comes about your first few attempts, this may just be that you need build a stronger connection with your subconscious mind. Maybe you need to follow the process a few times, taking notes and comparing them from each experience. So not only is this a great way to relax, but you are building a connection from your present everyday self with the parts of you that are spread out in various time periods.

If you want to go deeper, a trained professional can help you to explore certain events to a more detailed extent. Sometimes, you may need to unravel 'unresolved issues' which may be causing complications within this lifetime. You should probably find an independent, trained professional to help you resolve these difficulties. The journey above is presented as a means of bringing about <u>awareness of the past</u>, not to resolve any lingering issues. So, to answer the final part of the question:

'Does it matter who I was?'

By learning about past lives can sometimes help you to realise why you are experiencing and having certain lessons in this life. As I mentioned above, you may have unresolved issues from a past life that are causing complications in this one. As you pass through lives, each individual life and the experiences that life had slowly melds together to form a consciousness. The subconscious computer within you is by far the most powerful part of who you are. It remembers everything that has ever happened to you, and that it knows why your life may not be working as well as it should. Each re-incarnation has its own values and qualities and importance in the overall arc of a person's journey. There are a lot of wonderful things to experience and enjoy on Earth as well as some tough situations to learn from. Souls continue to learn even when they are nearly or fully ascended. So, we will keep coming back to fulfil our mission. Maybe if we have insight into who we were before, then it may give us a form of understanding why we have chosen certain lessons this time around.

GROWING SPIRITUALLY

An approach to growing spiritually starts with being willing to explore the possibility that the spiritual world is real. Also acknowledging that our inner spirit arrives in us with a plan to promote the growth of our souls and believing that our plan has been designed specifically for each one of us. Spiritual growth for this lifetime is by acceptance. *Accepting* that there is a plan for your life and realizing that there is something beyond this material life. *You are here to reach your spiritual goals and values, such as goodness, truth and inner beauty.* Some of us have been fortunate enough to have spiritual mentors and guidance. For those of you that haven't, I hope that you will find some answers within this book. What is so appealing about living a spiritual life, and growing spiritually? As human beings we need to be loved. Our spirit team sees us all as very young children who are learning what life is all about. They know our special gifts and who we are able to become as we mature. They do not see offences that must be forgiven, but instead they see *mistakes* to *be overcome.* They love us unconditionally and want to help us to find love and happiness in our earthly lives. All of us are spiritual children growing in love. Before us lies the possibility of pursuing: 'wisdom, integrity, courage, creativity, peace, empathy, generosity, honesty, compassion, joy, strength, originality, forgiveness, loyalty, truth, beauty, goodness, and much more'. *Each of us is a spiritual being, living his/her life in a material body.* This material life is the beginning of an ongoing spiritual adventure in the discovery and experience of love. The universe does not have clocks or calendars but a sequence of events. It is a living consciousness. Space, time energy and matter are created by a universal consciousness. The universe is energy in motion. Consciousness continues after the death of the body and exists through multiple lifetimes.

So, what happens when it is time to bid farewell?

When your soul leaves the physical body and begins it journey to the other world, it is never really alone at any stage. Family members and friends who have departed earlier, guardian angels, spirit guides, they're all there to be with you, give you strength throughout the time of transition. You're leaving and being separated not only from a physical body you've occupied and cared for during a whole lifetime, but also from all that and all those you loved, all that you're familiar with. I believe we have five exit points where our soul can choose to leave the body. We can choose to exit depending on what we have attained or are still wanting to learn in our life. You will have chosen five definite decisions before incarnating. Suicide is not an option. If someone decides to die slowly, it may be so that others can learn from their existence and experience the emotions. It may be to learn patience and very often, grief. Souls choose to die in different ways for different reasons. So, whatever serves your life, and your purpose determines when the soul will make its exit.

Just an example: My brother-in-law had *five major operations* towards the end of his life. He battled two types of cancer along with a heart attack. At any time during these operations his soul could have decided to exit this world, but it chose not to. After the first four, he lived a fairly normal life. It was only on the fifth operation that he obviously decided that he would take this exit. For some people death is a welcome ending to a life well-lived, for others death is reluctantly accepted by the ego, even though the '*soul*' has chosen the exit. The Soul is a permanent entity. It is the ego that is born, and it is the ego that dies. *The Soul does not die at all.* Some people that are in hospital and in pain, a couple of days before they pass, usually feel much better. They suddenly see people that have passed over, family and friends. These souls come to re-assure the dying person. They let them know that they will be on the other side to help them pass over. Consciousness may exist, but the '*energy body*' is preparing to exit. The mind will tune into a slightly higher vibration and the soul will be within a different reality. I talked about the planes of existence earlier in the book. So, to reiterate, the soul will find that it is in a beautiful place, very like the Earth, but the colours are much more vibrant. The sense of love and light is all empowering. Any pain that you may have experienced before you pass, will have disappeared before you actually leave the body, and it will never return. In the afterlife there is no pain as there is no physical body. There is comfort, happiness, joy and above all LOVE. Death is nothing to fear.

Do not stand at my grave and weep-I am not there, I do not sleep. I am a thousand winds that blow-I am the diamond glints on snow, I am the sun on ripened grain -I am the gentle autumn rain.
When you awaken in the morning's hush, I am the swift uplifting rush. Of quiet birds in circled flight. I am the soft stars that shine at night. Do not stand at my grave and cry, I am not there; I did not die.

Poem by Mary Elizabeth Frye

SUMMING UP

So, summing up: As I have said a' million times' now. *we choose to come back to Earth to grow spiritually, and so we return again and again, experiencing, pleasure and pain.* We are so eager to get on with the growing that we forget how hard it is on Earth. We plan our journey, and we hope that we will reach our destination having completed *all the tasks and assignments that we have set for ourselves.* This new life is a new opportunity to complete '*missed opportunities*' from our last incarnation. We know that when we return to spirit there is no judgement from any authoritative being. I have explained that we judge ourselves. So, let's make this time around the best opportunity to '*get things right*'. To accept the tests, experiences that we have *chosen* as our contract. Once we understand the reasons for us being here and the reasons *why* we have chosen to be with the people that are a part of our lives, we can stop battling and resisting. Life on the Earth is so brief compared to that in the afterlife. It is everyone's choice what to believe and I am not trying to convert people to my beliefs. Free will is paramount and all will decide for themselves what resonates with them. Whatever you choose to believe in this life.... *Is your own choice! We all learn at our own pace and accept when we are ready to accept*, so please just take *whatever resonates with you and whatever is your truth, is yours to decide*. I think if we remain open, we learn from each other.

We learn from each other's experiences, and we can learn to *listen* to others. To *accept others for who they are* and whatever pathway they have chosen. If we can be less judgemental of others and give *Love and acceptance* rather than hurt and hatred, (*even when others have hurt us*), we can reach our soul enlightenment all the quicker. Just seek out what makes you happy and comfortable. Remember that I said that forgiving others is essential for spiritual growth. Your experience of someone who has hurt you, while painful, is now nothing more than a thought or feeling that you carry around. These thoughts of resentment, anger, and hatred represent slow, debilitating energies that will dis-empower you if you continue to let these thoughts occupy space in your head. If you could release them, you would know more peace. Whenever you're upset over the conduct of others, take the focus off those you're holding responsible for your inner distress. Shift your mental energy to allowing yourself to be with whatever you're feeling — let the experience be as it may, *without blaming others for your feelings*. Don't blame yourself either! Just allow the experience to unfold and tell yourself that **no- one** has the power to make you uneasy without your consent, and that you're unwilling to grant that authority to this person right now. We all know that *resentment, anger and bitter feelings* can do us a lot of harm. If you are not aware that this is the case, you just need to become honestly aware of the effect that such feelings have on your body to see that they are not good for you. This is especially true if hatred or loathing come into the mix. The sickly, poisonous sensations which come with bitter, resentful feelings – especially if you are thinking of vengeance as a way to express your resentful feelings – ought to be a warning to not go any further with the line of thinking that you are on. If you were drinking or eating something and it had the same effect on your body us such feelings, you would most likely spit is out again very quickly. you would recognize it as toxic. *These thoughts create very low energy.* I believe that our world is going through a very low form of energy from fear and negativity and needs cleansing. The latest wars that we have had going on in different parts of the world, have created more fear and destruction. Maybe as a nation we need to wake up to the fact that we have to do more to save our planet. We need to raise our vibrations away from fear, and fear-based religions, to Love. I stated that our mind *is the most powerful tool.* If we can all use that tool to project Love for our fellow beings, then that will, in turn help raise the vibrations that are so desperately needed to help reverse some of the negative effects that have created the devastation in the world today. I am going to add a chapter on 'food for thought' to include what I feel about how the pandemic has made a lot of us more caring as a nation. A form of cleansing is to practice forgiveness. This will help to raise our vibrations to a higher level. Forgiveness is one of the hardest lessons.

As you think, you vibrate. As you vibrate, you attract. A vibration is a state of being, the atmosphere, or the energetic quality of a person, place, thought, or thing. When you are vibrating at a higher level, you feel lighter, happier, and more at ease. So, when we give *gratitude, generosity, empathy, forgiveness and love* we can reduce negativity, and each will higher our rate of vibration. Each thought you think creates your future. If the thoughts you think are pessimistic, overtly anxious, or in any way negative, you will likely find just that! Your life will be negative and unhappy. Gratitude draws more happiness into your life. Impatience, jealousy, and unworthiness are negative energies and will leave you feeling heavy and burdened. Be diligent about what thoughts you give your attention to, since it can take just a few seconds for a thought to attract another one and activate the Law of Attraction.

Push away negative energy and choose positive thoughts, for they are the key to positive change. We are all interconnected and taking the time to focus your attention towards pure, loving thoughts for someone else is healing. Your team of angels and spirit guides are always available to assist you and the people you care about to create more positive changes into the light of day. Sending love and light is a form of distant energy healing. Our world needs 'love and Light' to help the healing process, so let's begin now with a collective intention to heal the planet for the sake of our children and grandchildren. Fill your heart and soul with pure light and then send it out to the world for the highest and greatest good. Let your light flow within you and around you, knowing that you are loved.

Love is actual energy. When we feel Love, we've attuned to the vibration of the energy of Love. It is the most potent source of all vibrations; it can change a moment in time from chaos to peace. Love is the highest vibrational energy.

Light, in a spiritual sense is the energy and frequency of all-knowing wisdom. To live in the Light means that the vibration of the all-knowing, and all-wise shines from within. When you send someone Light, or someone offers you Light, it means the frequency of wisdom is offered to you. Therefore, When You Are

Offering Someone "Love and Light," You Are Offering the Ideal Energy of The Universe and Wisdom.

Throughout this book I have said things over and over again a number of times, to emphasise a point or two and to clarify. We can sometimes read or hear something and not really take it in. Then it appears again later, and it resonates with us. I want to now add that when we let go of things that no longer serve us, we can bring in new thoughts and vibrations. When we truly understand that there is more to us that just our body you can look deeper within and see who you really are. So, to be your 'best self':

Think bigger. Great minds think very big. ...
Motivate yourself. You will realize that motivation has a great influence on you. ...
Believe in yourself. ...
Set goals for yourself. ...
Spend your time wisely. ...
Take up new challenges. ...
Let go of past failures. ...
Take time to discover your strengths.

Food for thought- 2022

My ex-husband and myself met with the spiritual teachers that I mentioned earlier, every week for some while. Malcolm would channel with his guides to give us updates and information. One of the guides, 'Edward' told us that many people on planet earth were saying and believing that earth would end in 2012! He told us that this was not a truth, but what would happen beyond that time was a sort of death of a consciousness on the planet. This being death of old ways and habits. He told us that the world would go through a profound and overwhelming energy shift. So then, here we are now going through a different energy in our world! Our planet and ourselves need healing more now than ever before. We, as a whole, have experienced a loss of so many things that we had taken for granted before the pandemic. The loss of being with our friends and family. The restrictions of travel to name but a few. Some people have suffered more in the ways that it has affected them emotionally. We then are turning more and more to the health of ourselves and also the planet. The need for sustaining the planet has come to the surface and made us more aware. What our friends were saying to us, was that our world would go through a transformation. (I feel, it will be a cleansing and healing) After many months of quarantine and social distancing, our physical and mental health have been continually tested. Parenting, working from home, losing a job, losing our livelihood, caring for sick family members, being forced out of parks and gyms, and being estranged from our community: the new normal has taken its toll on our health and well-being. So, we ask ourselves where is our sense of purpose! I feel that we need to look deeper into our purpose in this life. Trials show that people with a greater sense of purpose show reduced rates of depression and a slower rate of cognitive decline. So, what gets us out of bed each day? We can begin by showing acts of kindness to people that are in need. Show appreciation. Offer words of encouragement to those that are feeling lonely and anxious. As human beings we tend to go into emergency mode in times of crisis, but by focussing on others we find a purpose in life. We are having to let go of a lot of the 'old ways' that have been the focus in our lives, and we are now having to adapt to a new way of living. A positive attitude is that we are probably changing spiritually, in that fact that we are thinking more about others that have suffered and are still suffering in their ways. We are now working from the heart and soul. We are re-wiring our responsibilities. I have been on my own personal spiritual journey for a while now, and I try to manage my energy in the best possible ways that I am able. The world is going through a massive transformation, and so are we. I can think back now to the message that 'Edward' gave us and can see what he meant by the impact that this time has had on our health and energy. So, this in itself is interesting to know that it was foreseen that the world would go through some challenging changes. So many emotions have been thrown into the mix due to us not being around our loved ones and having to isolate. People want to know 'when it will get better'. Well, it's all relevant with who we are, and what journey we are on. Maybe it's time to look at what we want to achieve in our lives and also being grateful what we do have already. Let go of all the negative self-talk, fear and doubt, and move into a new chapter.

Ego v Intuition

We all have that little voice in our head that can stop us from moving forward. Ego works on the past, feelings that we have had that have stopped us acting out possibilities. It has put the brakes on because it has remembered things from the past where someone has maybe told you that you are not good enough. Your inner voice (ego) will override your wants with fear and doubt. Your Intuition is what is telling you to move forward. It is telling you that there are changes that you need to bring forth. We have the vision, but then as we begin to walk towards it, the ego can take over and stop us in our tracks. What you need to do is recognise why our ego, the voice inside our head is saying no… you won't succeed and recognise the 'wounds' that have held us back. Ask yourself "what purpose does it serve me now". "Do I want to stay stuck, or do I want to move forward." If you keep having the thought come into your head about what you want to achieve, or a certain something that you want to do, or feel the need to do, then your soul is wanting you to see the new pathway and is showing you that it is time to move forward. Of course, the choice is always yours, but your intuition is letting you see what can be. Our intuition doesn't care about our fear, it is often asking us to overcome our fear. Your intuition shows you ways to move forward, and for a moment you feel, yes that feels good. Then the ego kicks in, and you start to find reasons why you can't go ahead with the image that the intuition gave you. You can, however, rationalise our ego thoughts, and pay attention to your intuition. Maybe you need to start in a small way, and just step out of your comfort zone. Keep committing to your intuition, thus improving your awareness to what you want to eventually achieve. Visions and instincts are the starting points. The old saying "*trust you gut*" refers to trusting your feelings of intuition, often as a way to stay true to yourself. Following your instinct can certainly direct you toward the best path for you. Overthinking in order to rationalize or justify something means that your thought process is not flowing freely. The flood of possibilities and considerations that overthinking generates can overwhelm and confuse, leaving you in a dizzying circle without clear direction. Our intuition is so deeply instinctual that even if we've been out of touch with it for our entire lives, it's still there inside of us, waiting for us to summon its wisdom.

Q: *"What is the ego?"*

A: "Psychology defines the ego as the part of the mind that is responsible for analysing your reality and affirming your sense of personal identity".

The ego's primary function is to ensure your basic survival needs are met having food to eat, securing shelter and assessing your environment to assure you're not in danger. The ego analyses the future and pushes you to plan for something that hasn't happened yet. It revisits memories from the past to determine if you could have done something differently in attempt to improve your future. This often leads to stress, anxiety and depression.

Q: *"Can you explain the difference between the ego and intuition?"*

A: "Your intuition originates from your soul". "Your soul is the energetic part of you that is temporarily residing in your body, and it's connected to a higher intelligence". "Your soul only knows how to experience love and wants to see you grow and enjoy your life."

It sends you messages to assist you on your path and gently guides you toward your greatest good. It can be experienced as a gut feeling, a gentle nudge, a tingling sensation, an inner knowing or an audible voice that you hear speaking. Through practice, you can recognize the differences between the voice of the ego and the voice of your intuition.

When your ego gets the better of you.

If you're trying to find ways to justify your actions, even though you know that you're wrong, this may be a sign that you have an ego problem! Have you ever been in an argument where you won't stop until you have the last word? You get angry or your feelings are hurt when things don't go your way? Are you offended when someone corrects your mistakes? You might want to check-in with your ego and figure out '*why*' you're feeling this way. A person with ego issues will often sulk and will have a hard time accepting that they may be wrong. You may hate the fact that you feel someone else has more than you have. This can be an insecurity issue. To take control of our ego instead of it controlling us, we can practice self-awareness: This means being aware of your actions, acknowledging your thoughts feelings, and behaviour. When you're more aware of how you act, think, or speak, you may be able to have the right discernment on how you can improve yourself. Learn how to accept your mistakes. We all make them! Having the courage to apologize is a step to self-improvement, and self-awareness.

Reflection

So, as we enter 2022 let's look back at where we have been, what has gone before and what we wish to achieve. What would you like to create within your life? We have experienced some challenging times, especially over the last two years. Maybe this year you can begin to feel clear about what you want and how you want your life to be. Life has been out of our control in a way. Maybe it's time to take back control over our lives. Maybe we need to change our ways of thinking about things. 'Self-reflection' is deliberate time set aside to slow down your life. You could look back on your day, month or year in an attempt to learn from your experiences, desires, and feelings. Find a place where you can be still. Use whatever will help you to prepare for your reflection time. If you like, play some music or if you prefer to sit in silence. Look honestly at your feelings over the last day, the highs, the lows and the level ground. The more closely we are connected to the people we love, the happier we feel and the more personal satisfaction we have in our lives. Most people rate moments of connection and shared enjoyment with their loved ones as their most important life experiences. However, creating and maintaining happy personal relationships and belonging to positive communities is not straightforward. During the uncertain times, like the coronavirus pandemic, we might have found it difficult to hold on to our positive outlook. Many may ask "What do we have to look forward to?"

Look forward to the future

Setting our sights on a positive future is in itself an act of courage and optimism. I would wager everyone reading this has done their fair share of looking ahead and feeling worried, anxious and doubtful. I have experienced some challenging emotions over the past however many months. However, if we can try to encourage ourselves to balance our thinking and look forward to a more positive tomorrow, we will reap the benefits. We can look forward to vacations, family gatherings and celebrations. We need to feed our minds with positive thinking, positive affirmations. So many people have lost loved ones to the pandemic and may wonder how they can regain their positivity and find happiness again. Maybe a way of dealing with some of the grief is to try to be grateful for having that person in your life. Trying to focus on the good memories. If you are feeling that you would like to become more spiritual now, then you can still connect with them. Positive affirmations may help, such as: It's ok for me to heal. I am able to feel close to my loved one whenever I choose. I choose to feel better. I am willing to find happiness again. In order for you to feel better, it's very important that you begin to focus on how your deceased loved ones lived, not how they died, on the blessings in your life, on the happy times, on the things you love, and on positive goals ahead of you. At first it may seem very difficult to do, given all that has happened, but after a while of deliberately changing your thoughts to more positive ones, it will get easier and easier. Writing down your blessings, goals and memories is a great way to start. Repeating affirmations throughout the day also helps immensely. It doesn't matter how you choose to do it, just that you make the choice to feel better! Remember, according to the Law of Attraction, you get what you think about most of the time. So, it makes sense to begin to focus on more positive, loving thoughts throughout each day. If you are a caregiver, this can have a great impact on your life and so it is important to look after yourself. Take time to meditate, exercise and find fun and laughter. We need to practice mindfulness to keep ourselves afloat. We have our human lessons to learn and deal with, but we can connect with our higher selves and spirit team to ask for guidance. Another way is to connect with nature. Grief can be a negative experience, making us not want to connect with the world. We may be grieving from the loss of a person or the loss of being able to do the things that we became accustomed to before isolation brought things to a halt. There has been a collective grief throughout the world. Maybe what we have been going through is an awakening. How do we respond to the challenges that the changes have brought? All experiences are part of our awakening. Challenges are tests for us. It is finding out what the challenges bring for you. Do you react in a negative way, or are you able to rise above the challenges? We can worry and wonder how we are going to deal with all of these challenges in our everyday life. This is carrying your burden around with you and not allowing you to see the beauty that is in nature and in life. We are all having to move and change, it is inevitable. It is how we deal with problems and changes within our lives, that help us to grow. We are all having a human experience and we are intertwined with each other. Each giving and receiving. All learning for one another. Many have become disillusioned with life and are maybe not prepared to try to understand that life comes with challenges and life lessons. I feel that healing will come more into the light to help with the feelings of anxiety and maybe depression that the pandemic has created. A major transformation is taking place right now. We all need healing on some sort of level. Maybe it is letting go of old limiting beliefs! Pay attention to your thoughts. Nothing will change for you if you don't consciously change it. Change your thought patterns. If something isn't working for you, change it, or change the way that you think about it. We need to work with the positive energies. Welcome people into your life that help you make the changes that you feel you need. You need the desire for change, for change to happen. We don't have a magic wand that will make changes happen instantly. We can all think that having riches will make us happier, and so many limits to what we feel we need to make us happy. When we rely on these things to make us happy, we become disillusioned with life. I feel that if we can lead our lives in a more spiritual way (not confusing this with religion) by being more loving, more understanding of others we can create healing amongst and within ourselves.

Suffering through the pandemic

Physical suffering is often only part of the difficulty that a person faces during a traumatic event or life-threatening illness. There can also be emotional and mental anguish — and spiritual distress or struggle. The last arises when a person's basic belief system is shaken. People in spiritual distress often no longer believe the world is a safe place. They might lose hope and have a difficult time finding meaning and purpose in what's happening to them. Serious illness and tragic events can challenge these anchors and throw a person into turmoil. Having to quarantine and social distance has tested our mental health. Parenting, working from home, losing a job, losing our livelihood, caring for sick family members, being forced out of parks and gyms has taken its toll on our health and well-being. But out of this we have found that people have found a greater sense of purpose by helping those in need. A collective coming together for a greater purpose. So many acts of kindness and comfort have been shown. When life throws you a curve ball, it is the universe trying to get your attention. You may resist and keep trying to take the left-hand lane when you should be in the right- hand lane. You will keep swerving in and out until something happens to put you on the right-hand side and ready to face the lesson intended for your soul growth. If you don't know what you want and are beginning to question, then this is where you are ready to open up. When there is tragedy in the world, it is extraordinary how everyone rallies round to help one another. This shows the true values of being human. Love and togetherness keep us growing and learning and awakening in a spiritual sense. This then is a time to reflect and give serious thought to how your actions and motives have affected your life thus far. So many of us continue through life doing the same things and wondering why we don't get a different outcome. It's essential to understand yourself at a deeper level. Self-awareness and a little soul searching are critical to success in all areas of life. Think what it is that you want out of this life. If it is joy and happiness, then look to ways to find this. There are no rules to spirituality, just look within and connect with your inner being. When you feel love and peace within, you will find outer joy and happiness. The loss that everyone is feeling in these times have made us disorientated and for some, feeling bitterness. If you want to shut yourself off from the world for a while, then do it. Accept what it is that you are struggling with and let yourself grieve if necessary. Allow all of the feelings to take place. Don't try to fight them. We are all unique and all have a different way of dealing with things. When you are ready and want to see a change in your life, look at what you can change. Just making tiny adjustments here and there is a step towards your change. If you are noticing a lot of synchronicities then you are becoming more aware of spirit, you begin to harmonise with the environment around you. You are vibrating at a higher rate. When you recognise this and allow yourself to connect you will feel that ideas to help you to make the changes that you want can probably come into focus. You may have these synchronicities for a while and then nothing. Your 'self' still has to come into play with what it has chosen and so you will still encounter challenges, BUT you will be able to deal with them in a more positive, productive way. You may be worried about making changes or maybe you don't really know what you want or maybe you are afraid to choose what may be '*the wrong*' decision. We can all fear change but change in inevitable as we move along life. Try to see the challenges as lessons and see how you can work through them with a positive mental attitude. As I have said before, try to let go of old limiting beliefs from the past that hold you back. We can often stay stuck with an emotion, so let yourself become aware of the feelings within, and give yourself time to *reflect*. The world is changing around us, and this brings changes within. I do feel that with the changes, more people will start to look within and want to see changes for themselves. We can all be judgemental and blame, maybe the government for their choices during the pandemic, however this is not helpful. It isn't going to change what has happened. We all react differently and have our own perception on things. We can't change how other people deal with things, but we can adjust our way of thinking. Even though we all make up our own minds on this, I feel that we just need to find support for ourselves, and just to be mindful of what we ourselves need in the way of care. When we focus on what we cannot control, the more likely we are to feel anxiety, anger or disappointment. How we respond to our thoughts influence the feelings within us. For me, I have found that being spiritually aware, I now pay attention to my reactions, and can often stand back and look at what is happening from a distance and give more clarity to what I feel is happening. This gives more time to evaluate a situation and think about how to react in the best possible way. Everyone is entitled to their opinions; it is the way we react to them that can be a positive or a negative outcome for us. The consciousness of the planet is changing, and we need to change with it. We are all on a journey through this life, the life that we have chosen to come into. Being a human being can create chaos within us. Sometimes we need direction and sometimes we need to sit and reflect. The world around us has become chaotic and we can lose ourselves in it. We are told to believe so many things that can cause a negative reaction within us. There is a mind field of energy chaos, and this can be overwhelming, and we can become traumatised by the way the news and social media panic. None of us know when our time is up! We may have gone through a lot of grief and stress and because of this, we may be feeding our minds with so much negativity and losing ourselves in it. So then, we should all try to take time out for ourselves. Let's do something that makes 'US' happy and try to find a balance. I have been through many stressful times and have got lost in a black hole of negativity, but my spiritual beliefs get me back on track. Writing this book has been uplifting for me. I have found joy in it and self-satisfaction. Life and life's challenges will always affect us, one way or another. Trust your heart to help you find your way. Maybe we should be looking to create a better world, rather than dwelling on the negative of what has been. We cannot be everything to everyone, but we can all strive to do our best in whatever way we are able. Maybe we need to accept that some things are out of our control, as I mentioned earlier. So should we hold on to the fear, the anxieties and unrest that we have experienced or indeed still experiencing, or should we look to find things and people that will help us to feel better. There are many counsellors ready to listen and help, and give support, plus other higher energy healers that can help to balance your energies. Alternatively, you can choose to help others that are in need of some sort of 'healing' be it in just a hug or listening. The more happiness we can create, the more everyone benefits. We need to find peace within. Beautiful music can help lift the vibrations to a higher level and this in itself can bring you peace. There are many stages on our healing journey. We may only be able to make small changes, but if we can re-train our minds to process life as it is, rather than what we feel it should be, maybe we can stop battling with life. We are all in a different phase of life. Throughout our life, our patterns change and with each change we need to find balance.

So then to end on reflection: At least once a day, try to reflect on your, on your life, and on what you feel that you have been doing right, and also what isn't working for you. Reflect on every aspect of your life, and from this habit of *reflection*, you should be able to continuously improve. By doing this it can help you learn from what you may term as mistakes. If we don't reflect on these, we usually have to repeat them. However, if we *reflect* on those mistakes, figure out what went wrong, see how we can prevent them in the future, we can use our mistakes to improve. Mistakes, then, are a valuable learning tool, instead of something to feel upset about. Reflection is an important way to do that. If then, you reflect on the things you feel you did right, that allows you to celebrate every little success. It allows you to realize how much you've done right, the good things you've done in your life. Without *reflection*, it's too easy to forget these things, and focus instead on our failures. *Reflection* gives you perspective. If we take a minute to step back, and reflect on these problems, and how in the grand scheme of things they don't mean all that much, it can calm us down and lower our stress levels. We gain perspective, and that's a good thing. We can reflect on how the pandemic has changed things for us. Evaluate things and look at what we want to change for ourselves, within ourselves. We have all been turned upside down and now some people may want to find out more about '*who they are*', '*why they are here*' and also '*where they are going.*' I hope that through my own experiences, I have been able to offer some guidance or insight into our life journey. If you are sceptical about anything that I have written, then that's ok for you to feel that way. Your journey is unique to you, and you will seek your own knowledge and truth when you are ready. I would like to end this chapter by sending love and light to all. We're all aware of the love and light meaning. We may struggle to put it into words or explain it to others, but it exists within our minds and within our souls. In these times of our human existence where our wellness is at risk given the increasing anxiety and depression, among other issues, I feel that we can share this now more than ever. So finally, listen to your heart, and connect to yourself. Let go of old wounds and limiting beliefs. Self -reflection is serious thought about your own character, actions and motives. It is about taking a step back and reflecting on your life. If self-reflection isn't a regular part of your life right now, this is your wake-up call. It's time for you to take a step back. Time to hop off the treadmill of life. Time to reflect.

GOOD LUCK

"As we grow in our consciousness, there will be more compassion and more love, and then the barriers between people, between religions, between nations will begin to fall. We have to beat down the separateness."

"Love yourself to love others. Be yourself to understand others".

"Be the light to show the way to others. Be peaceful to bring peace to the world"

Judge nothing …. You will be happy

Forgive everything…… You will be happier

Love everything…… You will be the happiest

Peace – Love and Light

Myself V My spiritual self

Spirituality can mean so much to some people and really very little to others. To those who hold spirituality as something important in their lives, then it is usually one of the most important things to them. They usually form their every thought, actions, and desires around how it better serves and contributes to their overall spirituality. Spirituality for me, means giving life perspective. It means that I am seeking to live my authentic self, by understanding who I really am. I have reflected upon the previous lives that I know that I have had and have also understood the healing that I have needed in this incarnation. Part of that realisation has brought clarity to some of the challenges I have had and hopefully for the ones I have yet to face. When I was writing the chapter on Empath's, I already acknowledged that I am one. I actually asked myself 'why' I would have chosen to be an empath in this life as it can be very energy draining. I have explained that we come into each life with 'baggage' that has not been sorted in previous lives. One aspect of being an empath is to do service, by giving and understanding others, but another I have discovered is a possible a need within the empath to be liked. So, this takes me back to the life that I had in China as a soldier. I have already explained that I think I went through a troubled experience and maybe I committed acts that were not especially kind? If this was true, then maybe I am dealing with that baggage in this life and feeling a subconscious need to be liked. I am now doing service to maybe compensate and balance Karma. This is just my theory, but it is the understanding of how we balance Karmic debts. An interesting comment that came to me via someone else was that when I think I am connecting with my loved ones and spirit guides, that I am actually talking to the devil! What I needed to ask myself, was *how did It make me feel* and *what did it trigger within me*. When people make you question your character, intelligence, beliefs, decisions or preferences it can trigger a negative response because you feel that you are being judged. In the past, before I became satisfied with who I am, I may have felt that she was just being UN-reasonable, and 'how dare she trash talk me'! However, today I understand that this person obviously has her own faith and what she believes in is totally different to mine. That's ok. We are all entitled to our beliefs, and we are all on different pathways throughout life. Of cause, certain people are going to be suspicious of what I believe, and again, that is everyone's free will to believe what they want to believe. I trust in what I feel and receive, and that is my truth. I am comfortable with my beliefs and who I am in this lifetime. I have had people make fun and scoff at my beliefs, and I could have felt cross with them, and it could have given me self-doubts, however, I think I has just made me stronger. I no longer worry about what other people think. Once you feel strong within yourself and are happy with who you are, then the negative remarks bounce off. There was a time when I did not believe in myself, and I can tell you, that lack of faith in myself was the source of many problems in my life. I would let negative remarks upset me and I would retaliate in a similar negative way. We all have something to offer, and I accept now that I have been given the gift of insight. I have found the strength to embrace the qualities that I now understand to be part of my journey through this life. So often we can get bogged down by other people's opinions of us, and voices in our head that may have told us that we are not good enough. It is realising that opinions of others are just that '*their opinions*'. Moving from self-doubt to self- belief can take time, especially if you have held on to that "I'm not good enough" zone for a long time. Your mind may tell you things — things that stem from long-held limiting belies, but that doesn't mean those thoughts are true, either. I examined my beliefs about myself and came to the conclusions that I feel today. As I mentioned in a previous chapter, one of the greatest lessons you'll learn in your life is to find happiness *within yourself.* That means choosing to believe in yourself. It also means embracing self-acceptance rather than self-criticism. You need to choose to believe in yourself even when life is hard and you're facing uphill battles. You are more powerful than you realize … you can do more than you're telling yourself you can do. So let go of self-limiting beliefs and stop worrying about what others may think of you. You don't have to be perfect, just be yourself. I have finally changed my perspectives about myself and have decided that I am in the driving seat of my own success. This has given me personal power which is like a protection shield against negative comments and thoughts. All past experiences have laid the foundations for me coming to an understanding about myself and the opportunities that are her for me in this lifetime. Once again, I have share this with you to show that we can take control of our own lives and accept who we are.

Feel your peace within

A lot of us have found peace during the isolation periods that we maybe wouldn't have had time for in our busy lives. More time to listen to music, or maybe just sitting and being quiet. I have found peace in writing this book. I started it before the pandemic, but I have had more time to reflect and focus on things that are important to me. As I have mentioned a few times throughout this book, we are spiritual beings having a human life, and that comes with challenges. We are changing and transforming every day of our lives. What I feel we need to address, is '*what matters to you*'. Figure out what is important to you, and what is not important to you. We have been given this time to reflect on what matters to us during the times that we have been 'home alone.' We maybe all needing some emotional healing from what we have been going through. To do this we have to clear some of the 'mind baggage' that we have been lugging around. Maybe have a sort out as you would do with house clearing. Only keep what really matters to you and let go of what doesn't serve you anymore. Look at what will bring you inner peace, and little by little, make some changes.

Un-clutter your mind - Slow down - find a relaxing technique that suits you - Accept and let go

"The simplification of life is one of the steps to inner peace. A persistent simplification will create an inner and outer well-being that places harmony in one's life".

Thanks, and Gratitude

I would like to thank everyone that is a part of my life and who have helped me on my path of discovery of 'who I am' and 'why I am here'. I am grateful for the challenges that have been offered helping me to make the choices and decisions that have put me on the right pathway, thus making me a stronger person.

I give grateful thanks to my (deceased) parents for their unconditional love.

My wonderful family and friends have helped be my inspiration for 'self' discovery and so I give thanks for having them in my life.

A spiritual awakening can mean so many different things to so many different people. The way I like to think of it is a coming home to one's true self, a realization of greater truths, and a recognition that we are part of something far greater than just this personality in this life. This search for purpose and deeper connection is just the beginning of our journey. I am truly grateful for the spiritual knowledge that I have that has taught me self-realization and spiritual enlightenment.

Unconditional love is not so much about how we receive and endure each other, as it is about the deep vow to never, under any condition, stop bringing the flawed truth of who we are to each other.

Thank you for taking the time to read my book.

Florette. x

Florette is a retired grandmother that lives on the North Devon coast

She is a spiritual medium

Counsellor

E.F.T. therapist

She has the gift of empathy and understanding

This book outlines inspiration and encouragement

for all things spiritual and to help you to understand the meaning and purpose of life and connect with your true 'self' list subjects as the appear throughout the book

Who am I and why am I here?

Basics including Karma

What is the Souls purpose – pre life Journey: - *see also*

(Life's journey - The subtle body and the soul)

Body and Soul -*see also* - (Soul Energy)

Basic Laws on Life

Trusting your life choices

Inner Guidance/Intuition *see also* Limiting beliefs and Karma

Forgiveness and Karma

Love is the ultimate goal

What we give out – we get back including (disease and disharmony)

Limiting beliefs – Karma

The Contract

The soul is pure Energy -*see also* (Soul energy and reincarnation)

Spirit Guides/helpers/ choosing to listen to your guides/ -*see also* (Spirit guides and protection) and (Life guides and guardian Angels) (Guides and messages)

Mediumship and Empathy

A few Life Lessons

Spiritual Vibrations/Energy

The Astral Plane

More about Guides and messages

Soulmates

Why we have difficult people in our lives

Surroundings in the spirit world and what happens there

The subtle body and the soul

Re-cap on Life's journey

Making connection with our loved ones in the spirit realms

Meditation

Proof of communication and spirit connections

Negative energies and protection -*see also* (negativity v positivity) *and also* (negative beliefs and manifestations)

More about Spirit Guides and protection

Who or What is God?

Soul Energy and reincarnation

Some of my past reincarnations and family connections

More about the spiritual dimensions

Stories from Spirit

Life is like a play

Love is the ultimate goal

Healing within

About the 'Self' *see also* (My life V my spiritual life)

Ways in which our guides contact us

Opening up

Chakras and well-being

Healing therapies

Soul ages

Life Guides and Guardian Angels

Negativity V Positivity

Anger amongst Siblings

Writing for better health /Journaling

Fears and Phobia's

Active listening

Perfectionism

Gratitude

Negative beliefs and manifestations

Re-cap on reincarnations - [Life & Death]

Accidental Death

Mediumship and messages

How to channel and find peace

The benefits of becoming a medium

Coincidences

Gut Instincts V Anxiety

Psychometry and spiritual knowledge

Questions and Answers

Life on Earth is a Team Game

Disharmony and Intentions

Listen to your intuition *see also* (Food for thought)

Questions and Answers (including star signs)

Receiving answers from above

Types of dreams and how to recognise them

Psychic protection

More about the Aura and how it protects us *Including -*

(The human Energy field)

More questions and Answers

Angels and feathers -Feathers and their meanings

Discovering that Earth is a school of learning

Spiritual Enlightenment

More messages and connections with our spirit guides

Intuition *see also* (ego V Intuition)

The circle of life

Doing service

What is EFT and how does it work

Self-esteem and the blaming game

Types of clairvoyance and trust

The power of mind over matter

How do I find out who I am and who I was in a former life?

Growing Spiritually

What happens when it is time to bid farewell?

Summing up

Food for thought (including ego V intuition)

Reflection

My self V my spiritual self

Thanks, and gratitude

Printed in Great Britain
by Amazon